VOLUME TWO

ALL STORIES WRITTEN BY **JOHN BROOME** AND ART PENCILLED BY **GIL KANE** AND
INKED BY **JOE GIELLA**, UNLESS OTHERWISE NOTED.

Dan DiDio SVP – EXECUTIVE EDITOR ☆ Julius Schwartz EDITOR – ORIGINAL SERIES
Georg Brewer VP – DESIGN & DC DIRECT CREATIVE ☆ Bob Harras GROUP EDITOR – COLLECTED EDITIONS
Bob Joy EDITOR ☆ Robbin Brosterman DESIGN DIRECTOR – BOOKS

DC COMICS

Paul Levitz PRESIDENT & PUBLISHER ☆ Richard Bruning SVP – CREATIVE DIRECTOR ☆ Patrick Caldon EVP – FINANCE & OPERATIONS
Amy Genkins SVP – BUSINESS & LEGAL AFFAIRS ☆ Jim Lee EDITORIAL DIRECTOR-WILDSTORM
Gregory Noveck SVP – CREATIVE AFFAIRS ☆ Steve Rotterdam SVP – SALES & MARKETING ☆ Cheryl Rubin SVP – BRAND MANAGEMENT

DC Comics, 1700 Broadway, New York, NY 10019
A Warner Bros. Entertainment Company
First Printing.

ISBN: 978-1-4012-2499-8
Printed by World Color Press, Inc., St-Romuald, QC, Canada 11/25/09

Cover art by Gil Kane and Joe Giella

SUSTAINABLE FORESTRY INITIATIVE

Certified Fiber
Sourcing
www.sfiprogram.org
Fiber used in this product line meets the sourcing requirements
of the SFI program. www.sfiprogram.org PWC-5FICOC-260

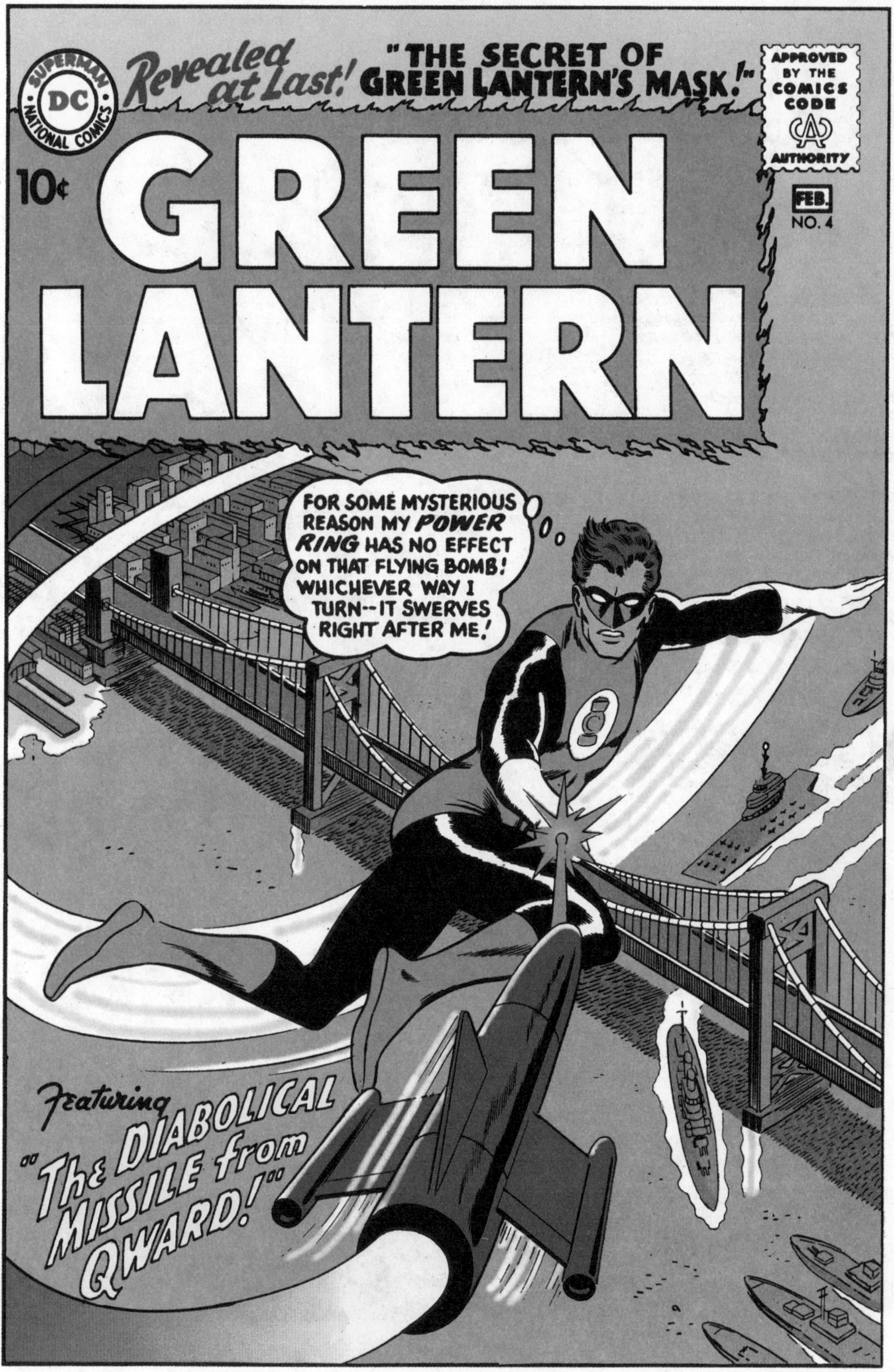
SUPERMAN DC NATIONAL COMICS
Revealed at Last! "THE SECRET OF GREEN LANTERN'S MASK!"
APPROVED BY THE COMICS CODE AUTHORITY
10¢
GREEN LANTERN
FEB. NO. 4
FOR SOME MYSTERIOUS REASON MY POWER RING HAS NO EFFECT ON THAT FLYING BOMB! WHICHEVER WAY I TURN--IT SWERVES RIGHT AFTER ME!
Featuring "The DIABOLICAL MISSILE from QWARD!"

GREEN LANTERN

IT WAS A VERY URGENT MISSION THAT FORCED **GREEN LANTERN** TO RETURN TO THE PERILOUS ANTI-MATTER UNIVERSE OF **QWARD**--TO CONFRONT DESTINY IN THE FORM OF A MALEVOLENT ROBOT!
BACK ON EARTH HIS FRIEND **PIEFACE** LAY IN MORTAL DANGER--A DANGER FROM WHICH ONLY THE **QWARDIANS** COULD SAVE THE LITTLE MECHANIC!
BUT THEY ASKED A **HIGH PRICE**!

The DIABOLICAL MISSILE FROM QWARD!

IT'S A TERRIBLE ANTAGONIST I HAVE IN THIS **QWARDIAN** ARENA--A GIANT ROBOT WITH SUPER-SCIENTIFIC POWERS! I MUST DEFEAT IT!

ON THE ANTI-MATTER UNIVERSE OF *QWARD*, THE EXACT OPPOSITE OF OURS IN EVERY WAY, A SECRET MEETING OF THE *CHIEF WEAPONERS*, THE PLANETARY OVERLORDS...

FELLOW *WEAPONERS*, THERE IS IN THE COSMOS AN UNENDING BATTLE BETWEEN THE FORCES OF *GOOD* AND *EVIL*! AS FOR US, WE LIVE BY THE PRINCIPLES OF *EVIL*...

...JUST AS OUR NEIGHBORING UNIVERSE WITH THE PLANET *EARTH* IN IT LIVES BY THE PRINCIPLES OF *GOODNESS*--WHICH WE ABHOR! BUT IN ORDER TO DESTROY OUR MORTAL ENEMIES WE MUST FIRST DESTROY ALL THE *POWER LAMPS*...

...SUCH AS THE ONE POSSESSED BY THE EARTHMAN *GREEN LANTERN*! THEREFORE I AM PLEASED TO REPORT TO YOU TODAY THAT A GREAT STEP HAS BEEN TAKEN ON THE ROAD TO OUR EVIL DESTINY! *GREEN LANTERN IS ABOUT TO BE DESTROYED!*

RECENTLY OUR SCIENTISTS COMPLETED THIS ROBOT! IT IS PERFECT IN EVERY WAY--INCLUDING ITS DISTORTED, EVIL MIND! AND THIS ROBOT--CALLED *GNAXOS*--SOLVED OUR MOST PERPLEXING PROBLEM...

WE GAVE IT THE ASSIGNMENT OF FIGURING OUT A SURE WAY TO ELIMINATE *GREEN LANTERN*--AND IN NO TIME AT ALL ITS SUBTLE BRAIN COMPLETED THE TASK! EVEN AT THIS VERY MOMENT...

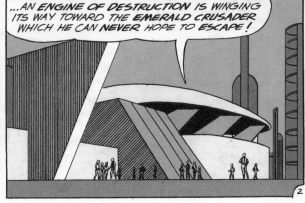

...AN *ENGINE OF DESTRUCTION* IS WINGING ITS WAY TOWARD THE *EMERALD CRUSADER* WHICH HE CAN *NEVER* HOPE TO ESCAPE!

2

AND AT THE **FERRIS AIRCRAFT COMPANY** WHERE HAL JORDAN, ACE TEST PILOT, IS EMPLOYED...

HAL, YOU SEEM A BIT WORRIED TODAY! IS ANYTHING WRONG?

I'M NOT SURE, PIEFACE! YOU SEE...

...MY **POWER RING**--WHICH I KEEP HERE IN THIS POCKET WHEN I'M NOT WEARING IT--HAS BEEN EMITTING A PECULIAR TYPE OF ENERGY FOR THE PAST HOUR! IT'S AS IF...AS IF IT'S TRYING TO WARN ME OF SOME **DANGER!**

GREAT FISH-HOOKS!

AND THAT REMINDS ME, I'D BETTER RECHARGE MY RING--JUST IN CASE! YOU KEEP AN EYE OUT, WILL YOU, PIEFACE?

SURE THING, HAL! DON'T WORRY--NO ONE WILL GET PAST **ME!**

Editor's Note:

PIEFACE--OR THOMAS KALMAKU, HAL'S CRACK ESKIMO AIRPLANE MECHANIC, TO GIVE HIM HIS REAL NAME -- IS THE ONLY PERSON ON EARTH WHO KNOWS THAT HAL JORDAN IS IN REALITY **GREEN LANTERN!** WHICH EXPLAINS THE TEST PILOT'S FREEDOM IN DISCUSSING SUCH **TOP SECRET** MATTERS AS HIS RING AND ITS POWERS!

BEHIND CLOSED DOORS IN HAL'S DRESSING ROOM AT THE HANGAR, A SOLEMN OATH IS REPEATED...

IN BRIGHTEST DAY, IN BLACKEST NIGHT, NO EVIL SHALL ESCAPE MY SIGHT! LET THOSE WHO WORSHIP EVIL'S MIGHT BEWARE MY POWER--**GREEN LANTERN'S LIGHT!**

AND AS THE **GREEN GLADIATOR** EMERGES...

I'VE DECIDED TO HAVE A LOOK AROUND, PIEFACE-- EH?

GL! WH--WHAT'S THAT?

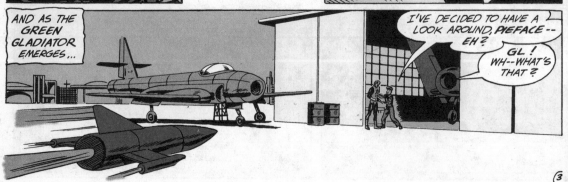

(3)

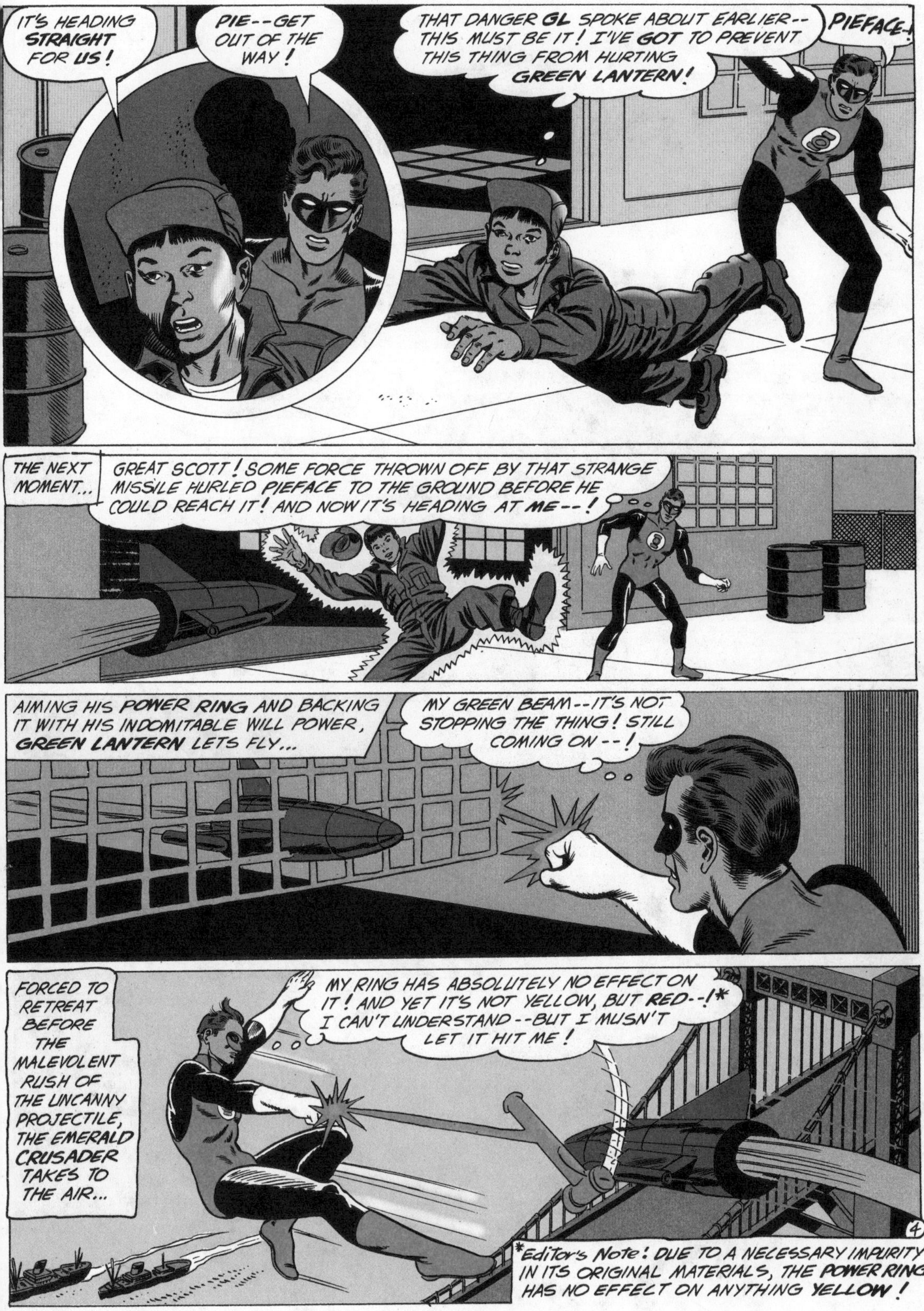
IT'S HEADING STRAIGHT FOR US!
PIE--GET OUT OF THE WAY!
THAT DANGER GL SPOKE ABOUT EARLIER-- THIS MUST BE IT! I'VE GOT TO PREVENT THIS THING FROM HURTING GREEN LANTERN!
PIEFACE-!
THE NEXT MOMENT...
GREAT SCOTT! SOME FORCE THROWN OFF BY THAT STRANGE MISSILE HURLED PIEFACE TO THE GROUND BEFORE HE COULD REACH IT! AND NOW IT'S HEADING AT ME--!
AIMING HIS POWER RING AND BACKING IT WITH HIS INDOMITABLE WILL POWER, GREEN LANTERN LETS FLY...
MY GREEN BEAM--IT'S NOT STOPPING THE THING! STILL COMING ON--!
FORCED TO RETREAT BEFORE THE MALEVOLENT RUSH OF THE UNCANNY PROJECTILE, THE EMERALD CRUSADER TAKES TO THE AIR...
MY RING HAS ABSOLUTELY NO EFFECT ON IT! AND YET IT'S NOT YELLOW, BUT RED--!* I CAN'T UNDERSTAND--BUT I MUSN'T LET IT HIT ME!
4
*Editor's Note: DUE TO A NECESSARY IMPURITY IN ITS ORIGINAL MATERIALS, THE POWER RING HAS NO EFFECT ON ANYTHING YELLOW!

WHICHEVER WAY I TURN--IT SWERVES RIGHT AFTER ME! AND IT'S COMING CLOSER ALL THE TIME!

THEN AN IDEA COMES TO THE *GREEN GLADIATOR*...

I'VE GOT TO OUTMANEUVER IT... AND MAYBE I KNOW THE WAY! THAT OLD BARN!

IF I'M RIGHT, IT'S TAKING THE MISSILE A FRACTION OF A SECOND LONGER THAN IT TAKES ME TO SWERVE! I'VE GOT TO BANK ON THAT--AND HERE GOES!

POWER-DIVING AT THE BARN, *GREEN LANTERN* TURNS ASIDE. AT THE VERY LAST INSTANT...

NOW TO SEE IF THIS WORKS!

THAT DOES IT!

CRAAASH!

5

8

AS GL RUSHES BACK TO HIS MECHANIC...

WHAT'S WRONG, PAL?

HE'S IN SOME KIND OF SHOCK! THE CONTACT WITH THE MISSILE--IT'S DONE SOMETHING TO HIM! HE DOESN'T SEEM BADLY HURT, AND YET--

THAT AURA OF YELLOW RADIATION AROUND HIM-- MY RING CAN'T GET THROUGH IT TO ROUSE HIM! NO TIME TO GO FOR A DOCTOR! I'VE GOT TO FIND OUT FOR MYSELF IF HE'S ALIVE--!

ON IMPULSE THE RING-WIELDER TURNS HIS GREAT GREEN BEAM INTO A HUGE STETHOSCOPE...

THERE! I HEAR HIS HEART ALL RIGHT! HE'S STILL ALIVE! BUT WAIT A SECOND--!

AS A DREAD FACT DAWNS ON THE EMERALD CRUSADER...

GREAT SCOTT! UNLESS I'M MISTAKEN HIS HEART IS SLOWING DOWN! YES... LITTLE BY LITTLE IT'S BEATING MORE SLOWLY!

THUMP! THUMP!

THUMP!

IN GRIM DESPERATION AT THE PLIGHT OF HIS PLUCKY LITTLE FRIEND, THE EMERALD CRUSADER PLUNGES INTO ACTION...

THERE ISN'T MUCH TIME! I'VE GOT TO WORK FAST! I'M CONVINCED IT'S THAT STRANGE RADIATION AROUND HIM THAT'S ENDANGERING PIEFACE'S LIFE--THE RADIATION GIVEN OFF BY THAT MISSILE!

IF MY RING CAN'T PIERCE THAT RADIATION, NO POWER ON EARTH CAN! BUT WHOEVER MADE THIS MISSILE MAY KNOW THE ANTI-DOTE! IT'S MY ONLY HOPE! I'VE GOT TO FIND OUT WHERE IT CAME FROM!

As GL's all-powerful ring examines the shattered projectile, a startling fact becomes clear...

GREAT SCOTT! THE MISSILE IS REALLY YELLOW! BUT A BATTERY OF RED LIGHTS IN ITS INTERIOR WAS SET UP TO SHINE THROUGH ITS TRANSPARENT METAL SKIN--SO AS TO MAKE IT SEEM RED!!

SO THAT'S WHY MY RING HAD NO EFFECT ON IT! WHAT A DIABOLICAL SCHEME! SOMEONE SET IT UP THIS WAY IN ORDER TO DESTROY ME--BY THROWING ME OFF MY GUARD! AND IT CAME WITHIN AN INCH OF SUCCEEDING! BUT WHERE--

OF COURSE! THIS MISSILE MUST HAVE COME FROM QWARD! I SHOULD HAVE REALIZED! ONLY MY DEADLY ENEMIES--THE WEAPONERS OF QWARD--HAVE THE SUPER-SCIENTIFIC KNOW-HOW NECESSARY TO CONSTRUCT SUCH A MECHANISM! AND THAT MEANS--

SNAP!

--I'VE GOT TO GO INTO QWARD TO GET THE ANTIDOTE TO THE RADIATION THAT IS KILLING PIEFACE! NOT A MOMENT TO LOSE--!

His ring cleaving the way, the GREEN-CLAD GLADIATOR streaks through the air, as his thoughts revolve around his strange objective...

THE UNIVERSE OF QWARD--WHAT AN INCREDIBLE PLACE! THOSE THAT TRY TO DO GOOD THERE ARE HOUNDED, THROWN BEHIND BARS! EVIL IS THE ACCEPTED WAY OF LIFE!

TRUTH IS SCORNED! THEY TRY TO OUT-DO EACH OTHER IN WICKEDNESS--AND I HAVE REASON TO BELIEVE THAT LATELY I...GREEN LANTERN...HAVE BECOME PUBLIC ENEMY NUMBER ONE THERE-- WHICH IS OKAY WITH ME!

7

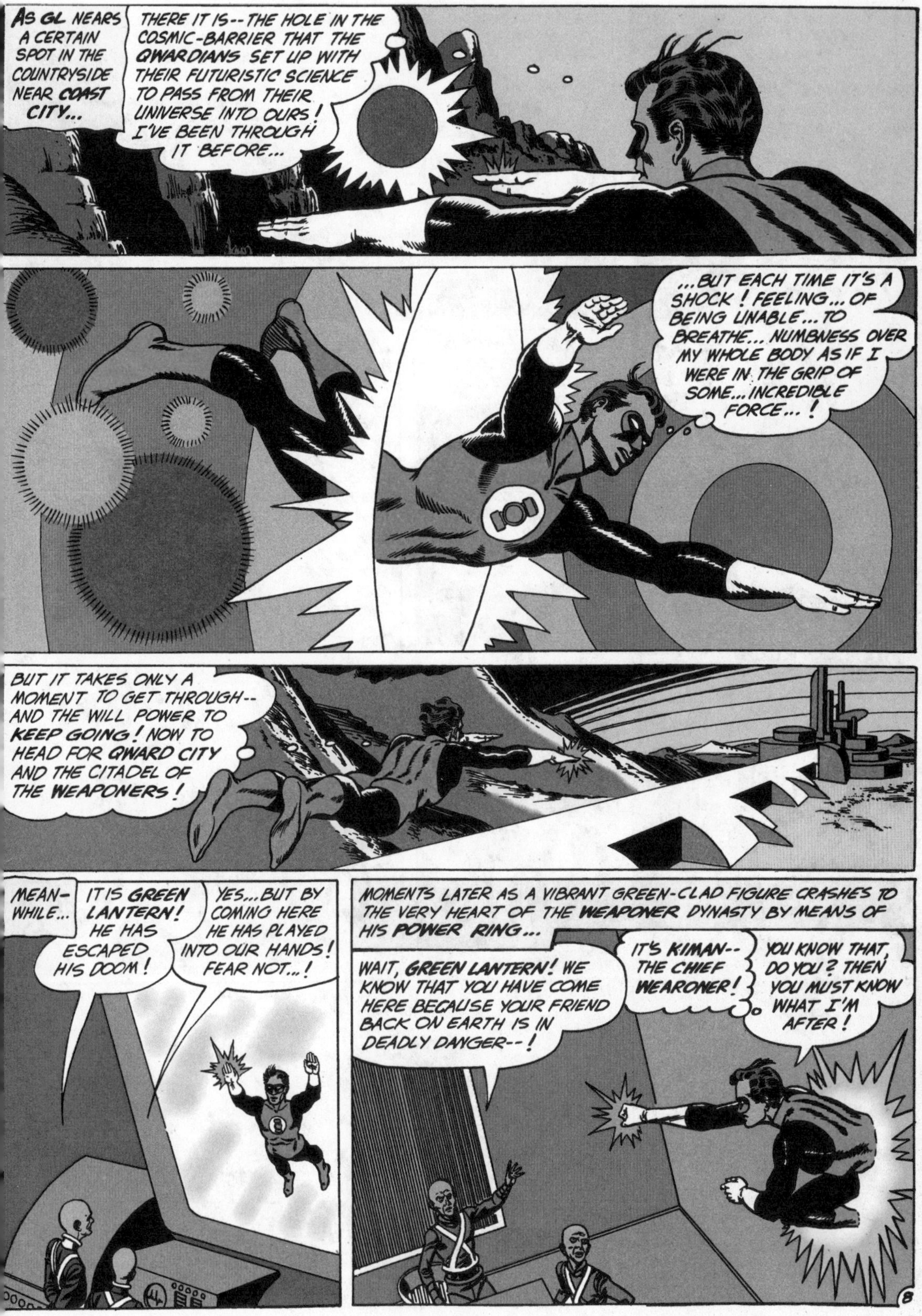
AS GL NEARS A CERTAIN SPOT IN THE COUNTRYSIDE NEAR COAST CITY...
THERE IT IS--THE HOLE IN THE COSMIC-BARRIER THAT THE QWARDIANS SET UP WITH THEIR FUTURISTIC SCIENCE TO PASS FROM THEIR UNIVERSE INTO OURS! I'VE BEEN THROUGH IT BEFORE...
...BUT EACH TIME IT'S A SHOCK! FEELING... OF BEING UNABLE... TO BREATHE... NUMBNESS OVER MY WHOLE BODY AS IF I WERE IN THE GRIP OF SOME... INCREDIBLE FORCE...!
BUT IT TAKES ONLY A MOMENT TO GET THROUGH--AND THE WILL POWER TO KEEP GOING! NOW TO HEAD FOR QWARD CITY AND THE CITADEL OF THE WEAPONERS!
MEAN-WHILE...
IT IS GREEN LANTERN! HE HAS ESCAPED HIS DOOM!
YES...BUT BY COMING HERE HE HAS PLAYED INTO OUR HANDS! FEAR NOT...!
MOMENTS LATER AS A VIBRANT GREEN-CLAD FIGURE CRASHES TO THE VERY HEART OF THE WEAPONER DYNASTY BY MEANS OF HIS POWER RING...
WAIT, GREEN LANTERN! WE KNOW THAT YOU HAVE COME HERE BECAUSE YOUR FRIEND BACK ON EARTH IS IN DEADLY DANGER--!
IT'S KIMAN--THE CHIEF WEAPONER!
YOU KNOW THAT, DO YOU? THEN YOU MUST KNOW WHAT I'M AFTER!
8

AS THE GREAT GREEN BEAM LASHES OUT...

GIVE ME THE MEANS TO REMOVE THE RADIATION FROM *PIEFACE*! OR THAT BEAM—HAND AROUND YOU WILL NEVER LOSE ITS GRIP!

YOU MAY DESTROY ME...

...AND YOU MAY DESTROY HALF OUR CITY BEFORE WE DESTROY YOU, *GREEN LANTERN*! BUT THAT WILL NOT SAVE YOUR FRIEND!

HE'S RIGHT! MUCH AS I HATE TO DO IT, I'VE GOT TO PARLEY WITH THESE EVIL-WORSHIPPERS!

ALL RIGHT! WHAT DEAL ARE YOU OFFERING FOR *PIEFACE'S* LIFE? WHATEVER IT IS, I'LL MEET IT!

WELL SPOKEN, *GREEN LANTERN*! BUT IT IS NOT SO BAD A DEAL...

QWARDIANS LOVE VIOLENCE--THE EXCITING CLASH OF A GREAT COMBAT! WHAT WE PROPOSE IS SIMPLY THIS: THAT YOU MEET OUR CHAMPION IN SINGLE COMBAT! IF YOU WIN, YOU DEPART UNHARMED AND WITH THE ANTIDOTE FOR THE RADIATION!

AND IF I FAIL?

NO--DON'T ANSWER THAT! I'M NOT GOING TO FAIL! BRING ON YOUR CHAMPION--WHOEVER HE IS!

GOOD! COME WITH US!

IN AN ARENA-LIKE AMPHI-THEATER...

THEY PUT ME IN THE CENTER HERE, BUT NO SIGN YET OF THEIR CHAMPION--EH?

ON YOUR GUARD, GREEN LANTERN!

9

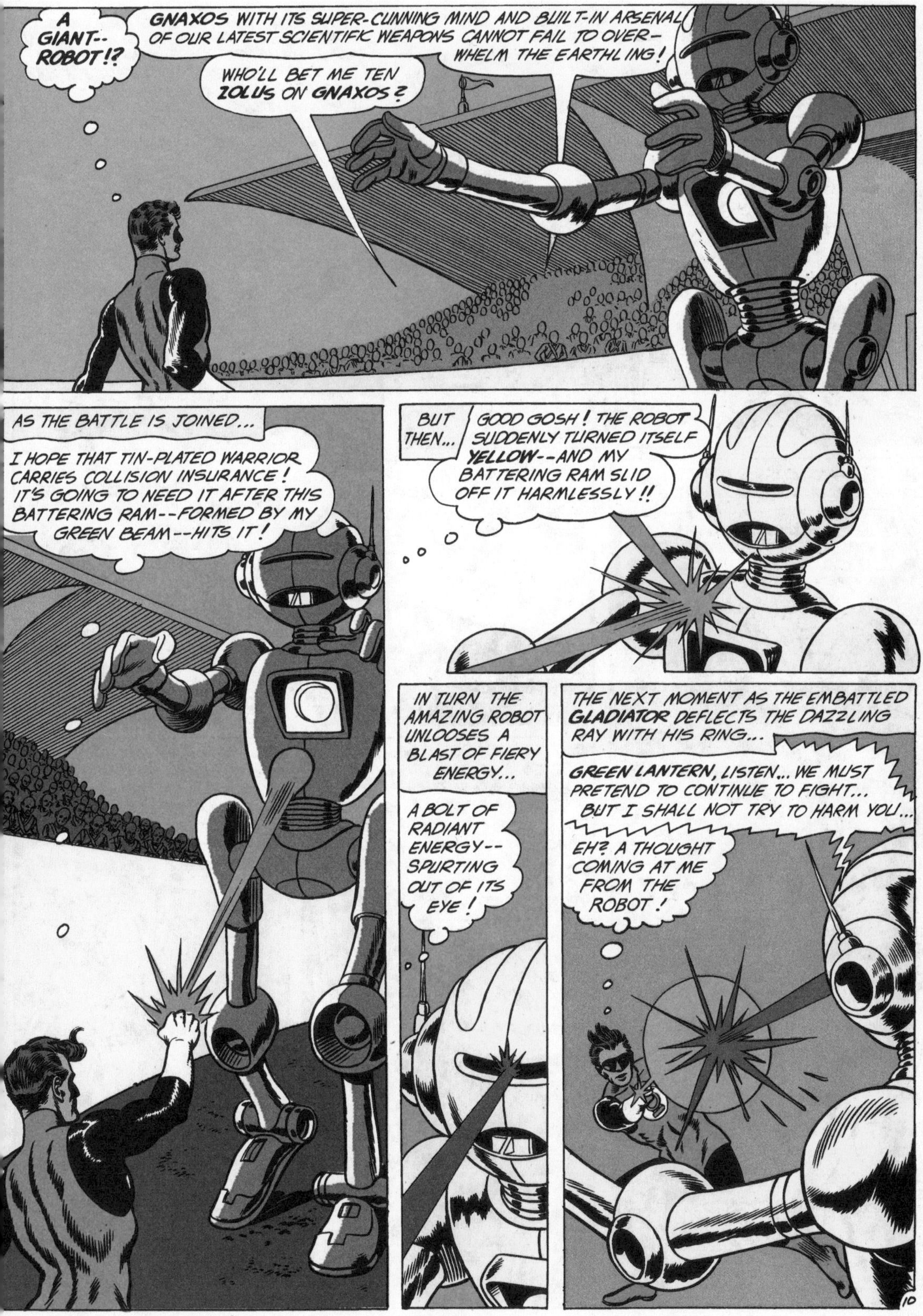
A GIANT--ROBOT!?
GNAXOS WITH ITS SUPER-CUNNING MIND AND BUILT-IN ARSENAL OF OUR LATEST SCIENTIFIC WEAPONS CANNOT FAIL TO OVER-WHELM THE EARTHLING!
WHO'LL BET ME TEN ZOLUS ON GNAXOS?
AS THE BATTLE IS JOINED...
I HOPE THAT TIN-PLATED WARRIOR CARRIES COLLISION INSURANCE! IT'S GOING TO NEED IT AFTER THIS BATTERING RAM--FORMED BY MY GREEN BEAM--HITS IT!
BUT THEN...
GOOD GOSH! THE ROBOT SUDDENLY TURNED ITSELF YELLOW--AND MY BATTERING RAM SLID OFF IT HARMLESSLY!!
IN TURN THE AMAZING ROBOT UNLOOSES A BLAST OF FIERY ENERGY...
A BOLT OF RADIANT ENERGY--SPURTING OUT OF ITS EYE!
THE NEXT MOMENT AS THE EMBATTLED GLADIATOR DEFLECTS THE DAZZLING RAY WITH HIS RING...
GREEN LANTERN, LISTEN... WE MUST PRETEND TO CONTINUE TO FIGHT... BUT I SHALL NOT TRY TO HARM YOU...
EH? A THOUGHT COMING AT ME FROM THE ROBOT!
10

THEN, ANOTHER BOLT--AND ANOTHER THOUGHT MESSAGE FLASHES AT THE EMERALD CRUSADER...

LISTEN, GREEN LANTERN! EVEN THOUGH I HAVE HAD ONLY A SHORT LIFE UP TO NOW, I HAVE LEARNED THE DIFFERENCE BETWEEN GOOD AND EVIL! THOSE HUMANS WHO MADE ME--THE QWARDIANS--ARE EVIL!

I, GNAXOS, WAS MADE TO BE EVIL BUT SOMETHING HAPPENED TO MY BRAIN AND I HAVE BECOME GOOD--AND I WANT TO HELP YOU BECAUSE I HAVE LEARNED FROM PROBING YOUR MIND THAT YOU TOO ARE GOOD!

JUMPIN' JUPITER! I--I'VE FOUND AN ALLY!

AS THE TWO CLOSE WITH EACH OTHER IN MORTAL COMBAT...

TAKE THIS, GREEN LANTERN! IT WILL COUNTERACT THE DEADLY RADIATION THAT IS AFFECTING YOUR FRIEND! TAKE IT-- AND FLEE!

BUT WHAT ABOUT YOU, GNAXOS? THE QWARDIANS ARE ALREADY BECOMING SUSPICIOUS! THEY'LL DISCOVER WHAT YOU'VE DONE-- THEY'LL DESTROY YOU!

PERHAPS-- IF THEY CAN!

BUT IF THEY DO, I SHALL PERISH THE WAY I WANT TO PERISH--FIGHTING FOR GOOD AND AGAINST EVIL! GO, GREEN LANTERN! I WILL HOLD THEM BACK--PREVENT THEM FROM ATTACKING YOU!

THE QWARDIANS KNOW SOMETHING IS UP NOW! THEY'RE RISING-- PULLING OUT WEAPONS--!

NO, GNAXOS! I'M NOT LEAVING YOU TO DEAL WITH THIS MOB ALONE! WE'LL BOTH FIGHT THEM--AND WE'LL BOTH GET OUT OF HERE TOGETHER--! COME ON--!

"WE"!?

14

BUT IN THE MELEE THAT FOLLOWS...

THEY'VE DOWNED THE ROBOT! I TRIED TO PROTECT IT WITH MY RING--BUT A HIGH-ENERGY SHOT SLIPPED THROUGH AND FINISHED IT!

I FEEL LIKE I'VE LOST A FRIEND! BUT I CAN'T MOURN FOR HIM ANY LONGER--I HAVE ANOTHER FRIEND TO THINK ABOUT...AND ENEMIES HERE TO SETTLE WITH!

WITH THE FURY OF VENGEANCE AND BACKED BY HIS INDOMITABLE WILL, GL SENDS A GREAT GREEN WAVE SURGING FROM HIS RING WITH OVERWHELMING FORCE...

MAYBE THEY DON'T HAVE TIDAL WAVES HERE IN THIS UNIVERSE--BUT THE QWARDIANS SURE KNOW WHAT ONE FEELS LIKE NOW!

SOON, OUT OF THE HALF-WRECKED CITADEL OF THE WEAPONERS...

WELL, IF I WASN'T PUBLIC ENEMY NUMBER ONE AROUND HERE BEFORE--I SURE AM NOW! BUT FROM HERE ON IN I'VE GOT TO TRAVEL --

THROTTLING UP HIS GREEN BEAM TO ITS HIGHEST VELOCITY, THE GREEN GLADIATOR STREAKS BACK THE WAY HE CAME! AND SOON...

HAVE I COME IN TIME? I'LL SOON FIND OUT...!

12

HIS HEART IS STILL BEATING, BUT SO SLOW IT SEEMS ABOUT TO STOP!

THUMP!

HURRIEDLY, *GL* APPLIES THE COUNTER RADIATION HE HAS BROUGHT...

WILL IT WORK? IT'S *GOT* TO!

THEN, AFTER A BREATHLESS MOMENT...

THE RADIATION IS GONE! *PIEFACE* IS GOING TO BE ALL RIGHT!

-GROAN!-

AND SOON... *GREEN LANTERN!* WHAT HAPPENED?

THE ANTIDOTE GIVEN TO ME BY *GNAXOS* SAVED HIM!

TAKE IT EASY, FELLER-- YOU'RE OKAY NOW!

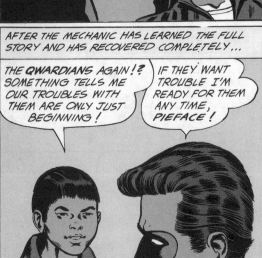

AFTER THE MECHANIC HAS LEARNED THE FULL STORY AND HAS RECOVERED COMPLETELY...

THE *QWARDIANS* AGAIN!? SOMETHING TELLS ME OUR TROUBLES WITH THEM ARE ONLY JUST BEGINNING!

IF THEY WANT TROUBLE I'M READY FOR THEM ANY TIME, *PIEFACE!*

WHAT DO YOU MEAN *YOU'RE* READY-- YOU MEAN *WE'RE* READY, DON'T YOU, *GL?!*

PIEFACE IS A GOOD FRIEND, BUT I GUESS I'LL ALWAYS KEEP IN THE BACK OF MY MIND THE MEMORY OF ONE WHO COULD HAVE BEEN MY FRIEND--IF IT HADN'T PERISHED TRYING TO SAVE ME!

The End

GREEN LANTERN

CAROL, YOU'VE UNMASKED GREEN LANTERN!

SO THAT'S WHAT HE REALLY LOOKS LIKE!

I--I CAN HARDLY BELIEVE IT!

YOU ARE INVITED TO JOIN THE GUESTS AT CAROL FERRIS'S COUNTRY ESTATE AS THEY TAKE OFF ON A GREAT SCAVENGER HUNT! THE OBJECT OF THEIR SEARCH-- GREEN LANTERN'S MASK! AND WHEN THEY GAIN THEIR OBJECTIVE, YOU WILL DISCOVER THE ASTONISHING ...

SECRET OF GREEN LANTERN'S MASK!

As TEST PILOT HAL JORDAN AND HIS ESKIMO MECHANIC *PIEFACE* SWEEP INTO A SUMPTUOUS SUBURBAN ESTATE...

NICE OF YOU TO DRIVE ME OUT HERE TO CAROL'S PLACE, *PIEFACE!*

I STILL SAY YOU'RE TAKING A CHANCE, HAL...

IT'S *GREEN LANTERN* WHO'S INVITED TO CAROL'S SOCIETY SHINDIG--NOT *YOU!* THEY'LL PROBABLY GIVE YOU THE BUM'S RUSH!

COULD BE--

--EXCEPT I'VE GOT A NIFTY PLAN WORKED OUT! THANKS A MILLION FOR THE LIFT, *PIEFACE!* BE SEEING YOU!

YEAH--SOONER THAN YOU THINK!

AFTER THE LOYAL LITTLE GREASE-MONKEY HAS DRIVEN OFF...

I'M DETERMINED TO "CRASH" THIS PARTY! IT'S THE ONLY WAY I COULD THINK OF TO SEE CAROL SOCIALLY! SINCE HER FATHER WENT OFF ON HIS ROUND-THE-WORLD TRIP,* SHE'S REFUSED TO DATE ME...

*Editor's Note: LEAVING CAROL IN SOLE CHARGE OF THE FERRIS AIRCRAFT COMPANY, WHERE HAL WORKS, ON THE PROMISE THAT SHE WOULD ENGAGE IN NO ROMANCE WHILE HE WAS GONE...

LATER, CAROL'S FATHER GAVE HER SPECIAL PERMISSION TO GO OUT WITH *GREEN LANTERN!* BUT IT'S AS *MYSELF*--AS *HAL JORDAN*--THAT I WANT TO WIN CAROL--NOT AS *GL* WHOM SHE SEEMS TO *PREFER!*

SHORTLY, INSIDE THE SUMPTUOUS MANSION...

er--YES, CAROL! *GREEN LANTERN* LEFT THIS NOTE FOR YOU AT THE PLANT! I DECIDED TO BRING IT OUT HERE MYSELF!

A NOTE--FROM *GREEN LANTERN!?*

AS PRETTY CAROL FERRIS READS THE MISSIVE...

HE CAN'T COME! OH, HOW ANNOYING!

*Dear Carol...
Sorry to disappoint you but an emergency has come up that I must take care of!
Green Lantern*

MY GUESTS AND I WERE COUNTING ON *GREEN LANTERN* BEING HERE!

BUSINESS BEFORE PLEASURE, CAROL! IN ANY EVENT, IT GAVE ME THE IDEA OF DELIVERING THE NOTE PERSONALLY!

THANKS! AND NOW IF YOU'LL EXCUSE ME...

NOT SO FAST, CAROL! AFTER ALL, WITHOUT *GREEN LANTERN,* YOU'LL BE A MAN SHORT, AND SINCE I'M NOT DOING ANYTHING TONIGHT--

YOU WOULDN'T TURN ME AWAY, WOULD YOU, CAROL? I CAN BE VERY AMUSING! I COULD DO A FEW CARD TRICKS--

CARD TRICKS?! HOW CAN YOU POSSIBLY COMPARE *THAT* WITH WHAT *GREEN LANTERN* CAN DO?

HOWEVER, NOW THAT YOU'RE HERE, I SUPPOSE YOU MIGHT AS WELL STAY!

~Whew!~ FOR A MINUTE I THOUGHT I WAS GOING TO NOSE-DIVE! BUT I'M IN!

MEET MY FRIEND, HAL JORDAN, EVERYBODY! HE--er--DOES CARD TRICKS!

MEANWHILE, IN A ROOM ASSIGNED TO A TRIO OF WAITERS ESPECIALLY HIRED FOR THE FESTIVE OCCASION...

I JUST HEARD THAT *GREEN LANTERN* ISN'T COMING AFTER ALL! SO WE CAN GO THROUGH WITH OUR PLAN!

GREAT! I'LL GET RIGHT INTO UNIFORM THEN!

AND SOON...

HOW DO I LOOK?

PERFECT, *WOOZY! GREEN LANTERN'S* OWN MOTHER WOULD BE FOOLED! NOW PUT ON YOUR MASK AND LET'S GET STARTED!

OUT IN THE DRAWING ROOM WHERE THE NEW ARRIVAL IS ENTERTAINING THE COMPANY...

HAL JORDAN TELLS THE MOST AMUSING STORIES, CAROL! HE'S REALLY FUN!

HAL *IS* OUTDOING HIMSELF TODAY! I'VE NEVER SEEN HIM LIKE THIS!

I GUESS IT'S BECAUSE HE'S TRYING TO TAKE *GREEN LANTERN'S* PLACE! BUT THAT'S IMPOSSIBLE! HE COULD NEVER IN A MILLION YEARS MATCH--EH?

LOOK-- IT'S *GREEN LANTERN!*

THIS TINY GREEN FLASHLIGHT I HAD MADE IN THE FORM OF A RING IS WORKING LIKE A CHARM!

HI, EVERY-BODY!

GREEN LANTERN, YOU'RE HERE! HOW WONDERFUL!

I FOUND I COULD MAKE IT, CAROL--SO I JUST OPENED THE THROTTLE ON MY GREEN BEAM-- AND HERE I AM! BUT DON'T LET ME INTERRUPT THINGS!

WHAT'S GOING ON HERE?

HAL JORDAN WAS GOING TO SHOW US SOME MAGIC CARD TRICKS, WEREN'T YOU, HAL?

I'VE GOT A BETTER IDEA, CAROL! WHY NOT--er--GET *GREEN LANTERN* TO DO SOME REAL MAGIC TRICKS WITH HIS *POWER RING*?

THIS JOKER IS ABOUT TO BE EXPOSED! BUT I WONDER WHO HE IS-- AND WHAT HE'S UP TO?

WELL, IF YOU ALL INSIST--!

LET'S SAY I WANT TO OPEN THAT DOOR BY REMOTE CONTROL! ALL I HAVE TO DO IS AIM MY RING AND--

AMAZING! IT'S THE FIRST TIME I'VE PERSONALLY SEEN *GREEN LANTERN* IN ACTION!

BEHIND THE DOOR...

HEH--HEH! THIS MUST LOOK LIKE *MAGIC*--FROM THE OTHER ROOM!

WONDERFUL!

DO SOMETHING ELSE!

ALL RIGHT! NOW WATCH THAT WAITER AS I FLASH MY GREEN BEAM AT HIM...

...AND CRY OUT THE MAGIC WORDS *PRESTO--CHANGEO--!*

THAT PHONEY GREEN BEAM CAN'T POSSIBLY HAVE ANY EFFECT ON THE WAITER!

THE NEXT MOMENT...

HA! HA! I JUMPED UP HERE FROM THE FLOOR--BUT THE *POWER OF SUGGESTION* IS TERRIFIC! TO THESE SAPS IT SEEMS I WAS LIFTED UP HERE!

LOOK AT THAT!! HE LIFTED THE WAITER UP...!

AS THE EMERALD-CLAD IMPOSTOR ADDRESSES HIS AUDIENCE...

NOW, MY FRIENDS, IF YOU'LL EXCUSE ME FOR A FEW MINUTES, I JUST REMEMBERED I MUST RECHARGE *MY RING!* IT WON'T TAKE ME LONG! GO ON WITH YOUR FUN! I'LL BE RIGHT BACK!

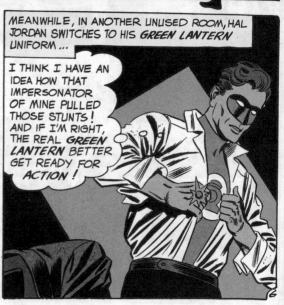

SOON, BEHIND CLOSED DOORS...

WHAT ARE WE WAITING FOR, *WOOZY?* LET'S GET ON WITH THE BIG *JOB!*

I KNOW WHAT I'M DOING, *CHIP!* I'M GAINING THEIR *CONFIDENCE*...

IF I MOVE TOO FAST--THEY MAY GET SUSPICIOUS, SEE? LEAVE EVERYTHING TO ME-- AND DON'T WORRY!

WELL, ALL RIGHT-- BUT DON'T STALL *TOO* LONG!

MEANWHILE, IN ANOTHER UNUSED ROOM, HAL JORDAN SWITCHES TO HIS *GREEN LANTERN* UNIFORM...

I THINK I HAVE AN IDEA HOW THAT IMPERSONATOR OF MINE PULLED THOSE STUNTS! AND IF I'M RIGHT, THE REAL *GREEN LANTERN* BETTER GET READY FOR *ACTION!*

BACK AT THE PARTY...

A SCAVENGER HUNT? THAT'S A TERRIFIC IDEA, CAROL! BUT WHAT WILL WE GO AFTER?

THERE'S ONE OBJECT I'VE ALWAYS BEEN CURIOUS ABOUT--

HOW ABOUT THIS-- THE WINNER OF OUR GAME WILL BE WHOEVER MANAGES TO BRING BACK *GREEN LANTERN'S* MASK!

HOW ORIGINAL!

AS BOY AND GIRL TEAMS SCATTER TO SEARCH FOR THEIR PREY, THE *GREEN GLADIATOR*...

MAYBE THIS WAY I'LL GET WHAT I'VE WANTED FOR A LONG TIME-- A LOOK AT *GREEN LANTERN'S* FACE!

HE MAY BE OUT IN THE GARDEN--!

CAROL! THERE HE IS!

LET'S GET HIM, FRED! HURRY-- BEFORE HE CAN USE HIS *POWER RING* TO ESCAPE US!

WHAT IN THUNDER--?

FASTER, FRED! HE'S GETTING AWAY!

SUDDENLY...

OH, MY! HE FELL...SLIPPED ON THE FLOOR...KNOCKED HIMSELF OUT!

7

THEN... HE'LL COME TO IN A MOMENT! HE'S NOT REALLY HURT!

...AND MEANWHILE AT LEAST I'M ABOUT TO SEE THE FACE OF MY BELOVED!

WITH A QUICK HAND CAROL FERRIS REACHES OUT...

OHHHHH... WH--WHAT HAPPENED?

HMMMM! HE'S NOT AT ALL LIKE WHAT I THOUGHT HE'D BE! IN FACT--!

I DON'T THINK I LIKE HIM ANY-MORE! NOT WITH *THAT* FACE!

YOUR MASK IS THE TREASURE IN A SCAVENGER HUNT WE STARTED *GREEN LANTERN!* HOPE YOU DON'T MIND!

THEY GOT MY MASK! BUT THEY DIDN'T RECOGNIZE ME--SO I GUESS EVERYTHING'S STILL OKAY! LUCKILY, NO ONE EVER NOTICES A WAITER'S FACE!

AFTER THE *"EMERALD CRUSADER"* HAS BEEN GIVEN BACK HIS MASK...

WELL, CAROL AND FRED WON THE SCAVENGER HUNT! NOW -WHAT--

LISTEN, EVERY-ONE! I'VE GOT *ANOTHER IDEA* THAT MAY AMUSE YOU...

WHAT IS IT, *GREEN LANTERN?*

WELL, YOU'VE SEEN THAT MY **POWER RING** IS CAPABLE OF INCREDIBLE STUNTS, HAVEN'T YOU? NOW I'M GOING TO SHOW YOU ONE TRICK THAT WILL REALLY STARTLE YOU...

8

HERE'S MY IDEA! EVERY-BODY PUT HIS JEWELS AND WATCHES ON THIS TABLE HERE! THEN, WITH MY RING I'LL SEND THEM INTO SPACE, ORBIT THEM AROUND THE MOON -- AND BRING THEM BACK HERE IN LESS THAN ONE MINUTE!

SENSATIONAL!

I CAN HAVE A WATCH THAT *GREEN LANTERN* SENT AROUND THE MOON!

THAT'S FOR ME! MY PEARLS WILL BE *MORE VALU-ABLE* THAN EVER!

ME TOO!

(they're falling for it! Get ready, CHIP!)

(I'm all set!)

THEN..

NOW... AS I SPEAK THE MAGICAL WORDS -- *ALIGAROO GAZAM*... AND FLASH OUT MY GREAT GREEN BEAM...

SUDDENLY IN THE MIDST OF THE "MYSTIC INCANTATION"...

HEY!! THE LIGHTS WENT OUT!

WHAT HAPPENED?

AND WHEN FINALLY LIGHT IS RESTORED...

LOOK! OUR JEWELS ARE GONE!

AND SO'S *GREEN LANTERN!*

9

OUTSIDE...

HA! HA! LIKE STEALING THE CANDY AT A BABY CONTEST!

HOP IN, *WOOZY!* LET'S TRAVEL!

BUT NEARBY... I COULD HAVE EXPOSED THAT PHONEY *GL* EARLIER--BUT I WAITED UNTIL I COULD CATCH HIM--AND HIS ACCOMPLICES--WITH THE GOODS!

AS THE GETAWAY CAR *ZOOMS* OFF...

WHERE'D THAT CAR COME FROM? LOOK OUT, CHIP--!!

HEADING STRAIGHT FOR US!

THE NEXT MOMENT...

YOU DIMWIT! YOU PLOWED INTO THESE HEDGES! WE'RE STUCK!

I HAD TO AVOID THAT CAR!

SKREEEEE!

LOOK! IT'S *GREEN LANTERN*--THE *REAL GREEN LANTERN!*

YES! AND WITH A REAL *POWER RING* TOO--MY WILY FRIENDS!

10

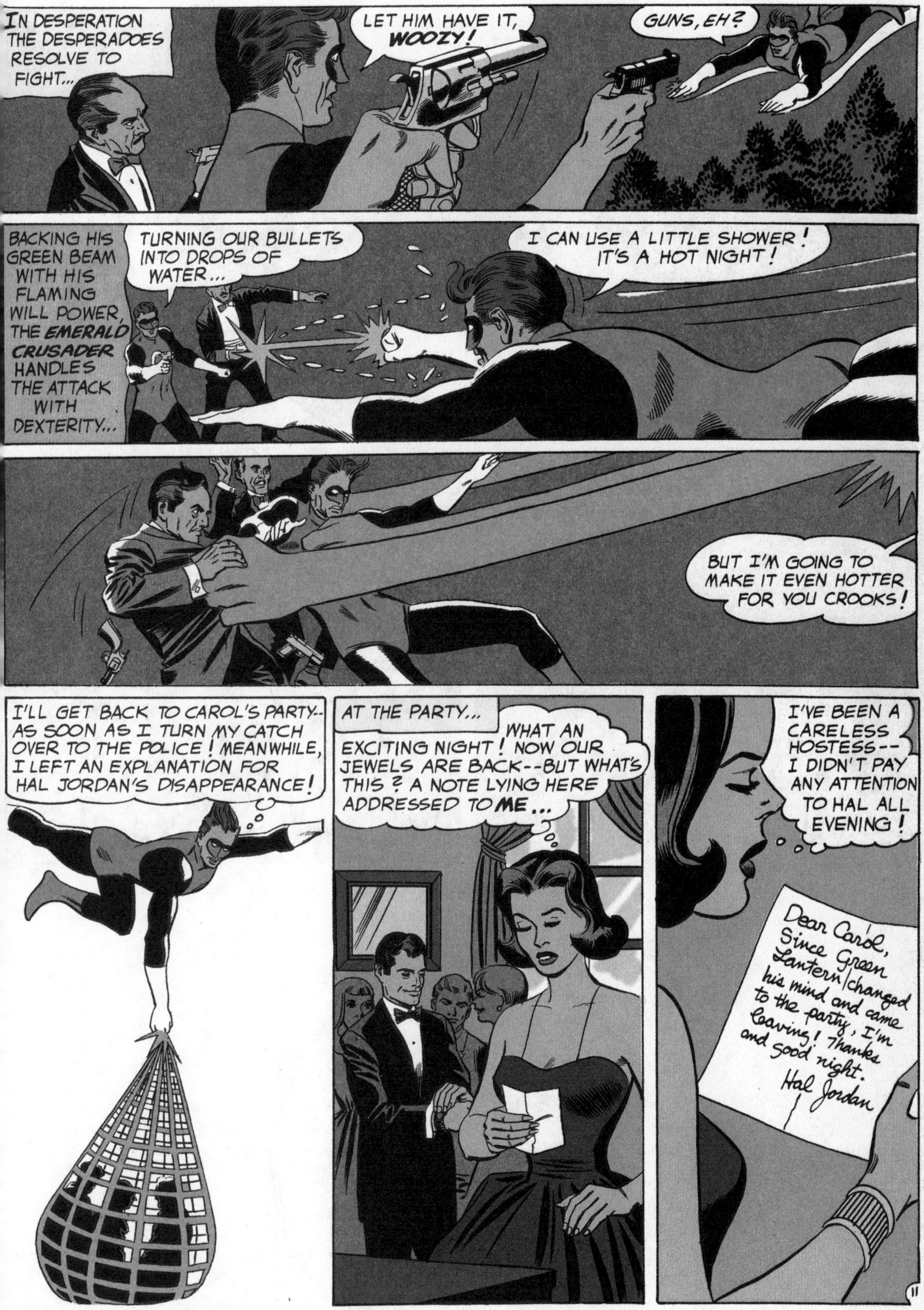

IN DESPERATION THE DESPERADOES RESOLVE TO FIGHT...
LET HIM HAVE IT, WOOZY!
GUNS, EH?
BACKING HIS GREEN BEAM WITH HIS FLAMING WILL POWER, THE EMERALD CRUSADER HANDLES THE ATTACK WITH DEXTERITY...
TURNING OUR BULLETS INTO DROPS OF WATER...
I CAN USE A LITTLE SHOWER! IT'S A HOT NIGHT!
BUT I'M GOING TO MAKE IT EVEN HOTTER FOR YOU CROOKS!
I'LL GET BACK TO CAROL'S PARTY-- AS SOON AS I TURN MY CATCH OVER TO THE POLICE! MEANWHILE, I LEFT AN EXPLANATION FOR HAL JORDAN'S DISAPPEARANCE!
AT THE PARTY...
WHAT AN EXCITING NIGHT! NOW OUR JEWELS ARE BACK--BUT WHAT'S THIS? A NOTE LYING HERE ADDRESSED TO ME...
I'VE BEEN A CARELESS HOSTESS-- I DIDN'T PAY ANY ATTENTION TO HAL ALL EVENING!
Dear Carol, Since Green Lantern changed his mind and came to the party, I'm leaving! Thanks and good night. Hal Jordan
11

LATER, AFTER *GREEN LANTERN* HAS RETURNED TO EXPLAIN ALL...

THE FIRST *GREEN LANTERN* WAS AN IMPOSTOR? THEN IT WASN'T YOUR *FACE* I SAW?

NO, CAROL! AND I SUPPOSE YOU'RE--er--STILL CURIOUS!

SUDDENLY, CAROL'S HAND WHIPS OUT AT *GL'S* MASK...

YES, I AM! AND THIS TIME I'M GOING TO GET THE MASK OFF THE REAL *GREEN LANTERN*-- EH?

IT WON'T COME-- IT WON'T COME OFF!

NO! MY STRINGLESS MASK IS FIXED ON BY THE FORCE OF MY *POWER RING,* CAROL! NO POWER ON EARTH CAN GET IT OFF AGAINST MY WILL!

NOW--SHALL WE JOIN THE PARTY, CAROL?

I STILL HAVEN'T SEEN THE FACE OF MY BELOVED! BUT I HAVE THE STRONGEST FEELING--THAT *SOME DAY* I WILL!

The End

12

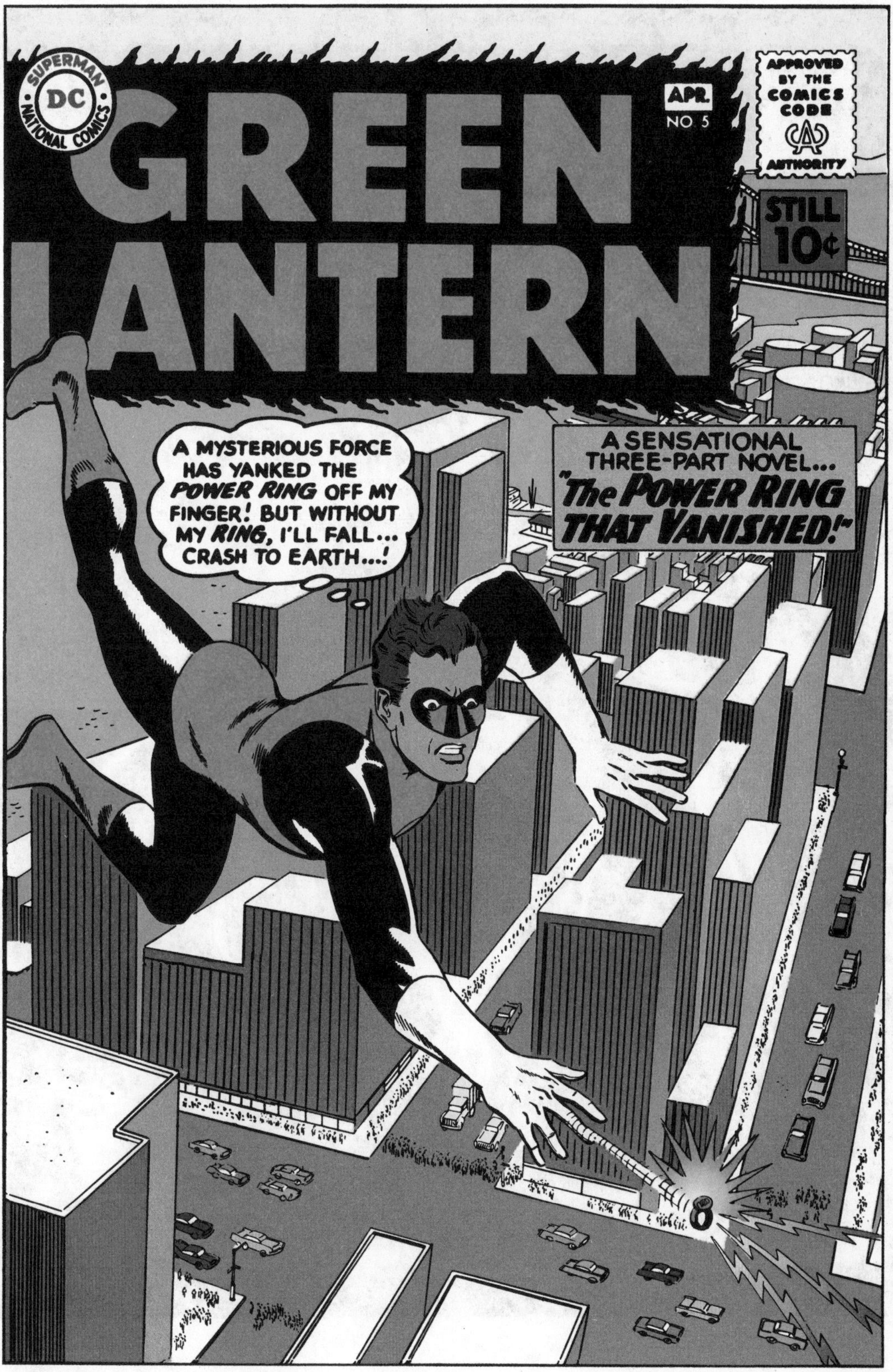
SUPERMAN
DC
NATIONAL COMICS
GREEN
ANTERN
APR.
NO 5
APPROVED BY THE COMICS CODE AUTHORITY
STILL 10¢
A MYSTERIOUS FORCE HAS YANKED THE *POWER RING* OFF MY FINGER! BUT WITHOUT MY *RING*, I'LL FALL... CRASH TO EARTH...!
A SENSATIONAL THREE-PART NOVEL... *"The POWER RING THAT VANISHED!"*

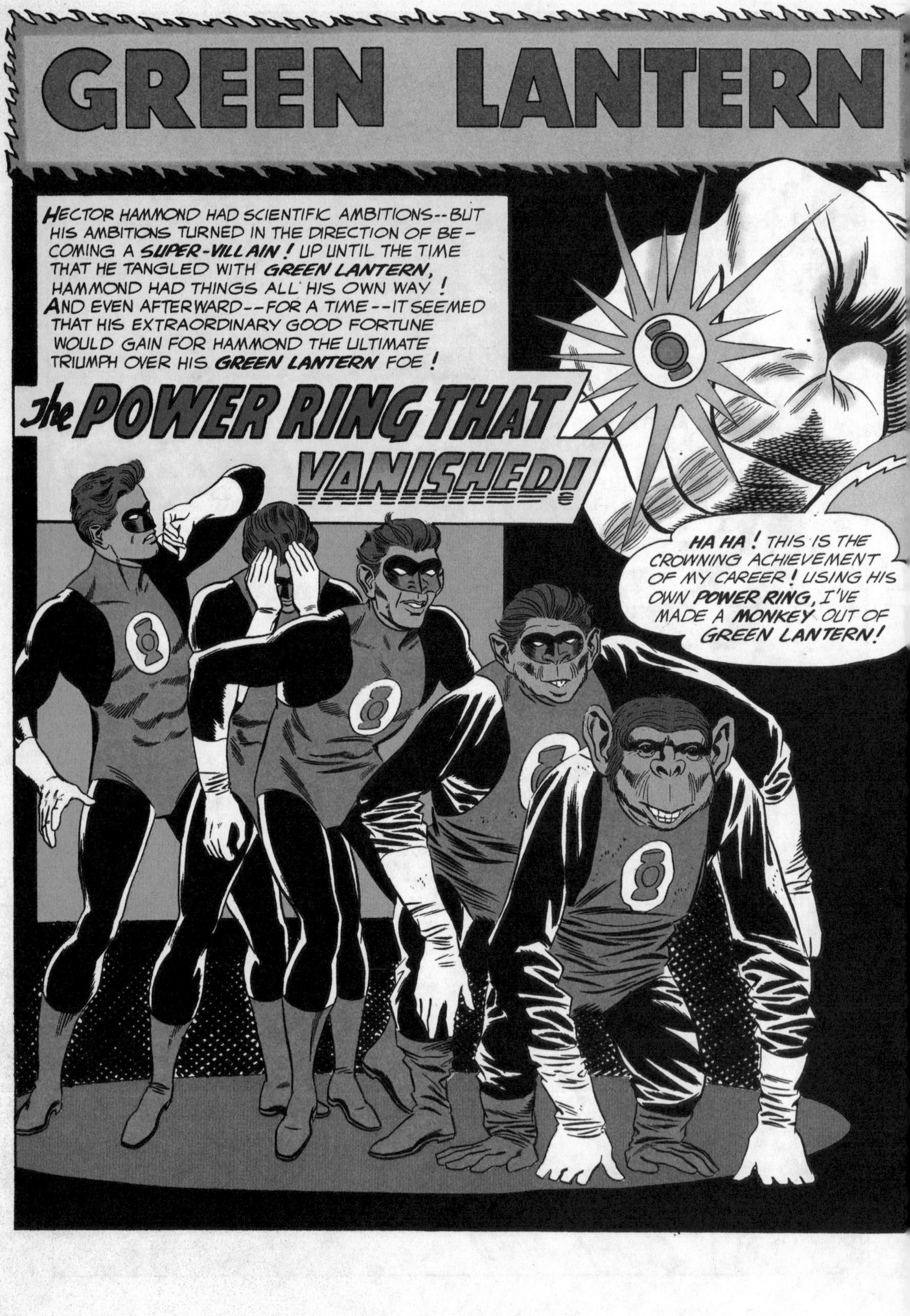
GREEN LANTERN
HECTOR HAMMOND HAD SCIENTIFIC AMBITIONS--BUT HIS AMBITIONS TURNED IN THE DIRECTION OF BE-COMING A SUPER-VILLAIN! UP UNTIL THE TIME THAT HE TANGLED WITH GREEN LANTERN, HAMMOND HAD THINGS ALL HIS OWN WAY! AND EVEN AFTERWARD--FOR A TIME--IT SEEMED THAT HIS EXTRAORDINARY GOOD FORTUNE WOULD GAIN FOR HAMMOND THE ULTIMATE TRIUMPH OVER HIS GREEN LANTERN FOE!
The POWER RING THAT VANISHED!
HA HA! THIS IS THE CROWNING ACHIEVEMENT OF MY CAREER! USING HIS OWN POWER RING, I'VE MADE A MONKEY OUT OF GREEN LANTERN!

As a familiar figure flies high over COAST CITY...

IT'S GREEN LANTERN!

BOY! THAT POWER RING OF HIS-- LOOK AT HIM GO WITH IT!

BUT THE FOLLOWING INSTANT...

EH? SOME INVISIBLE FORCE HAS STRUCK ME--YANKING THE POWER RING RIGHT OFF MY FINGER!

AND A MOMENT LATER...

I'M FALLING--IN A LONG ARC DOWNWARD LIKE A GLIDER! BUT WITHOUT MY RING I'LL CRASH--THERE ISN'T A CHANCE FOR ME!

WE KNOW WHAT YOU'RE THINKING, READER! WHO COULD POSSIBLY STRIP THE EMERALD CRUSADER OF HIS INVINCIBLE POWER RING? HOW DID THIS INCREDIBLE SITUATION COME ABOUT? FOR THE STARTLING DETAILS THAT LED UP TO THIS DRAMATIC MOMENT, LET US TURN BACK THE CLOCK BEFORE WE GO ANY FURTHER...

...TO A SCENE IN AN EXCLUSIVE SUBURBAN ESTATE WHERE A GAY GATHERING HAS COLLECTED SOME TIME EARLIER...

THIS HECTOR HAMMOND HAS BECOME THE LION OF SOCIETY!

AND TO THINK--ONLY A MONTH AGO HARDLY ANYONE HAD EVER HEARD OF THE FELLOW!

THEY SAY HIS KNOWL- EDGE OF SCIENCE IS UNCANNY!

I DON'T LIKE HIM! 2

AT LUNCHEON SOON AFTER...

OH, MY! THAT WAITER SPILLED A BOWL OF SOUP OVER HAMMOND!

WATCH HIM LOSE HIS GOOD HUMOR *NOW*!

BUT TO THE AMAZEMENT OF ALL, THE CELEBRITY REMAINS CALM...

PLEASE BRING ME A FRESH NAPKIN, WAITER!

OF C-COURSE, SIR!

YOU SEE, I HAD THIS SUIT MADE BY A SPECIAL *CHEMICAL FORMULA* OF MY OWN! ANY *STAIN* CAN MERELY BE WIPED RIGHT OFF IT!

WELL, HOW DO YOU LIKE THAT!

AND LATER...

HECTOR HAMMOND HAS INVITED US ALL TO CONTINUE THE PARTY AT HIS HOUSE! YOU'LL COME, WON'T YOU, CAROL?

OF COURSE, SUE!

AS *CAROL FERRIS*, DAUGHTER OF THE OWNER OF THE *FERRIS AIRCRAFT COMPANY*＊, PREPARES TO LEAVE WITH THE OTHERS...

I FIND MR. HAMMOND FASCINATING! HE'S THE FIRST MAN I'VE MET WHO MIGHT VERY WELL MAKE ME FORGET *GREEN LANTERN*!

*Editor's Note: AND NOW SOLE MANAGER SINCE HER FATHER LEFT HER IN CHARGE ON EMBARKING ON A RECENT ROUND-THE-WORLD TOUR!

ON THE WAY...

I'VE HEARD FASCINATING STORIES ABOUT THIS *NEW* HOUSE OF YOURS, MR. HAMMOND! IS IT REALLY SO UNUSUAL?

WAIT TILL YOU SEE IT, MISS FERRIS! I DON'T LIKE TO *BOAST*!

SOON, ON THE OUTSKIRTS OF THE METROPOLIS...

THERE IT IS!

WELL, THE HOUSE CERTAINLY IS STRIKING-LOOKING! BUT SO FAR I DON'T SEE ANY-THING UNUSUAL ABOUT IT...

LET'S ALL GO IN! IT'S A CLOUDY DAY--BUT I THINK A GALA PARTY LIKE THIS DESERVES BRIGHT SUNLIGHT! IT'LL BE MY PLEASURE TO DO SOMETHING ABOUT THAT!

WHAT CAN HE MEAN?

THEN, AFTER ALL THE GUESTS ARE INSIDE THE HOUSE, AN INCREDIBLE OCCURRENCE...

WE'RE GOING UP--RISING LIKE A BALLOON!

YES! IT'S MY OWN INVENTION--A HOUSE THAT CAN RISE ABOVE THE CLOUDS TO FINE WEATHER ANY TIME I WISH! AT THE TURN OF A SWITCH!

IT'S UTTERLY FANTASTIC!

YET QUITE SIMPLE, MISS FERRIS! THIS HOUSE IS BUILT OF A RARE LIGHT STRUCTURAL METAL OF MY OWN DISCOVERY! AND IT RISES WHEN A CERTAIN GAS IS RELEASED IN HIDDEN POCKETS IN THE WALLS!

WE REALLY ARE ABOVE THE CLOUDS!

YES! I ALWAYS PICK THE KIND OF WEATHER THAT SUITS MY MOOD! BUT LET ME SHOW YOU AROUND THE HOUSE!

4

AS THE WONDERS OF HAMMOND'S SCIENTIFIC DOMICILE ARE REVEALED...

THIS IS MY PRIVATE ASTRONOMICAL LABORATORY! I'VE MADE DISCOVERIES THAT SCIENCE IS NOT EVEN AWARE OF YET!

HOW MARVELOUS!

WHILE CAROL FERRIS DOES NOT KNOW WHICH TO ADMIRE MORE, THE ASTONISHING HOUSE-- OR THE MAN WHO BUILT IT...

MORE AND MORE I FEEL MYSELF DRAWN TO HECTOR HAMMOND! I WONDER IF I'M GOING FOR HIM ROMANTICALLY-- AND WHAT *GREEN LANTERN* WOULD SAY IF HE KNEW IT!

MEANWHILE, AT THE *FERRIS* PLANT, *GREEN LANTERN'S* ALTER EGO HAL JORDAN DOES KNOW A THING OR TWO...

NO, IT'S NOT JUST JEALOUSY WHICH HAS CAUSED ME TO CHECK UP ON THIS HECTOR HAMMOND, *PIEFACE*-- EVEN THOUGH I KNEW HE AND CAROL HAVE BEEN SEEING A LOT OF EACH OTHER LATELY!

THEN WHAT IS IT, HAL?

AS THE ACE TEST PILOT EXPLAINS TO HIS TRUSTED MECHANIC...

MY FINDINGS SHOW THAT HAMMOND HAS EXTRAORDINARY TALENTS IN *FOUR SCIENCES* --CHEMISTRY, PHYSICS, ASTRONOMY, AND BIOLOGY! NOW BY A STRANGE COINCIDENCE...

...THOSE HAPPEN TO BE THE *SPECIALTIES* OF THE *FOUR SCIENTISTS* WHO DISAPPEARED FROM THIS AREA SOME MONTHS AGO WITHOUT LEAVING A TRACE!*

JUMPING FISHHOOKS, HAL! THAT'S *RIGHT*!

*Editor's Note: A CASE WHICH HAS UTTERLY BAFFLED THE POLICE!

BUT YOU DON'T THINK THAT HAMMOND--

I DON'T THINK ANYTHING, YET, *PIE*! I JUST SAY IT'S A STRANGE COINCIDENCE! BUT ONE THAT *BEARS INVESTIGATION*! NOW LISTEN, THIS IS WHAT I PROPOSE TO DO...

SOON AFTER, BEHIND LOCKED DOORS IN HAL'S DRESSING ROOM AT THE HANGAR, A MYSTIC RITE TAKES PLACE...

IN BRIGHTEST DAY, IN BLACKEST NIGHT, NO EVIL SHALL ESCAPE MY SIGHT! LET THOSE WHO WORSHIP EVIL'S MIGHT BEWARE MY POWER-- GREEN LANTERN'S LIGHT!

G-GOLLY! THAT'S THE FIRST TIME I'VE EVER SEEN YOU CHARGE YOUR-RING AND TAKE YOUR OATH, GREEN LANTERN!

IT'S ONLY FITTING THAT YOU SHOULD SEE ME NOW, PIE...

...SINCE YOU ARE GOING TO IMPERSONATE ME DURING THE NEXT DAY OR SO! ARE YOU SURE YOU CAN CARRY OUT YOUR PART OF OUR SCHEME?

JUST GIVE ME A CHANCE, THAT'S ALL I ASK!

*Editor's Note: BY CHARGING HIS RING AT HIS AMAZING LAMP, GREEN LANTERN GETS POWER FOR TWENTY-FOUR HOURS!

AND SHORTLY AS AN EMERALD-GLINTING FIGURE SLIPS UNSEEN FROM THE CITY...

SO FAR SO GOOD! USING MY RING, I'VE TURNED PIEFACE INTO AN ABSOLUTE REPLICA OF ME-- INCLUDING THE POWER RING! AND HE KNOWS HIS MISSION--WHICH IS TO KEEP HIMSELF CONTINUOUSLY ON DISPLAY IN THE CITY...

...SO THAT HECTOR HAMMOND WON'T BE AWARE I'M NOT THERE! AND WHILE PIE-FACE IS DOING THAT, I'LL BE COMBING EVERY INCH OF THIS ENTIRE COAST FOR THE FOUR MISSING SCIENTISTS!

ACCORDING TO MY HUNCH, THOSE SCIENTISTS ARE SOMEWHERE IN THIS VICINITY-- PROBABLY CAPTIVES! MY POWER RING CAN ACT AS AN X-RAY, PROBING THESE HILLS FOR HIDDEN CAVES OR CAM-OUFLAGED SHACKS...!

6

IF HECTOR HAMMOND HAD ANYTHING TO DO WITH THE DISAPPEARANCES, I DON'T WANT HIM TO SUSPECT I'M SEARCHING FOR THE MEN--NOT YET! AND BY IMPERSONATING ME, *PIEFACE* WILL TAKE CARE OF THAT ANGLE!

BACK IN *COAST CITY*, A REMARKABLE TRANSFORMATION HAS TAKEN PLACE...

WOOOEEE! I LOOK LIKE *GREEN LANTERN!* I AM *GREEN LANTERN!* I'VE EVEN GOT A *POWER RING!* I CAN HARDLY WAIT TO TRY IT OUT!

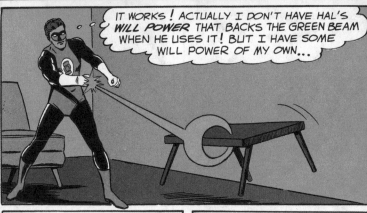

IT WORKS! ACTUALLY I DON'T HAVE HAL'S *WILL POWER* THAT BACKS THE GREEN BEAM WHEN HE USES IT! BUT I HAVE SOME WILL POWER OF MY OWN...

...ENOUGH TO SLIP THROUGH THE HANGAR WALL AND FLY IN THE AIR! *JUMPING FISHHOOKS!* WHAT A SENSATION--!!

FREE AS A BIRD, THE TRANSFORMED GREASEMONKEY CAN'T GET ENOUGH OF HIS WONDERFUL NEW ABILITIES...

FLYING THIS HIGH WITH NOTHING UNDER ME GIVES ME A FUNNY TICKLY FEELING IN THE STOMACH!

LOOK AT *GREEN LANTERN!*

HE SEEMS TO HAVE GOTTEN SPRING FEVER!

MEANWHILE, OTHER EYES ARE ON THE SWOOPING GREEN FIGURE...

GREEN LANTERN IS PUTTING ON *QUITE A SHOW!* I SUPPOSE IT'S HIS JUVENILE WAY OF TRYING TO IMPRESS CAROL FERRIS! BUT I THINK HE MAY BE TOO LATE ON THAT SCORE!

HIS PARTY OVER, HECTOR HAMMOND IS ALONE...

CAROL IS A JEWEL! SHE'S SO LOVELY--AND SUCH A DELIGHT-FUL PERSON! PERHAPS I'LL EVEN MARRY HER! I MUST GIVE THAT MATTER A LITTLE MORE *SCIENTIFIC* THOUGHT! BUT RIGHT NOW...

...IT'S TIME I PAID A VISIT TO MY *FOUR WISE OLD MEN!* THAT'S SOMETHING THAT WOULD INTEREST *GREEN LANTERN*-- IF HE WASN'T SO BUSY SHOWING OFF! HA HA!

AT THAT MOMENT ON A CRAGGY AND ISOLATED ISLE OFF THE COAST...

WE MUST HURRY! THE *MASTER* MAY BE HERE SOON!

DO YOU THINK IT WILL WORK, DR. EVART?

IT MUST WORK, PROFESSOR PAULSON! DON'T FORGET, THE *MASTER* HAS EVOLVED US--BY HIS DIABOLIC METHODS--INTO HUMANS SUCH AS WILL EXIST ON EARTH *100,000* YEARS FROM NOW!

TRUE! AND OUR BRAINS ARE CAPABLE OF THE MOST *COMPLEX* THOUGHT AND DISCOVERY!

YES! AND IT IS BY MEANS OF OUR BRAINS THAT WE HAVE CONSTRUCTED A WAY TO ESCAPE FROM HERE! TURN ON THE *TELE-VIEWER,* HORTON!

⑧

As a dial is turned...

THERE HE IS AGAIN-- THE ONLY ONE WHO CAN SAVE US!

WE MUST BRING *GREEN LANTERN* HERE! TURN ON THE OTHER SWITCH, HORTON!

WITH THE PUSH OF A TINY LEVER, A BOLT OF *SIGMA ENERGY*, CREATED BY THE SUPER-ADVANCED MINDS OF THE FOUR CAPTIVE SCIENTISTS, SPURTS FROM THE MACHINE...

THERE IT GOES!

BE SURE IT'S AIMED RIGHT!

3000 BEV'S! IT WILL TAKE A MINUTE OR TWO MORE TO BUILD UP THE NECESSARY FORCE!

OUR *LIVES* DEPEND ON IT!

3000
2500
2000

MEANWHILE, ALL UNAWARE, THE TRANSFORMED *PIEFACE* IS STILL ENJOYING HIMSELF...

I DON'T HAVE A THING TO WORRY ABOUT! *GL* SAID THAT HE FIXED MY RING SO THAT IF HECTOR HAMMOND TRIED TO LEAVE THE CITY, IT WOULD *GIVE THE ALARM!*

HE ALSO SAID THAT MY RING WOULD BE JUST THE SAME AS HIS--EXCEPT THAT IT *CAN'T BE CHARGED UP* ONCE IT RUNS OUT OF POWER AFTER TWENTY-FOUR HOURS! I MUST REMEMBER THAT--EH?

SUDDENLY...

JUMPING FISH-HOOKS! MY RING IS QUIVERING-- EMITTING A GLOW! THAT'S THE SIGNAL-- IT MEANS HAMMOND IS LEAVING THE CITY AND *I'VE GOT TO FOLLOW HIM--!*

BUT BEFORE *GREEN LANTERN'S* DUPLICATE CAN EVEN TURN, ANOTHER EXTRAORDINARY THING HAPPENS...

AND THE NEXT MOMENT...

MY RING--YANKED OFF MY FINGER! I'M FALLING... BUT STILL IN THE GRIP OF THAT MYSTERIOUS FORCE!

S-SOMETHING IS GRABBING HOLD OF ME! STARTING TO PULL ME THROUGH THE AIR! I--I'M POWERLESS AGAINST IT--!

BACK ON THE ISLAND PRISON OF THE FOUR SCIENTISTS...

OUR *SIGMA-RAY* PULLED THE *POWER RING* OFF *GREEN LANTERN'S* FINGER!

I CAN EXPLAIN THAT, DR. EVART!

THE FREQUENCY OF VIBRATION OF THE *RING* IS DIFFERENT FROM THE REST OF *GREEN LANTERN'S BODY!* THEREFORE OUR *SIGMA-RAY* HAS A SLIGHTLY GREATER EFFECT ON IT AND IS PULLING IT FASTER TO US THAN *GREEN LANTERN* HIMSELF!

CAREFUL, PROFESSOR-- BRING HIM IN SLOWLY-- OR HE'LL BE HURT!

THEN, AS *"GREEN LANTERN"* IS BROUGHT TO EARTH...

J-JUMPING FISHHOOKS! WHERE AM I?

PART TWO OF *"THE POWER RING THAT VANISHED"* BEGINS ON THE *FOLLOWING PAGE!*

10

THESE CREATURES MUST BE THE MISSING SCIENTISTS! THEY WERE *CHANGED* SOMEHOW BY *HECTOR HAMMOND* -- HE'S KEEPING THEM PRISONER HERE! AND THEY EXPECT *ME* TO HELP THEM *ESCAPE* --!

YOU *MUST* HELP US ESCAPE, *GREEN LANTERN!*

I HATE TO TELL THEM I'M *NOT* GREEN LANTERN! BUT THE TROUBLE IS, EVEN IF I WAS -- I COULDN'T HELP THEM ...

I HAVEN'T GOT MY RING!

YOUR RING --!?

THAT'S RIGHT! WE SAW IT FLY OUT OF HIS HAND --! BUT WITHOUT HIS RING HE CAN'T GET US PAST THE *BARRIER!*

WHAT *BARRIER* --?

IT'S AN *INVISIBLE FORCE* THAT HAMMOND SET UP TO KEEP US CAPTIVE HERE! OBJECTS CAN ENTER THROUGH IT--BUT NOTHING---EXCEPT HAMMOND HIMSELF--CAN GET OUT!

LET'S LOOK FOR THE RING! IT MAY HAVE FALLEN HERE WITHOUT OUR SEEING IT!

AT THAT MOMENT A LITTLE WAY OFF ON THE TINY ISLE...

WHAT'S *THIS*...?

AS HECTOR HAMMOND, THE JAILOR OF THE SCIENTISTS, EXAMINES HIS FIND MORE CLOSELY...

UNLESS I'M DEAD WRONG THIS IS *GREEN LANTERN'S POWER RING!* THERE'S A WAY OF MAKING SURE!

WITH GREAT INTEREST, HAMMOND DONS THE RING AND...

AMAZING! BY EXERTING MY *WILL* I CAN DO ANYTHING--SUCH AS SHRIVELING THAT WILD APPLE TREE INTO A DEAD AND ROTTING STUMP!

THIS RING HERE MEANS THAT *GREEN LANTERN* MAY BE HERE TOO! AND IF HE IS, HE'S HELPLESS AGAINST ME--SINCE HIS *POWER RING* IS NOW IN MY POSSESSION! HA HA! MY *LUCK* IS HOLDING FAST!

AS THE SUPER-VILLAIN STRIDES CONFIDENTLY FORWARD, HIS THOUGHTS ARE CONFIDENT TOO...

EVER SINCE I FIRST SPIED THE *METEOR*, MY INCREDIBLE *LUCK* HAS BEEN WITH ME ALL THE WAY! I'LL NEVER FORGET THAT MOMENT I SET EYES ON IT A YEAR AGO...

12

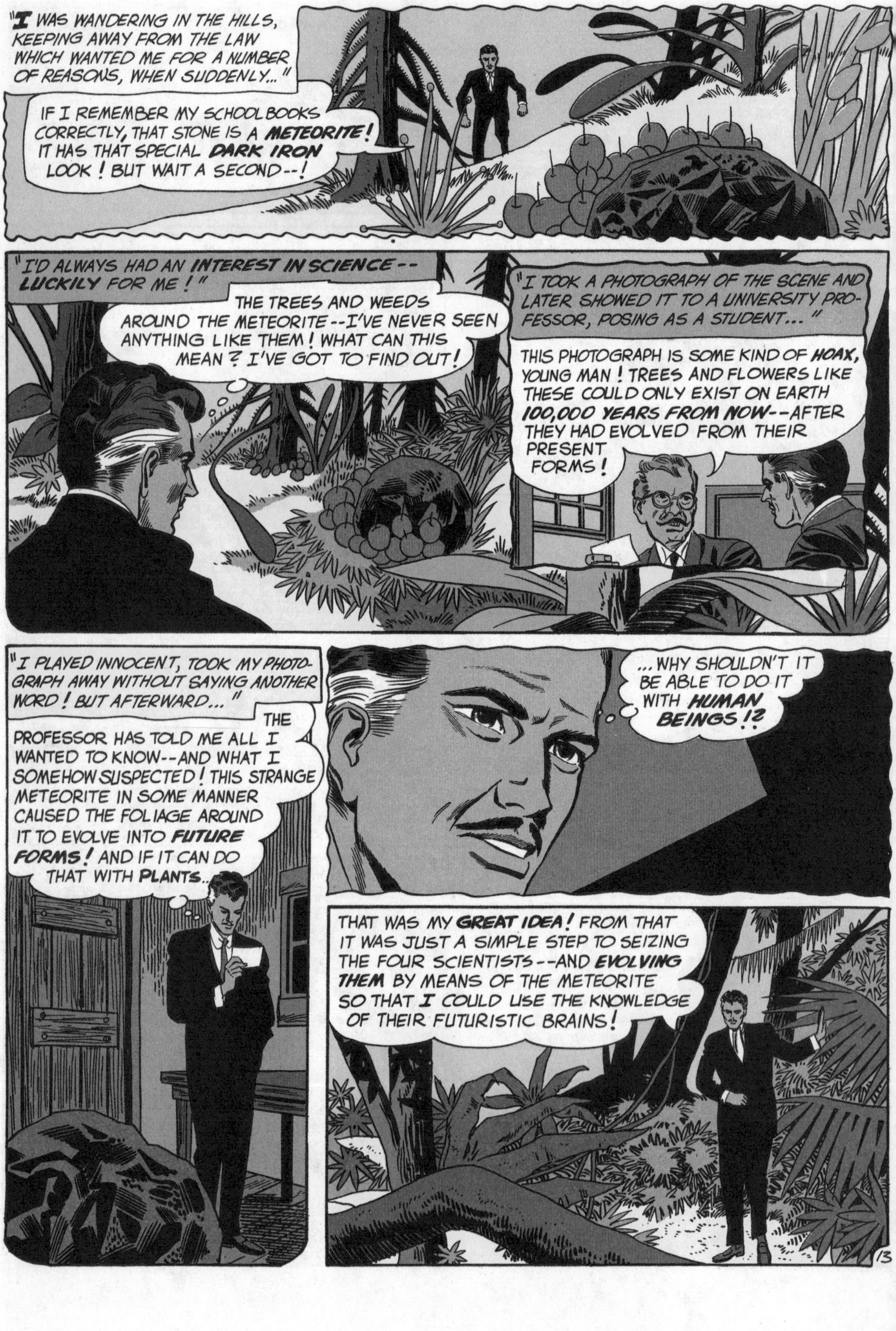
"I WAS WANDERING IN THE HILLS, KEEPING AWAY FROM THE LAW WHICH WANTED ME FOR A NUMBER OF REASONS, WHEN SUDDENLY..."
IF I REMEMBER MY SCHOOL BOOKS CORRECTLY, THAT STONE IS A METEORITE! IT HAS THAT SPECIAL DARK IRON LOOK! BUT WAIT A SECOND--!
"I'D ALWAYS HAD AN INTEREST IN SCIENCE--LUCKILY FOR ME!"
THE TREES AND WEEDS AROUND THE METEORITE--I'VE NEVER SEEN ANYTHING LIKE THEM! WHAT CAN THIS MEAN? I'VE GOT TO FIND OUT!
"I TOOK A PHOTOGRAPH OF THE SCENE AND LATER SHOWED IT TO A UNIVERSITY PROFESSOR, POSING AS A STUDENT..."
THIS PHOTOGRAPH IS SOME KIND OF HOAX, YOUNG MAN! TREES AND FLOWERS LIKE THESE COULD ONLY EXIST ON EARTH 100,000 YEARS FROM NOW--AFTER THEY HAD EVOLVED FROM THEIR PRESENT FORMS!
"I PLAYED INNOCENT, TOOK MY PHOTOGRAPH AWAY WITHOUT SAYING ANOTHER WORD! BUT AFTERWARD..."
THE PROFESSOR HAS TOLD ME ALL I WANTED TO KNOW--AND WHAT I SOMEHOW SUSPECTED! THIS STRANGE METEORITE IN SOME MANNER CAUSED THE FOLIAGE AROUND IT TO EVOLVE INTO FUTURE FORMS! AND IF IT CAN DO THAT WITH PLANTS...
...WHY SHOULDN'T IT BE ABLE TO DO IT WITH HUMAN BEINGS!?
THAT WAS MY GREAT IDEA! FROM THAT IT WAS JUST A SIMPLE STEP TO SEIZING THE FOUR SCIENTISTS--AND EVOLVING THEM BY MEANS OF THE METEORITE SO THAT I COULD USE THE KNOWLEDGE OF THEIR FUTURISTIC BRAINS!
13

"ALL I HAD TO DO AFTER CAPTURING THEM WAS LOCK THEM UP WITH THE METEORITE ON THIS LONELY ISLE..."

DAY BY DAY THEY'RE CHANGING INTO HUMANS OF THE FUTURE WITH *INCREDIBLE BRAIN-POWER*! THROUGH THEM I'LL LEARN THE ANSWERS TO ALL THE THINGS I WANT TO KNOW!

"BY SHEER *LUCK* THE SAME METEOR-RAY THAT EVOLVED THE SCIENTISTS WEAKENED THEIR WILL POWER! THEY COULD REFUSE ME NOTHING!"

I WANT TO THROW AN INVISIBLE FORCE-FIELD AROUND THIS LABORATORY! FIGURE IT OUT AND TELL ME HOW TO DO IT!

WE CANNOT HELP OUR-SELVES! WE MUST DO WHAT HE SAYS...!

"AND THAT WAS HOW AFTER CHANGING MY NAME TO FOOL THE POLICE, I BECAME THE *AMAZING HECTOR HAMMOND, WONDER MAN OF SCIENCE!* HA HA.."

I COULD HAVE EVOLVED *MYSELF* OF COURSE -- BUT I WANTED TO REMAIN A NORMAL-LOOKING HUMAN IN ORDER TO MINGLE WITH OTHER HUMANS AND ENJOY MY POWER! THIS WAY IS BETTER! AND NOW FOR A LOOK AT MY CAPTIVES...

AT THAT MOMENT...

HERE COMES HAMMOND NOW -- THROUGH THE BARRIER! WE MUST SUBDUE HIM -- ALL OF US TOGETHER! IT IS OUR ONLY CHANCE!

COUNT ME IN ON THIS, FELLERS!

CHARGE!

WHAT'S THIS? AN *ATTACK* -- LED BY *GREEN LANTERN*!? SO I WAS RIGHT -- HE *IS* HERE!

INSTANTLY THE KEEN-WITTED ARCH-VILLAIN WILLS THE *POWER RING* TO FORM A HUGE HOSE WHICH EMITS A POWERFUL JET OF COMPRESSED AIR AT HIS ATTACKERS...

HA HA! HITTING THEM IN THE LEGS THIS WAY WON'T HURT THEM TOO BADLY, BUT IT WILL TAKE ALL THE FIGHT OUT OF THEM, I'LL BET!

JUMPING FISHHOOKS! HE'S GOT MY *RING*!

14

AND SOON, WITH HIS FOES RENDERED HELPLESS BY THE MYSTICAL **GREEN BEAM**...

HOW DID **GREEN LANTERN** GET HERE? EXPLAIN!

WE CANNOT HELP OURSELVES--HIS **WILL POWER** IS TOO STRONG! WE MUST ANSWER!

AFTER THE TRUTH OF THE LITTLE PLOT HAS EMERGED...

HOW ABOUT THAT! I TURNED YOU INTO MEN OF THE FUTURE! YOU KNOW MORE THAN MANKIND WILL FOR CENTURIES! AND ALL I ASK IS THAT YOU STAY HERE AND SHARE YOUR KNOWLEDGE WITH ME! AND ARE YOU SATISFIED? NO...

YOU INSIST ON TRYING TO ESCAPE! FOOLS! THERE IS NO ESCAPE FOR YOU! YOU MUST ALWAYS REMAIN HIDDEN--SO THE WORLD WILL NEVER KNOW THE SOURCE OF MY SCIENTIFIC WONDERS! AND AS FOR **GREEN LANTERN**...

SOMEHOW I HAD EXPECTED MORE OF A **BATTLE** WHEN **GREEN LANTERN** AND I FINALLY CAME UP AGAINST EACH OTHER--AS I KNEW WE WOULD SOMEDAY! BUT I GUESS I **OVERRATED** YOU...

IF HE DIDN'T HAVE THAT RING...!

ONE THING IS SURE! YOU WILL NEVER BOTHER ME AGAIN! I'M GOING TO USE YOUR OWN **POWER RING** TO **CHANGE YOU, GREEN LANTERN!** BUT IN A **DIFFERENT** WAY FROM THE CHANGE I MADE IN THESE SCIENTISTS!

A STARTLING TRANSFORMATION BEGINS TO COME OVER THE DISGUISED **PIEFACE**...

WH--WHAT'S HAPPENING TO ME!?

(15)

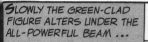

SLOWLY THE GREEN-CLAD FIGURE ALTERS UNDER THE ALL-POWERFUL BEAM...

THE DIFFERENCE, *GREEN LANTERN,* IS THAT I'M EVOLVING YOU *BACKWARD* INSTEAD OF FORWARD... FAR BACKWARD...

AS THE CHANGE BECOMES COMPLETE...

HA HA! LOOK AT THE MIGHTY *GREEN LANTERN!* FROM NOW ON I'M GOING TO KEEP YOU AROUND FOR LAUGHS!

J-JUMPING FISHHOOKS!

THE THINGS I DO FOR A PAL! I WAS JUST HELPING OUT THE *REAL GREEN LANTERN*--AND LOOK WHAT HAPPENS! THIS ODD-BALL MAKES A *MONKEY* OUTA ME!

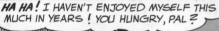

HA HA! I HAVEN'T ENJOYED MYSELF THIS MUCH IN YEARS! YOU HUNGRY, PAL?

OF COURSE I COULD TELL HAMMOND HE'S MADE A MISTAKE--THAT I'M NOT REALLY *GREEN LANTERN...*

...BUT WILD HORSES COULDN'T DRAG THAT INFORMATION OUT OF ME! AND WHEN THE REAL *GL* CATCHES UP WITH THIS GUY, HE'LL MAKE A "*MONKEY*" OUTA *HIM!*

HAVE A BANANA! HA HA!

BUT WHERE IS THE *REAL GREEN LANTERN?* AT THAT VERY MOMENT, HE IS HEADING OUT TO OPEN SEA...

MY RING HAS PICKED UP SOME *ODD VIBRATIONS,* AS FROM ANOTHER *POWER BEAM* AT WORK IN THIS DIRECTION! BUT I LEFT *PIEFACE* AND HIS *POWER RING* BACK IN *COAST CITY!* WHAT COULD BE CAUSING THE VIBRATIONS OUT HERE AT SEA--!?

FOR THE STARTLING CONCLUSION TO "*THE POWER RING THAT VANISHED*" TURN TO THE FOLLOWING PAGE!

16

The POWER RING THAT VANISHED! PART THREE

HOUR AFTER HOUR, A GRIM *GREEN LANTERN* SEARCHES FOR THE SOURCE OF THE MYSTERIOUS VIBRATIONS...

THE VIBRATIONS HAVE STOPPED..., AND THERE'S NOTHING OUT HERE BUT OCEAN! YET MY HUNCH IS I WAS ON THE *RIGHT TRACK*...!

ALL THROUGH THE NIGHT--AFTER PAUSING ONLY TO RECHARGE HIS RING--THE DAUNTLESS GLADIATOR CONTINUES HIS PATROL...

CAN'T REST FOR AN INSTANT! I'VE *GOT* TO KEEP ON THE ALERT FOR THOSE VIBRATIONS AGAIN! SOMETHING TELLS ME THIS IS THE MOST IMPORTANT TASK I'VE EVER UNDERTAKEN!

AND THEN, NEXT DAY...

THE SUN IS GLINTING ON SOMETHING--A TINY ISLAND! IT SEEMS UNINHABITED! BUT I'M GOING DOWN FOR A CLOSER LOOK! CAN'T LEAVE ANY STONE UNTURNED AT THIS STAGE--!

MEANWHILE, UNDER THE PROTECTIVE CAMOUFLAGE OF THE TINY ISLE...

HA, HA! WHAT A SENSATION IT WOULD CAUSE IF THE WORLD KNEW THAT I HAD TURNED YOU INTO A MONKEY, *GREEN LANTERN*--AND HAD YOU HERE IN A CAGE! BUT NO ONE MUST LEARN ABOUT IT YET...

HA HA YOURSELF WISE GUY! YOU'RE IN FOR A SURPRISE!

SOMETHING SEEMS TO HAVE CAPTURED THE MONKEY'S ATTENTION! WHAT--?

G-GREEN L-LANTERN?!

HECTOR HAMMOND! SO I WAS RIGHT ABOUT THIS ISLAND! I SMELL *SOMETHING CROOKED* GOING ON HERE RIGHT NOW!

BEFORE THE *EMERALD CRUSADER* CAN BRING HIS *POWER BEAM* INTO PLAY...

CAN'T UNDERSTAND THERE BEING *TWO GREEN LANTERNS*--BUT I BETTER HANDLE *THIS ONE TOO!*

THE *POWER RING!* HAMMOND HAS THE *POWER RING* I MADE FOR *PIEFACE!*

AS THE TWO *RING-WIELDERS* CLASH IN VIOLENT COMBAT...

THROWING A GREEN *JAVELIN* AT ME--CREATED BY HIS BEAM AND TRAVELING AT TERRIFIC SPEED!

INSTANTLY THE *GREEN GLADIATOR* REARS A DEFENSE...

¡WHEW!¡ ONLY A SHIELD MADE BY MY RING COULD HAVE PROTECTED ME-- I WHIPPED IT UP JUST IN TIME!

THUD!

AND A MOMENT LATER...

HE MADE A GREAT *BEAM-HAND* TO SEIZE ME--BUT I MADE ONE OF MY OWN TO PREVENT HIM! AND NOW THE QUESTION IS-- WHICH *POWER-HAND* CAN OVERPOWER THE OTHER!?

JUMPING FISHHOOKS! IT'S A KING-SIZE *HAND-WRESTLE!!*

18

SLOWLY, THE **GREEN GLADIATOR'S** CREATION GAINS THE "UPPER HAND"...

IT'S MY WILL POWER AGAINST HIS NOW! IF I CAN DEFEAT HIM I'LL SHATTER HIS **WILL TO RESIST**--

THEN, JUST WHEN THE FIGHT SEEMS TO GO AGAINST THE **SUPER-SCIENTIST**...

HE'S BROKEN OFF OUR **DUEL OF HANDS**-- AND IS STREAKING OUT OF HERE! I CAN'T LET HIM ESCAPE ME NOW!

THEN, OUTSIDE HAMMOND'S LABORATORY...

I NEED MORE TIME TO HANDLE THE **POWER RING** AS WELL AS **GREEN LANTERN** DOES! HE'S HAD MORE PRACTICE WITH IT, THAT'S ALL! SO TO GAIN TIME...

...I'LL SET UP THIS **JET-BLACK CLOUD** BEHIND ME, AND ESCAPE WHILE HE'S TRYING TO FIGHT HIS WAY THROUGH IT!

LIKE PLOWING THROUGH A SUPER-DENSE FOG...

AS THE DEVICE SERVES ITS PURPOSE, SLOWING DOWN THE **EMERALD WARRIOR**...

I'VE COME OUT OF THAT **BLACKNESS** HE SPREAD HERE OVER THE OCEAN! BUT WHERE IS **HE**?

AS THE SUPER-SENSITIVE RING ON **GL'S** FINGER PROVIDES A CLUE...

THOSE RING-VIBRATIONS-- I'M PICKING THEM UP AGAIN-- AND THEY TELL ME THAT **HAMMOND'S** HEADED FOR **COAST CITY**! I'VE GOT TO CORRAL HIM NOW! WITH THAT **POWER RING** HE COULD WREAK INCALCULABLE DAMAGE IN THE CITY!

THE RING TELLS ME *GREEN LANTERN'S* STILL ON *MY TRAIL!* I *MUST* DELAY HIM UNTIL I CAN FIND A WAY OF FINISHING HIM OFF! I'VE GOT TO CAUSE A DISTRACTION FOR HIM!

NEAR COAST CITY, A HUGE DAM REARS ITS WHITE EXPANSE...

TOO BAD THIS DAM HAS TO GO, BUT IT'S THE ONE WAY I CAN BE SURE OF GETTING *GREEN LANTERN* OFF MY HEELS--AT LEAST FOR A WHILE!

AS THE ALL-POWERFUL *GREEN BEAM* BLASTS DOWNWARD WITH TERRIBLE FORCE...

CRACK!

IN ABOUT HALF A MINUTE *COAST CITY* WILL BE STRUCK BY A GIGANTIC WAVE-- TRAVELING AT THE SPEED OF AN EXPRESS TRAIN! *THIS* WILL GIVE *GREEN LANTERN* SOMETHING TO THINK ABOUT BESIDES ME--!

AND SCARCELY SECONDS LATER...

THE DAM'S GIVEN WAY! ONLY THAT COULD HAVE CAUSED THAT *AVALANCHE OF WATER* TO POUR DOWN TOWARD *COAST CITY!*

20

As the aroused *GLADIATOR* tears toward the menacing water...

NO TIME NOW TO TRY TO REPAIR THE DAM-- I'VE GOT TO SAVE THE CITY! IT'LL BE DEMOLISHED IF THAT WATER HITS!

GOT TO THROW UP ANOTHER DAM TO HOLD BACK THE WATER-- AND DO IT FAST!

With his incredible *POWER RING*, GL completes in moments what it would take an army of workers months to accomplish...

NOW--WILL MY POWER-DAM HOLD BACK THE TREMENDOUS PRESSURE OF THAT WALL OF WATER? THE NEXT FEW SECONDS WILL TELL!

IT'S HOLDING! THE VALLEY BEYOND IS BEGINNING TO FILL UP WITH WATER-- THE CITY IS SAVED!

MEANWHILE, ON A CLIFFSIDE NOT FAR FROM THE CITY...

I'VE USED MY *POWER RING* TO CIRCLE THIS HILL WITH *MACHINE-GUN NESTS!* AND WITH MY *RING* I'LL BE ABLE TO FIRE THEM ALL AT ONCE -- AS SOON AS *GREEN LANTERN* SHOWS UP, AS I EXPECT HE WILL ANY TIME NOW!

MY AGILE FOE MAY BE ABLE TO DEFEND HIMSELF AGAINST MOST OF THE BULLETS, BUT *ONE* OR *TWO* FROM ODD ANGLES ARE BOUND TO *HIT HOME!* AND THAT WILL BE ENOUGH!

AND AT THAT VERY MOMENT...

I'M CONVINCED *HAMMOND* HAD SOMETHING TO DO WITH THAT BROKEN DAM! I'VE GOT TO LOCATE HIM AND PUT HIM OUT OF CIR-CULATION BEFORE HE CAN DO ANY MORE DAMAGE!

BUT AS FATE WOULD HAVE IT, A DRIED LIMB CHOOSES THIS INSTANT TO TOPPLE FROM A TALL TREE OVER THE *EMERALD CRUSADER*...

CLUNK

AND ON HIS FORTIFIED HILL, HAMMOND VIEWS A RARE SIGHT...

EH? EITHER I'M SEEING HAPPY MIRAGES, OR *GREEN LANTERN* HAS JUST BEEN KNOCKED HELPLESS RIGHT IN FRONT OF MY GUNS! TALK ABOUT MY LUCK!

22

AS THE SUPER-VILLAIN STARTS TO TAKE SWIFT ADVANTAGE...

I'LL FIRE ALL THE GUNS AT ONCE! FOR *GL* TO COME OUT OF THIS ALIVE, HE'LL HAVE TO BE A REAL *WONDER—WORKER!*

BUT THEN, AS WAS BOUND TO HAPPEN, HAMMOND'S LUCK FINALLY RUNS OUT...

THE *RING*—SUDDENLY IT'S LOST ITS *POWER!* I CAN'T SEEM TO MAKE IT WORK—NO MATTER HOW MUCH WILL POWER I SUMMON UP!

AND WHEN HAMMOND, IN DESPERATION, ABANDONS USE OF THE RING AND SCRAMBLES TOWARD ONE OF HIS GUNS...

I'LL BLAST HIM BY HAND! I--EH?

TOO LATE, MY FRIEND! THAT LITTLE DELAY WAS ALL I NEEDED TO COME TO MY SENSES--AND DISCOVER WHAT YOU WERE UP TO!

AS A GIANT BROOM WHISKS HAMMOND AWAY FROM THE GUN...

SOMEHOW YOU GOT HOLD OF MY DUPLICATE *POWER RING*—BUT YOU DIDN'T KNOW IT HAS TO BE *RECHARGED EVERY TWENTY—FOUR HOURS!* IT JUST RAN OUT OF POWER, THAT'S ALL!

BUT SINCE YOU DON'T HAVE A *POWER RING* ANY MORE, I WON'T USE MINE-- BECAUSE I DON'T NEED IT TO BRING YOU TO JUSTICE!

POW!

AND LATER, BACK ON THE ISLAND, AFTER *GREEN LANTERN* HAS USED HIS *RING* TO UNCOVER HAMMOND'S VILLAINY, AND TO SET CERTAIN MATTERS RIGHT AGAIN...

THANKS FOR BRINGING ME BACK TO MY OLD SELF AGAIN, *GREEN LANTERN!*

THAT'S NOT ALL I DID, *PIE*...

I RETURNED THE CAPTURED SCIENTISTS TO THEIR OLD SELVES AGAIN TOO--AND USED MY *GREEN BEAM* TO REMOVE ALL TRACES FROM THEIR MINDS OF THE *FUTURISTIC ADVANCES OF SCIENCE* THEY MADE HERE! AND I'VE DONE THE SAME FOR HAMMOND!

IT'S BETTER FOR EARTH-- SCIENCE TO PROGRESS GRADUALLY AND NOT MAKE ANY DISCOVERIES *AHEAD OF TIME*-- SO THAT UNSCRUPULOUS MEN LIKE HAMMOND CAN'T TAKE ADVANTAGE OF THEM!

I GUESS YOU'RE RIGHT, *GL!* THIS WAY IS BETTER...

LATER, AS CAROL FERRIS LEARNS OF HAMMOND'S EVIL PLOT...

HMMM...!

5¢ COAST NEWS 5¢

HECTOR HAMMOND EXPOSED AS CUNNING FRAUD!

CAPTURED BY GREEN LANTERN!

WHAT DID I EVER SEE IN THIS HECTOR HAMMOND? SOMETIMES I THINK I HAVE A FLIGHTY MIND...

BUT NOW I KNOW IT'S *GREEN LANTERN* I'M CRAZY ABOUT-- IT'S REALLY BEEN HIM ALL ALONG!

AND AT STATE PRISON IN DUE COURSE AN ADDITION IS MADE TO THE STAFF OF THE PRISON LIBRARY..

THIS IS A GOOD JOB FOR HAMMOND, WARDEN! HE ATTEMPTED TO GET KNOWLEDGE THE EASY WAY-- BY CAPTURING OTHER MEN AND USING THEIR BRAINS! NOW HE CAN TRY IT HERE THE *HARD WAY*-- BY HIMSELF!

BUT CAN HECTOR HAMMOND TAKE ADVANTAGE OF HIS OPPORTUNITY...

ALL KNOWLEDGE OF THE *PAST, PRESENT,* AND *FUTURE* IS CONTAINED IN THE *WORDS* OF THIS UN-ABRIDGED DICTIONARY-- BUT HOW DO I GO ABOUT STRINGING THE WORDS TOGETHER IN THE RIGHT ORDER TO GIVE ME THAT KNOWLEDGE?

The End

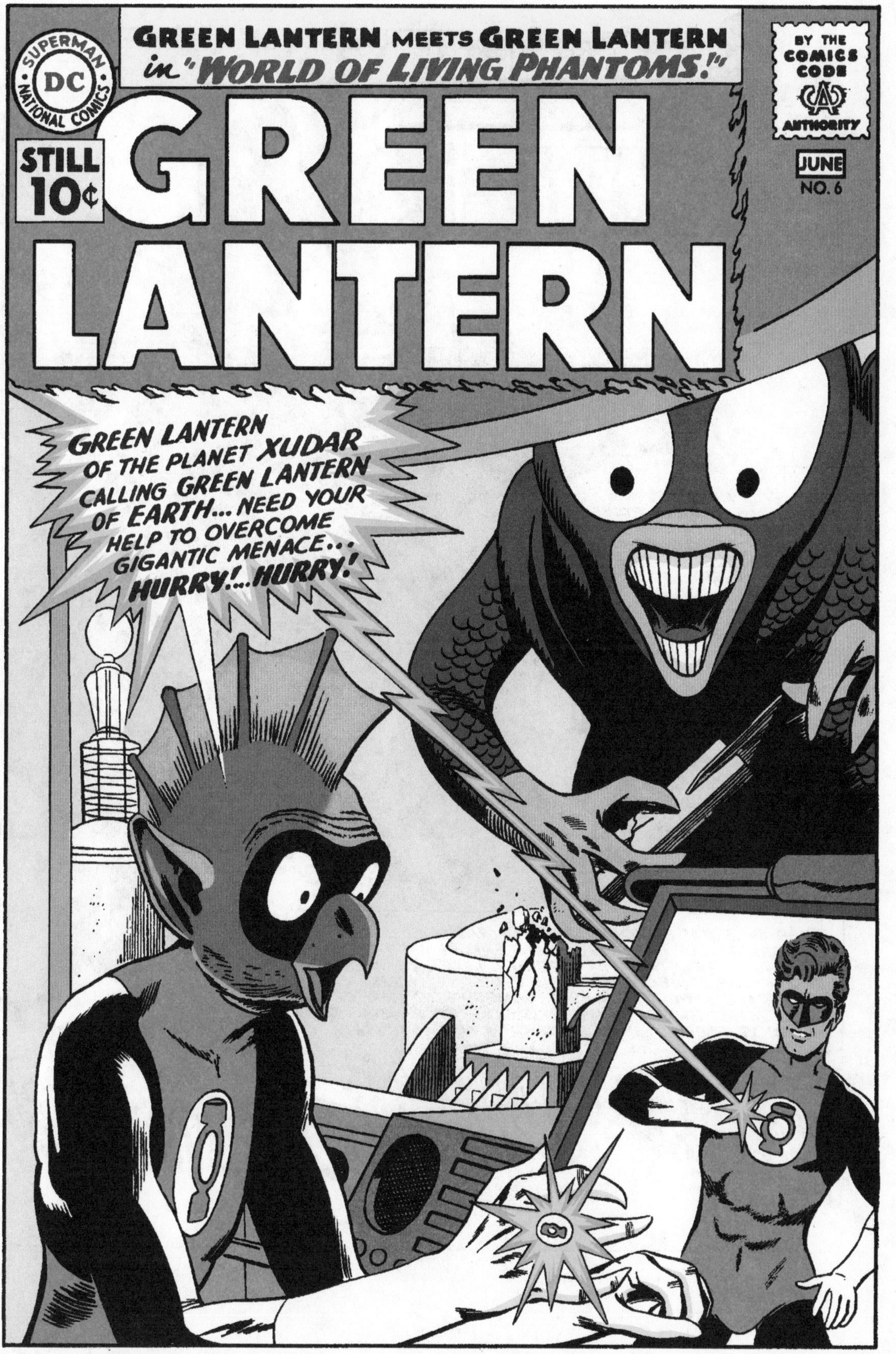
GREEN LANTERN MEETS GREEN LANTERN
in "WORLD OF LIVING PHANTOMS!"
SUPERMAN DC NATIONAL COMICS
STILL 10¢
GREEN LANTERN
BY THE COMICS CODE AUTHORITY
JUNE NO. 6
GREEN LANTERN OF THE PLANET XUDAR CALLING GREEN LANTERN OF EARTH... NEED YOUR HELP TO OVERCOME GIGANTIC MENACE... HURRY!... HURRY!

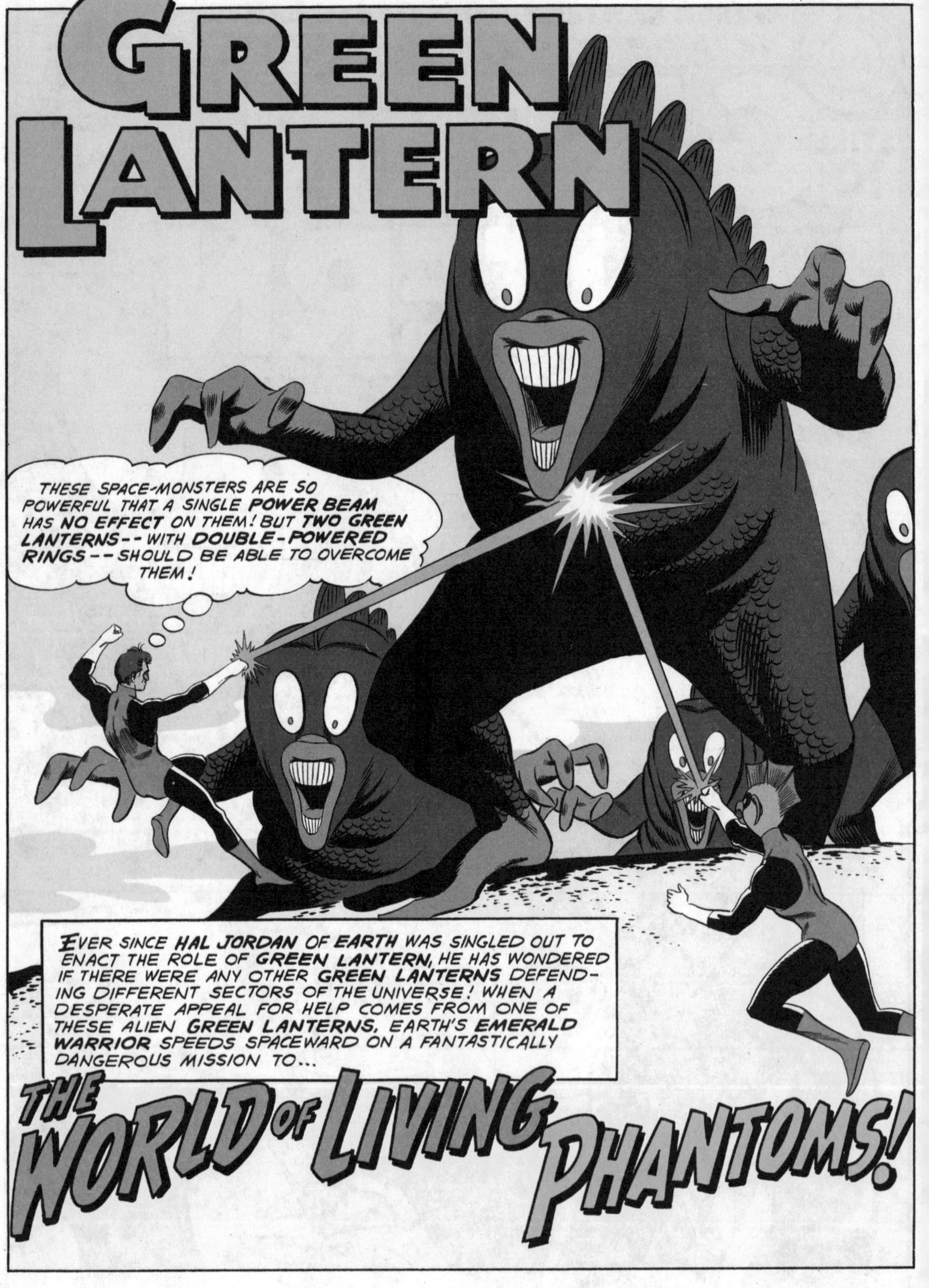
GREEN LANTERN
THESE SPACE-MONSTERS ARE SO POWERFUL THAT A SINGLE POWER BEAM HAS NO EFFECT ON THEM! BUT TWO GREEN LANTERNS--WITH DOUBLE-POWERED RINGS--SHOULD BE ABLE TO OVERCOME THEM!
EVER SINCE HAL JORDAN OF EARTH WAS SINGLED OUT TO ENACT THE ROLE OF GREEN LANTERN, HE HAS WONDERED IF THERE WERE ANY OTHER GREEN LANTERNS DEFENDING DIFFERENT SECTORS OF THE UNIVERSE! WHEN A DESPERATE APPEAL FOR HELP COMES FROM ONE OF THESE ALIEN GREEN LANTERNS, EARTH'S EMERALD WARRIOR SPEEDS SPACEWARD ON A FANTASTICALLY DANGEROUS MISSION TO...
THE WORLD OF LIVING PHANTOMS!

IN THE MILLIONS OF HABITABLE WORLDS OF THE UNIVERSE, LIFE HAS DEVELOPED ALONG COUNTLESS STRANGE LINES! BUT PERHAPS THE STRANGEST OF ALL CIVILIZATIONS EXISTS ON A PALE BLUE WORLD IN THE CONSTELLATION OF MONOCEROS...

A VISITOR TO THIS WORLD OF *AKU* WOULD AT FIRST SEE NOTHING VERY UNUSUAL...

...FOR IT APPEARS TO BE AN ADVANCED, SUPER-SCIENTIFIC CIVILIZATION...

BUT ACTUALLY THE *REAL* INHABITANTS OF *AKU* LIE UNDERGROUND IN SPECIAL CHAMBERS...

...IN A UNIQUE STATE RESEMBLING SLEEP AND SUSPENDED ANIMATION...

WHILE ABOVE IN THE CITY, THEIR THOUGHT-IMAGES CARRY ON THEIR DAILY LIVES!

I MUST HURRY! THERE IS AN EMERGENCY MEETING OF THE *DIRECTORATE* AND I MUST NOT BE LATE...

CENTURIES BEFORE, *IBR*—THE CHIEF SCIENTIST OF *AKU*—HAD EXPLAINED HIS GREAT PLAN TO THE *DIRECTORATE* OF THE PLANET...

...AND BY MY PLAN, EXCELLENCIES, THE *LIFE-ENERGY* OF EVERY CITIZEN OF *AKU* WOULD BE EXTENDED ALMOST INDEFINITELY! FOR WHILE WE LIE UNDERGROUND IN A STATE OF SUSPENDED ANIMATION, OUR *THOUGHT-IMAGES*, PROJECTED FROM OUR MINDS...

...WOULD CARRY ON OUR LIVES, *EXACTLY* AS WE WOULD OURSELVES, IN THE WORLD ABOVE US!

WONDERFUL, *IBR!* IT IS THE CLOSEST THING TO *IMMORTALITY!*

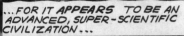

2

AND SO THE PLAN WAS PUT INTO EFFECT! AND FOR CENTURIES ALL WAS WELL, BUT THEN...

CLANG! CLANG!

THE ALARM...

THROUGH THE MINDS OF ALL THE SLEEPERS--HELPLESS THROUGH CENTURIES OF INACTIVITY--RUNS ONE AGONIZING THOUGHT...

THE ALARM CAN ONLY MEAN-- SOMETHING HAS GONE TERRIBLY WRONG IN THE WORLD ABOVE!

CLANG! CLANG!

ESPECIALLY IS THE MIND OF *IBR*, THE CHIEF SCIENTIST, AGONIZED...

HOW COULD THIS HAPPEN?! I THOUGHT WE HAD FORESEEN EVERY POSSIBILITY! EVERYTHING WAS ELECTRONICALLY CONTROLLED IN ADVANCE! IT'S IMPOSSIBLE! AND YET--

CLANG!

AND YET IT *IS* HAPPENING! AND THERE IS *NOTHING* WE CAN DO TO STOP IT! LYING HERE MOTIONLESS FOR AGES WE HAVE LOST ALL POWER OF MOVEMENT! WE ARE--*DOOMED!*

CLANG!

AND INDEED THE CITIZENS OF *AKU* WOULD BE DOOMED IF IT WERE NOT FOR THE FACT THAT ON THE NEARBY WORLD OF *XUDAR*...

...SITS AN INDIVIDUAL IN A STRANGELY-FAMILIAR UNIFORM!

YES! IT IS NONE OTHER THAN *TOMAR-RE*, THE *GREEN LANTERN* OF THIS PARTICULAR SECTOR OF THE UNIVERSE!

TROUBLE ON THE WORLD OF *AKU!* OF ALL THE UNFORTUNATE TIMES FOR THIS TO HAPPEN...!

③

58

IN TOMAR-RE'S SECTOR HE IS IN CHARGE OF A NUMBER OF WORLDS AND KEEPS A CONSTANT CHECK ON THEM THROUGH A UNIQUE CONTROL PANEL OF HIS OWN DESIGN...

THE ZATHON-RAY COMMUNICATOR WHICH ASSURES ME WHEN ALL IS WELL ON A WORLD HAS CHANGED ITS FREQUENCY! THIS MEANS THAT AKU--"THE WORLD OF SLEEPERS"--NEEDS HELP! BUT I HAVE JUST LEARNED...

...THAT AN INVASION OF SPACE-MONSTERS HAS JUST TAKEN PLACE AT THE SOUTHERN TIP OF MY OWN WORLD! I WAS JUST ABOUT TO LEAVE TO DEAL WITH THEM--SO I CANNOT POSSIBLY GO TO AKU!

IN HIS DILEMMA, THE BRILLIANT MIND OF THE ALIEN GREEN LANTERN WORKS SWIFTLY...

ONLY ONE THING TO DO! I MUST GET IN TOUCH WITH THE GREEN LANTERN IN THE NEAREST SECTOR--AND APPEAL TO HIM TO LEND ME A HAND IN THIS EMERGENCY! LET ME SEE... THROUGH MY ALL-WAVE RADIO RECEPTION I HAVE LEARNED...

...THAT THE NEAREST GREEN LANTERN IS ON THE PLANET CALLED EARTH, IN SECTOR 2814! I MUST CONTACT HIM AT ONCE...

AT THAT VERY MOMENT ON THE PLANET CALLED EARTH..."

I HOPE CAROL IS READY! I'VE WAITED SO LONG FOR THIS DATE OF OURS THAT I DON'T THINK I CAN WAIT EVEN ANOTHER MINUTE!

BRIINNNG!

4

As Hal Jordan, ace test pilot, nervously awaits the appearance of his "boss" Carol Ferris...

Ever since Carol's dad took off on a round-the-world tour leaving Carol in sole charge of FERRIS AIRCRAFT -- where I work -- she's refused to have any SOCIAL RELATIONS with an employee like ME! Though she has dated...

...GREEN LANTERN, my alter ego! But I guess persistence has finally triumphed -- because at long last she agreed to go out with me tonight! I'm going to make her forget GREEN LANTERN -- which won't be easy, because he's MYSELF!

But then, suddenly...

An image... springing from my POWER RING! An energy IMAGE of some kind--!

And out of the image a thought surges into the brain of the startled pilot...

This is TOMAR-RE, GREEN LANTERN of the planet XUDAR! You must come at once--

When Carol, having finally made up to suit herself, answers the door...

Well how do you like THAT!? Hal begs me for months -- for a date -- and now he's running off... as if he suddenly got cold feet!

Soon, in the dark privacy of Hal's dressing room at the hangar, a solemn oath is repeated...

In brightest day, in blackest night, no evil shall escape my sight! Let those who worship evil's might beware my power -- GREEN LANTERN'S LIGHT!

5

AND IN THE ROOM OF THE **ALIEN GREEN LANTERN** AT THIS MOMENT...

...AND THAT IS WHY YOU MUST GO TO **AKU, GREEN LANTERN** OF **EARTH**--WHILE I DEAL WITH THE **SPACE-MONSTERS** INVADING MY PLANET!

THERE IS ONE NOW!

I'M ON MY WAY, **TOMAR-RE!**

AS AN EMERALD LIGHTNING BOLT DARTS UPWARD FROM EARTH...

ACCORDING TO **TOMAR-RE**, SOME OF THE **LIVING THOUGHT-IMAGES** ON THE INCREDIBLE **WORLD OF AKU** HAVE BROKEN **OUT OF CONTROL** OF THE MINDS PROJECTING THEM-- AND ARE ENDANGERING THE ENTIRE CIVILIZATION THERE!

PROTECTED BY HIS ALL-POWERFUL GREEN BEAM-- AND POWERED BY IT-- **GREEN LANTERN** PIERCES THE COLD OF SPACE LIKE A JET-PROPELLED ARROW!

THE REBELLIOUS **THOUGHT-IMAGES** HAVE SOMEHOW FOUND A WAY OF SUPPLYING THEMSELVES WITH **ENERGY**-- AND ARE BENT ON TAKING CONTROL OF THEIR PLANET! THEY MUST BE STOPPED!

MEANWHILE, ON THE STRICKEN WORLD OF **AKU**...

DISASTER GROWS MORE CERTAIN EVERY MOMENT! I HAVE JUST REALIZED THAT THE LEADER OF THE REBELLIOUS **THOUGHT-IMAGES** IS NONE OTHER THAN **MY OWN IMAGE!!**

SOMEHOW WHATEVER WAS **EVIL** IN MY NATURE HAS BROKEN LOOSE IN THIS THOUGHT-COUNTERPART OF MYSELF! I CAN SEE HIM NOW--BY MEANS OF MY SUPERIOR MENTAL POWERS-- IN MY LABORATORY ABOVE, CARRYING OUT HIS **EVIL** DESIGNS...! I'LL ATTACK HIM **MENTALLY**...

I MUST REGAIN CONTROL OF HIM! I MUST...

YOU NEVER SHALL, **IBR!** I'LL STOP YOU...WITH **MENTAL FORCE!**

AS A DUEL OF ENERGY-FORCES RESULTS IN THE DEFEAT OF THE UNDERGROUND SCIENTIST...

YOU SHALL NEVER DIRECT ME AGAIN! I SHALL BE MY OWN MASTER--AS SOON AS I *DESTROY YOU!*

I CANNOT DO MORE! I AM HELPLESS..!

AND SOON AT A **WAR COUNCIL** OF THE LIVING PHANTOMS...

THE BEINGS FROM WHOSE MINDS WE SPRANG WILL NEVER STOP TRYING TO CONTROL US--UNTIL WE DESTROY THEM!

YES! TRUE!

ONLY *AFTER* WE HAVE ANNIHILATED EVERY ONE OF THEM WILL WE BE ABLE TO CARRY OUT OUR REAL AIM TO RULE THIS GALAXY-- **BY FORCE!**

BUT HOW CAN WE HARM THEM, "IBR"?

YOU KNOW, OF COURSE, THAT THE BEINGS WHO CREATED US LIE UNDERGROUND IN A SPECIALLY-BUILT CHAMBER WHICH NO KNOWN WEAPON CAN PENETRATE!

YES, I AM WELL AWARE OF THAT, KADMUN...

...BUT YOU FORGOT TO TAKE INTO ACCOUNT THAT I POSSESS THE IDENTICAL BRAIN AS THE **CHIEF SCIENTIST IBR**--THE MOST AMAZING BRAIN EVER KNOWN ON **AKU!** AND I HAVE DEVISED...

A NEW **RADIATION EXPLOSIVE** BASED ON **ANTAGONISTIC ATOMS!** IF IT WORKS, WE CAN DESTROY OUR FORMER MASTERS COMPLETELY! LET US PROCEED TO **TEST IT OUT...**

7

SOON, AT A SELECTED TEST SITE...

IF THE NEW EXPLOSIVE WORKS THE WAY I HOPE, IT WILL DESTROY THE UNDERGROUND CHAMBER WITHOUT HARMING US OR OUR CITY! IN OTHER WORDS, IT WILL WORK WITH TERRIBLE FORCE, BUT IN A RESTRICTED AREA...

NOW WE WILL SEE WHAT IT DOES TO THAT MOUNTAIN...AS I PRESS THIS ELECTRO-BEAD...

AND A MOMENT LATER, INCREDIBLY...

ASTONISHING! A WHOLE SECTION OF THE MOUNTAIN VANISHED!

LEAVING THE REST OF THE MOUNTAIN UNTOUCHED!

EXCELLENT! NOW WE CAN TAKE CARE OF OUR FORMER MASTERS!

BUT AS THE GROUP RETURNS TOWARD THE CITY...

SO THIS IS AKU..!?

IBR--SEE! WHAT MANNER OF CREATURE IS THAT!?

TURNING, THE EMERALD GLADIATOR SENSES DANGER!

EVIL THOUGHTS REACHING ME--! THESE MUST BE THE REBEL IMAGES THAT TOMAR-RE SPOKE ABOUT! THOUGH THEY LOOK REAL ENOUGH!

GOOD THOUGHTS REACHING US! HE IS OUR FOE!

POWERED BY HIS RING, A MIGHTY BEAM FLASHES AT THE PHANTOM-LIKE ENEMY...

RAISING A WEAPON AT ME!? BUT MY POWER RING WILL REACH HIM AND THE OTHERS FIRST..!

I MIGHT HAVE SUSPECTED THIS! THESE CREATURES ARE JUST PROJECTED IMAGES--THEY AREN'T MATERIAL BEINGS-- AND MY RAYS ARE PASSING RIGHT THROUGHT THEM--WITHOUT HARMING THEM IN THE LEAST!

HA, HA! HIS WEAPON CANNOT HURT US, KADMUN...

BUT OURS WILL TAKE CARE OF HIM...VERY EFFECTIVELY!

UHH!

HA HA! HE WILL NOT BOTHER US ANYMORE!

AN INSTANT AFTER...

INCREDIBLE...! EVERY SQUARE INCH SEEMS TO HAVE BECOME ENORMOUSLY HEAVY... AS IF I SUDDENLY WEIGH THOUSANDS OF POUNDS! CAN'T MOVE... CAN'T STIR A FINGER..!

9

MEANTIME BELOW GROUND, CHIEF SCIENTIST IBR HAS MENTALLY WITNESSED ALL THAT HAS HAPPENED ABOVE...

A CHAMPION FROM ANOTHER WORLD HAS COME TO HELP US! BUT THE PHANTOM REBELS HAVE RENDERED HIM POWERLESS! I MUST CONTACT THE STRANGER AT ONCE! UNLESS HE CAN AID US, WE ARE LOST..!

WHILE THE EMBATTLED GLADIATOR STRUGGLES AGAINST THE INVISIBLE FORCE CHAINING HIM TO THE SPOT...

I FEEL AS IF I WERE ON A PLANET WHERE THE SURFACE GRAVITY IS A MILLION TIMES STRONGER THAN ON EARTH! BUT I CAN STILL MAKE MY RING WORK... EVEN THOUGH I CAN'T MOVE A MUSCLE!

VALIANTLY, GREEN LANTERN SEEKS TO COMBAT THE TREMENDOUS WEIGHT THAT HAS HIM ROOTED TO THE GROUND! BUT DESPITE HEROIC EFFORTS...

NO USE! DESPITE ALL THE WILL POWER I CAN BRING TO BEAR THROUGH MY POWER BEAM, I CAN'T RID MYSELF OF THIS WEIGHT! CAN'T LIGHTEN THE LOAD THE LEAST BIT..!

AND THEN, IN A MOMENT OF WEAKNESS SUCH AS CAN HAPPEN TO ALL HUMANS...

I GUESS...THIS IS IT! LOOKS LIKE... I'LL NEVER SEE CAROL AGAIN... OR PIEFACE *... OR EARTH...

* EDITOR'S NOTE: HAL JORDAN'S ESKIMO GREASE-MONKEY AND PAL BACK AT THE FERRIS AIRCRAFT COMPANY IN COAST CITY.

BUT SUDDENLY IN THE MIDST OF GL'S BLACK DESPAIR...

EH? A THOUGHT...THE FACE OF SOMEONE... POPPING INTO MY BRAIN..!

GREEN LANTERN, LISTEN TO ME! THIS IS IBR, THE CHIEF SCIENTIST OF AKU, CONTACTING YOU...

I KNOW ALL ABOUT YOU, GREEN LANTERN, THROUGH MY TELEPATHIC ABILITY TO REACH OUT INTO YOUR BRAIN... EVEN THOUGH YOU ARE ON THE SURFACE OF MY WORLD AND I AM FAR UNDERGROUND... IN OUR SPECIAL "SLEEP-CHAMBER"...

10

RAPIDLY, THE THOUGHTS, THE WORDS, TUMBLE INTO **GREEN LANTERN'S** MIND...

...AND WHEN THE **REBEL IMAGES** OF OURSELVES CUT THEMSELVES OFF FROM US THEY NEEDED A **NEW SOURCE** OF ENERGY TO KEEP THEMSELVES-- "ALIVE"! FOR THIS PURPOSE THEY CREATED A GRAVITY HIVE...

A GRAVITY HIVE!?

"YES! A SUPERIOR SCIENTIFIC DEVICE WHICH TAPS THE **GRAVITY** OF OUR PLANET AND POURS ITS ENERGY INTO THEM THROUGH RADIATION..."

NOW WE ARE COMPLETELY INDEPENDENT OF OUR FORMER MASTERS! WE HAVE OUR OWN ENERGY SUPPLY--IN ENDLESS AMOUNTS!

I SEE, **IBR!** THEN THE WEAPON THAT THE **IMAGES** USED AGAINST ME WAS BASED ON THEIR CONTROL OF GRAVITY-- A SORT OF **GRAVITY GUN!**

EXACTLY, **GREEN LANTERN!** BUT YOU **MUST FREE** YOURSELF!

"EVEN NOW, AT THIS MOMENT, THE **REBELS** ARE SETTING THEIR **NEW EXPLOSIVE** AT THE DOOR OF OUR CHAMBER..."

"IN ANOTHER FEW MINUTES IT WILL BE SET OFF-- DESTROYING US UTTERLY..."

IT IS ALMOST READY, **KADMUN!** THE ADJUSTMENT OF THE **ANTAGONISTIC** ATOMS MUST BE PRECISE...

"YOU ARE THE ONLY ONE ON **AKU** WHO CAN HELP US, **GREEN LANTERN!** YOU **MUST** STOP THEM!"

AS THE TELEPATHIC VOICE OF THE CHIEF SCIENTIST, FILLED WITH DESPERATE APPEAL, TRAILS OFF...

...YOU **MUST** SAVE US...!

SAVE THEM? BUT HOW CAN I-- WHEN I MYSELF AM HELPLESS..?

AS THE SECONDS TICK BY IN THE UNDERGROUND "SLEEP CHAMBER" AND DOOM APPROACHES, SADNESS SETTLES ESPECIALLY ON TWO OF THE "SLEEPERS"-- STILL YOUNG DESPITE CENTURIES OF IMMOBILITY...

NOW I SHALL NEVER SEE ALYSSHA AGAIN! NEVER...

I HAD ALWAYS HOPED THAT SOMEHOW COSMO AND I... BUT NOW IT CAN NEVER BE!...IT IS TOO LATE...TOO LATE...

BUT THE INDOMITABLE CHAMPION FROM EARTH REFUSES TO BOW TO DISASTER...

WAIT... I JUST THOUGHT OF PIEFACE A WHILE AGO! SOME TIME BACK I USED MY POWER RING TO TURN PIE-FACE INTO A SECOND GREEN LANTERN-- A REPLICA OF MYSELF! *

*EDITOR'S NOTE: AS RE-COUNTED IN "THE POWER RING THAT VANISHED" IN THE APRIL, 1961 ISSUE OF GREEN LANTERN!

WHY CAN'T I USE MY RING TO DUPLICATE MYSELF--CREATE ANOTHER GREEN LANTERN THAT CAN MOVE--AND GO TO THE AID OF THE SLEEPERS! SOME QUALITY OF THIS PLANET SEEMS TO FAVOR THE PRODUCTION OF ENERGY-IMAGES!

INSTANTLY, THE GREAT GREEN BEAM FLARES FROM THE RING OF ITS MOTIONLESS WIELDER! AND...

DID IT! I'VE MADE AN EXACT DOUBLE OF MYSELF IN EVERY WAY--COMPLETE WITH POWER RING AND ALL!!

UH...NOT A MOMENT TO LOSE!

EDITOR'S NOTE: ONLY ON AKU, WITH ITS UNIQUE SUPER-MAGNETIC FIELD, COULD GREEN LANTERN CREATE AN IMAGE OF HIMSELF OUT OF THIN AIR! HE COULD NOT DO IT ANYWHERE ELSE!

GREEN LANTERN'S ENERGY-DOUBLE WHIZZES OFF...

WHAT A STRANGE FEELING! TO REMAIN HERE-AND WATCH MYSELF SPEED AWAY! AND YET IT'S FITTING--SINCE I'M FIGHTING IMAGES--TO MAKE AN IMAGE OF MYSELF TO DO IT!

12

AT THAT MOMENT, NEAR THE DOORWAY TO THE UNDERGROUND HIBERNATION CHAMBER...

NOW WE SEND THE SLEEPERS TO THE ETERNAL SLEEP, KADMUN!

EVEN THOUGH WE ARE SO CLOSE, MY AMAZING EXPLOSIVE WILL NOT HARM US AT ALL--AS IT DESTROYS THE UNDERGROUND CHAMBER!

BUT JUST AS THE TERRIBLE DEVICE IS IN THE VERY ACT OF BURSTING...

HEU! A STRANGE GREEN LIGHT COVERING THE BOMB!? WHAT--!?

INTO SIGHT, A DAZZLING FIGURE FLASHES...

I'M STOPPING THE EXPLOSION--MUFFLING IT--BUT IT'S TAKING EVERY OUNCE OF WILL POWER I'VE GOT TO TURN THE TRICK!!

HEU!?

ANOTHER INTRUDER--JUST LIKE THE ONE WE GRAVITIZED!!

HE HAS RUINED OUR BOMB! GRAV HIM!!

ONCE AGAIN, THE DREAD GRAVITY GUNS FIRE THEIR AWFUL RAY-CHARGE AT THE EMERALD GLADIATOR! BUT THIS TIME...

THIS TIME THEIR WEAPONS HAVE NO EFFECT ON ME! BECAUSE I'M NOT AN ACTUAL MATERIAL BEING--BUT ONLY A RING-MADE IMAGE OF MYSELF!

WHAT ON AKU--!

ZZZZZT!

13

AS THE DUPLICATE GREEN LANTERN ZOOMS UPWARD INTO THE CITY, PURSUED BY HIS RAGING FOES...

OUR WEAPONS NOW ARE USELESS AGAINST EACH OTHER! BUT I'VE GOT TO FINISH THEM OFF--BEFORE THEY CAN FIND A WAY OF FINISHING ME--

... AND I THINK I KNOW HOW TO DO IT!

HE IS INVULNERABLE TO OUR GUNS! BUT PERHAPS WE CAN OVERCOME HIM BY THE COMBINED POWER OF OUR MINDS! AT HIM-- ALL OF US!

OUT OF THE COMBINED THOUGHTS OF THE REBEL BAND POURS A FIERCE MENTAL ENERGY...

THEY'RE WEAKENING ME! BUT IF I LET DOWN NOW... ALL IS LOST! GOT TO KEEP MY WILLPOWER STRONG! STRONG ENOUGH TO USE MY RING... AGAINST THIS GRAVITY HIVE...

BATTLING AGAINST THE CROWDING THOUGHTS THAT THREATEN TO DRAIN HIM OF ENERGY, GL SENDS HIS RING SURGING FORTH...

THIS GRAVITY HIVE GIVES THE IMAGES THEIR ENERGY! I MUST STEP UP ITS GRAVITY OUTPUT... TO FANTASTIC HEIGHTS!

AND THEN AS THE INCREDIBLE BATTLE REACHES A SUDDEN CLIMAX...

IT'S AFFECTING THEM!! THEIR OWN ENERGY-SOURCE--THIS GRAVITY HIVE--IS POURING OUT SO MUCH GRAVITY NOW THAT IT'S BEGINNING TO WEIGH THEM DOWN! DESPITE THE FACT THAT THEY STARTED AS IMMATERIAL BEINGS, THEY'RE BECOMING ENORMOUSLY HEAVY!

14

SWIFTLY, THE GREEN-CLAD FIGURE PRESSES HIS ADVANTAGE...

GOT THEM! NOT A ONE OF THEM CAN MOVE SO MUCH AS A MUSCLE! EVEN THEIR BRAIN POWER HAS BEEN CUT DOWN TO ZERO...

THE STRANGER... OUR ENEMY... HAS... CONQUERED US!

MOMENTS LATER, AS THE ENERGY-GREEN LANTERN RETURNS TO HIS CREATOR...

HERE COMES MY RING-IMAGE BACK TO ME! AND I KNOW WE'RE BOTH THINKING THE SAME THING-- BY COMBINING OUR POWER RAYS WE MAY BE ABLE TO RETURN ME TO NORMAL!

AS THE TWO GREEN LANTERNS COMBINE FORCES TO TRY OUT THE IDEA...

NO... USE! IT STILL DOESN'T WORK! NOT EVEN TWO POWER RINGS CAN RID ME OF THIS COLOSSAL WEIGHT! BUT-- I HAVE ANOTHER IDEA...

IN DESPERATION, THE EMERALD GLADIATOR USES HIS MYSTIC RAY TO CREATE A SCORE OF GREEN LANTERNS-- EACH COMPLETE WITH POWER RING...!!

IF TWO GREEN BEAMS CAN'T DO THE TRICK, PERHAPS TWENTY CAN! THERE MUST BE A WAY-- I CAN'T GIVE UP!

MUST LIGHTEN THAT TERRIBLE GRAVITY! MUST DRIVE IT AWAY...!

15

AND FINALLY...

⸾WHEW!⸾ I'M MYSELF AGAIN! HOW GOOD IT FEELS JUST TO BE ABLE TO *MOVE!*

AS DETERMINED *WILL POWERS* STEP UP THE INTENSITY OF THE *POWER RAYS...*

I--I CAN FEEL THE WEIGHT DISSOLVING! I'M GETTING LIGHTER EVERY MOMENT--

WITH A COMMAND OF HIS RING, *GREEN LANTERN* DISSOLVES THE IMAGES THAT AIDED HIM...

NO NEED FOR *THEM* ANYMORE! AND NOW I'VE GOT TO RUSH TO THE *SLEEPERS* -- FIND OUT HOW THEY ARE!

MOMENTS LATER, BELOW GROUND...

YES, *GREEN LANTERN*, WE ARE ALL RIGHT, THANKS TO YOU! WE SAW EVERYTHING THAT HAPPENED ABOVE, BY OUR TELEPATHIC MINDS! THE REBEL *PHANTOMS* HAVE "SURRENDERED"...

DUE TO THE FACT THAT THEY WERE COMPOSED ONLY OF *MENTAL ENERGY*, THE ENORMOUS GRAVITY THAT ENTERED THEM WAS TOO MUCH FOR THEM AND THEY SUCCUMBED TO IT! PEACE HAS ONCE MORE COME TO *AKU...*

BUT WE *STILL* CAN'T UNDERSTAND WHAT WENT WRONG, *GREEN LANTERN!* *HOW* DID OUR OWN *THOUGHT-IMAGES* BREAK LOOSE FROM OUR CONTROL? IT IS A PROBLEM WE CANNOT SOLVE!

PERHAPS I CAN FIGURE IT OUT, *IBR* -- WITH THE AID OF MY *POWER RING!*

16

UNLOOSING HIS RAY, **GREEN LANTERN** PLAYS IT ON THE **MASTER SWITCHBOARD** IN THE **SLEEP CHAMBER**...

MY BEAM MAKES EVERYTHING CLEAR! THIS BOARD IS DESIGNED TO RECEIVE THE THOUGHT-ENERGY OF THE **MENTAL VOLTAGE** BEFORE TRANSMISSION TO THE DUPLICATE IMAGES ON THE SURFACE...

BUT THE THOUGHT-ENERGY OF **TWO** OF THE **SLEEPERS** BECAME ENTANGLED ELECTRONICALLY-- THROWING OFF THE ENTIRE SWITCHBOARD! LET ME SEE! I CAN FIND OUT WHICH TWO ARE TO BLAME BY TRACING THE ENERGY-LINES...

SOON, DETERMINED TO PLUMB TO THE BOTTOM OF THE MATTER, THE CHAMPION FROM SPACE SUMMONS THE GUILTY PAIR BEFORE HIM...

YES, **GREEN LANTERN!** YOU HAVE FOUND OUR SECRET! I LOVE HIM...!

I WAS ALWAYS THINKING OF HER! I COULDN'T HELP IT!

SO HERE'S THE TROUBLE! THESE TWO--IN LOVE-- AND UNABLE TO DO ANYTHING ABOUT IT! LYING HERE MOTIONLESS-- TORMENTED--HELPLESS ALL THESE YEARS!!

BUT IF I MERELY PUT THEM BACK IN THEIR PLACES NOW, THE **SAME THING** MAY HAPPEN AFTER I'M GONE--AND AGAIN DISRUPT THE WHOLE **MENTAL SWITCHBOARD** OF THIS PLANET! HMM! I HAVE AN IDEA...

LATER, AFTER THE PAIR HAS JOYOUSLY ACCEPTED THE **EMERALD GLADIATOR'S** DRAMATIC PROPOSAL...

THERE! MY **GREEN BEAM** HAS GIVEN THEM BACK THE **POWER OF MOTION**--THE SAME VIGOR THEY ENJOYED WHEN THEY WENT INTO THE SLEEP CHAMBER CENTURIES AGO!!

HEU!

17

SO NOW THERE WILL BE NOT ONLY *THOUGHT-PHANTOMS* MOVING ABOUT THE STRANGE WORLD OF *AKU*-- BUT ALSO A REAL FLESH-AND-BLOOD LIVING PAIR! AND WHO KNOWS...

...BUT SOME DAY A WHOLE NEW RACE--NOT OF *SLEEPERS* BUT OF *REAL PEOPLE*--MAY SPRING FROM THIS! I OFFERED TO DO THE SAME FOR ALL THE REST OF THE *SLEEPERS*, BUT NO ONE ELSE WOULD ACCEPT...

THEY ALL SAID THEY WERE *TOO OLD* TO START LIFE ANEW! MAYBE THEY'RE RIGHT...THEY'RE USED TO THIS WAY...OF LIVING THROUGH THEIR *THOUGHT-PHANTOMS!* I GUESS IT'S TOO LATE FOR THEM TO CHANGE...

RING-PROTECTED, *GREEN LANTERN* SPEEDS SPACEWARD...

BUT IT MAY NOT BE *TOO LATE* FOR ME TO AID MY COMRADE-IN-ARMS *TOMAR-RE*--IN HIS BATTLE AGAINST THE *SPACE-MONSTERS* THAT INVADED HIS PLANET! I'LL STOP THERE BEFORE HEADING BACK TO EARTH--!

AND AT THAT MOMENT, UNKNOWN TO THE *EMERALD WARRIOR*, HIS "COMRADE-IN-ARMS"--THE ALIEN *GREEN LANTERN*--IS IN TROUBLE...

MY RING...KNOCKS DOWN THESE INVADERS FROM SPACE...BUT THEY'RE SO HUGE AND POWERFUL THAT THEY PICK THEM-SELVES RIGHT UP AGAIN! THEY'RE FORCING ME BACK...BACK...!!

18

WORLD *of* LIVING PHANTOMS Chapter 3

IS IT POSSIBLE THESE CREATURES ARE *INVULNERABLE*? SUMMONING ALL THE POWER IN MY RING, I'M ABLE ONLY TO KNOCK THEM DOWN MOMENTARILY! I--I CAN'T HOLD THEM OFF MUCH LONGER--!

BESET BY HIS FOES, *TOMAR-RE--* THE *GREEN LANTERN* OF SECTOR 9 IN THE COSMOS-- FIGHTS A DESPERATE REAR-GUARD ACTION TO SAVE HIS WORLD FROM THE MONSTROUS INVADERS!

BUT THE NEXT MOMENT...

BY THE SEVEN SUNS OF SALOMAR! *ANOTHER POWER BEAM*--JUST LIKE MY OWN--HITTING THE COLOSSUS FROM BEHIND AS MY OWN RING-BEAM STRIKES IT IN FRONT!

UNDER THE *DUAL IMPACT,* THE GREAT CREATURE TOPPLES LIKE A STRICKEN FOREST GIANT!

DESTROYED IT! THE *TWO BEAMS* TOGETHER DID IT! BUT--?

19

AS THE **UNKNOWN** RING-WIELDER FLASHES INTO VIEW...

GREEN LANTERN OF EARTH--I SHOULD HAVE KNOWN IT WAS YOU!

LOOKS LIKE I GOT HERE JUST IN TIME, **TOMAR!**

YES! MY RING ALONE COULD NOT HANDLE THESE INVADERS-- BUT BY **DOUBLING** ITS POWER, IT CAN HANDLE THEM!

LET'S TEAM UP AND DRIVE THEM OFF!

BUT AS THE DUO SPURTS FORWARD...

GREAT TERRA! MY RING--IT'S RUNNING OUT OF POWER! **TWENTY-FOUR HOURS** HAVE PASSED SINCE I LAST CHARGED IT! IN ALL THE EXCITEMENT IT SLIPPED MY MIND--!

IN THE EMERGENCY, A QUICK CONFAB...

THE CREATURES ARE COMING AT US AGAIN! AND WITHOUT YOUR RING--IT LOOKS LIKE WE'RE BOTH LOST, **GREEN LANTERN!**

NOT NECES- SARILY, TOMAR!

LISTEN--YOU HAVE A **POWER BATTERY!** WHY CAN'T I CHARGE MY RING AT IT?

NO REASON, AT ALL! LET'S GO--

HOOKING HIS BEAM TO **GREEN LANTERN OF EARTH,** TOMAR STREAKS REARWARD, AS BEHIND THEM THE MONSTERS ADVANCE...

HANG ON, FELLOW- GREEN LANTERN...

20

AND SOON IN **TOMAR-RE'S** HEADQUARTERS...

THERE IT IS, **GREEN LANTERN!** GO TO IT--

IN BRIGHTEST DAY, IN BLACKEST NIGHT, NO EVIL SHALL ESCAPE MY SIGHT! LET THOSE WHO WORSHIP EVIL'S MIGHT BEWARE MY POWER-- **GREEN LANTERN'S LIGHT!**

THEN, AS THE DUO OF **GREEN LANTERNS** RETURNS TO THE FRAY...

I'M ALL CHARGED UP, **TOMAR-RE!** LET'S GET AT THOSE INVADERS!

THEY'VE REACHED OUR CITY--DESTROYING EVERYTHING IN THEIR PATH!

LIKE TWIN THUNDERBOLTS, THE **CRUSADERS** CATAPULT AT THEIR GIGANTIC FOES...

THAT'S ANOTHER THAT WON'T BOTHER US ANYMORE!

SUDDENLY...

TOMAR-RE! BEHIND US--!

21

QUICKLY WHIRLING, THE TWO GLADIATORS FOIL THE SNEAK ATTACK...

GOOD TEAMWORK, GREEN LANTERN!

AS THE TIDE OF BATTLE TURNS INTO A ROUT...

WE'VE GOT THEM ON THE RUN, TOMAR!

FOLLOW UP OUR ADVANTAGE! WE'VE GOT TO DRIVE THEM OFF FOR GOOD!

AND SOON, WITH THE BEATEN REMNANTS OF THE HUGE INVADERS FLEEING SPACEWARD IN THE SHIPS THAT BROUGHT THEM...

AFTER THIS I DON'T THINK THOSE ALIENS WILL EVER RETURN! THEIR INVASION ATTEMPT WAS TOO COSTLY! YOU'VE HELPED SAVE MY WORLD, GREEN LANTERN!

IT WAS A PLEASURE, TOMAR!

LATER, TWO CHAMPIONS OF JUSTICE WHO HAVE EARNED A REST TAKE IT AND MATCH NOTES...

THEN YOUR TIME-SCALE HERE ON YOUR WORLD IS DIFFERENT FROM OURS ON EARTH, TOMAR-- BUT AS NEAR AS WE CAN FIGURE OUT, WHEN YOU CHARGE YOUR RING IT GIVES YOU POWER FOR WHAT AMOUNTS TO 24 EARTH-HOURS!

THAT'S RIGHT...

APPARENTLY THE GUARDIANS OF THE UNIVERSE-- THE MYSTERIOUS BEINGS WHO SELECTED US AS POWER BATTERY POSSESSORS-- DECREED THAT WE SHOULD ALL BE EQUAL IN THAT RESPECT...

THE...GUARDIANS OF THE UNIVERSE...!

22

SUDDENLY, A TRAIN OF THOUGHT DARTS MEMORY-LIKE THROUGH THE MIND OF THE EARTH GREEN LANTERN...

ODD! IT'S AS IF I'VE ALWAYS KNOWN ABOUT THEM... THE *GUARDIANS!* BUT HOW COULD I--SINCE I NEVER HEARD THE NAME BEFORE?

EDITOR'S NOTE: UNKNOWN TO HAL (GREEN LANTERN) JORDAN, THE GUARDIANS OF THE UNIVERSE CONTACTED HIM EARLIER IN HIS CAREER TO DETERMINE HIS FITNESS AS A POSSESSOR OF A BATTERY OF POWER! BUT TRUE TO THEIR DESIRE TO REMAIN BEHIND THE SCENES AND IN OBSCURITY, THIS MEETING WAS AFTERWARDS WIPED COMPLETELY FROM GREEN LANTERN'S CONSCIOUS MIND! THUS IT IS ONLY AN UNCONSCIOUS MEMORY THAT IS NOW STIRRING HIM!

AS *TOMAR-RE* ADDS TO THE EARTHMAN'S MEAGER KNOWLEDGE OF THE MYSTERIOUS GROUP...

THE *GUARDIANS OF THE UNIVERSE* INHABIT A WORLD SOMEWHERE IN THE COSMOS--NO ONE KNOWS WHERE! AND THEY CONTACT US ONLY INDIRECTLY--THROUGH THE *POWER BATTERY!*

YES, THAT'S HAPPENED TO ME!

ONCE OR TWICE I'VE RECEIVED INSTRUCTIONS THROUGH MY *POWER BATTERY* TO GO TO THE AID OF SOME PLANET IN DISTRESS! BUT I NEVER KNEW WHERE THE MESSAGES CAME FROM--UNTIL NOW!

IT CAME FROM THE *GUARDIANS!*

THE *GUARDIANS* HAVE MYSTERIOUS WAYS OF OBTAINING INFORMATION--FROM ANYWHERE IN SPACE! THEY MUST POSSESS KNOWLEDGE THAT MAKES OUR SCIENCE--YOURS AND MINE--SEEM LIKE CHILDREN AT PLAY BY COMPARISON!

IS THERE ANYTHING MORE YOU CAN TELL ME ABOUT THEM?

ONLY THIS... THEY ALLOWED ME TO KNOW THE LOCATION OF SEVERAL OTHER *GREEN LANTERNS*--NO DOUBT BECAUSE MY SECTOR OF SPACE IS SO LARGE THAT I MIGHT SOMEDAY NEED HELP TO CONTROL IT-- JUST AS I NEEDED *YOU* THIS TIME!

23

LATER, AFTER **EARTH-GL** HAS GIVEN HIS COLLEAGUE A FULL REPORT OF THE EVENTS ON **AKU**...

GOOD! I'M GLAD THINGS ARE BACK TO NORMAL THERE! IT'S A STRANGE WORLD, AND I'VE HAD MY EYE ON IT FOR SOME TIME...

TOMAR-RE SURE HAS HIS HANDS FULL IN THIS SECTOR!

THEN, THE TIME FOR PARTING...

GOODBY, MY FRIEND--AND THANKS AGAIN!

NO NEED TO THANK ME, **TOMAR!** WE'RE BOTH IN THE SAME BUSINESS-- FIGHTING EVIL! PLEASE DON'T HESITATE TO CALL ON ME-- ANY TIME!

SOON, A SHIMMERING GREEN ROCKET HURTLES THROUGH SPACE...

AND IN DUE COURSE, BACK AT THE FERRIS AIRCRAFT COMPANY, WHERE PIEFACE PRESSES GREEN LANTERN TO EXPLAIN HIS ABSENCE...

WHERE HAVE YOU BEEN? CAROL HAS BEEN AROUND ASKING FOR YOU MORE THAN ONCE!

CAROL?! OH-OH!

I'LL EXPLAIN EVERYTHING LATER, **PIEFACE!** RIGHT NOW I'VE GOT TO ATTEND TO **SOMETHING IMPORTANT!**

JUMPING FISHHOOKS! YOU DON'T STAY PUT A MINUTE!

IT'S NOT TOO LATE! MAYBE I CAN STILL GET A DATE WITH CAROL TONIGHT! BUT I'LL HAVE TO HAVE A **GOOD** EXCUSE FOR WHAT HAPPENED THE OTHER NIGHT-- LEAVING HER IN THE LURCH THAT WAY!

24

LATER, AFTER THE JORDAN CHARM, AGAINST ODDS, HAS SECURED HIM A SECOND CHANCE...

CAROL, YOU JUST HAVE TO TRUST ME! I CAN'T TELL YOU WHY I HAD TO RUN OUT ON YOU SUDDENLY-- OR WHAT I'VE BEEN DOING SINCE THEN! ALL I CAN SAY IS THAT MY EXCUSE IS A LEGITIMATE ONE...

HE MUST BE DOING TOP SECRET WORK THAT HE CAN'T SPEAK ABOUT!

BUT I'LL SAY THIS! I'LL TELL YOU EVERYTHING SOME-DAY-- AFTER WE'RE MARRIED!

MARRIED!? HMM! YOU DO TAKE A LOT FOR GRANTED, HAL JORDAN! WHY, I SUPPOSE YOU THINK I SAT AROUND MOON-ING ABOUT YOU THAT NIGHT--

WELL, LET ME ASSURE YOU I DIDN'T! IT SO HAPPENS--ER--THAT GREEN LANTERN CALLED ME AND TOOK ME OUT THAT NIGHT! SO THERE!

GREEN LANTERN!?

25

OHO! IF CAROL FEELS IT NECESSARY TO TELL A LITTLE WHITE LIE TO MAKE ME JEALOUS OF GREEN LANTERN, MY OWN ALTER EGO-- THEN MY STOCK WITH HER IS REALLY GOING UP! THIS IS THE BEST DEVELOPMENT YET IN MY BATTLE TO WIN HER AFFECTIONS AS HAL JORDAN!

Ike
End.

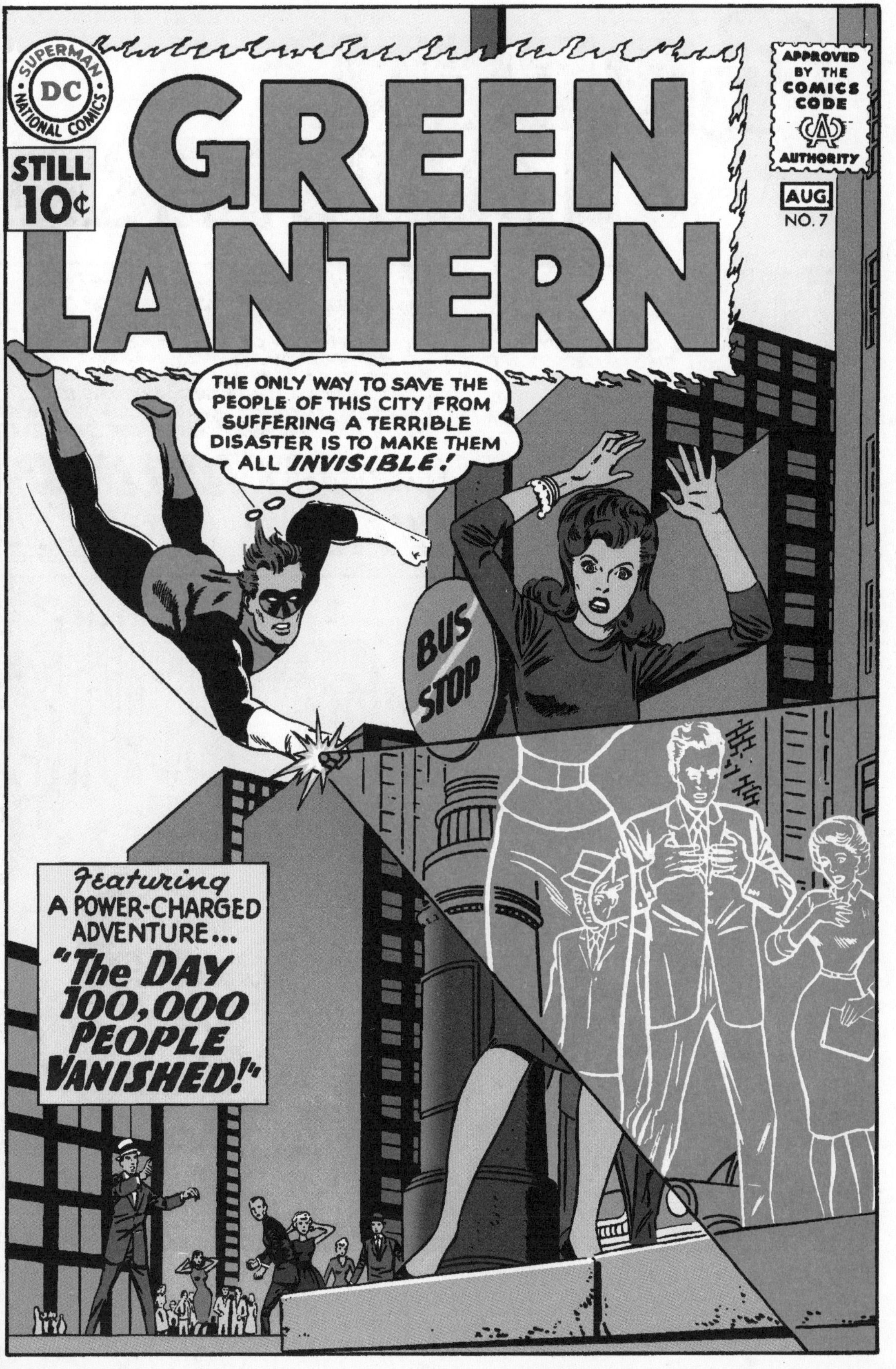
SUPERMAN DC NATIONAL COMICS
STILL 10¢
GREEN LANTERN
APPROVED BY THE COMICS CODE AUTHORITY
AUG. NO. 7
THE ONLY WAY TO SAVE THE PEOPLE OF THIS CITY FROM SUFFERING A TERRIBLE DISASTER IS TO MAKE THEM ALL INVISIBLE!
BUS STOP
Featuring A POWER-CHARGED ADVENTURE... "The DAY 100,000 PEOPLE VANISHED!"

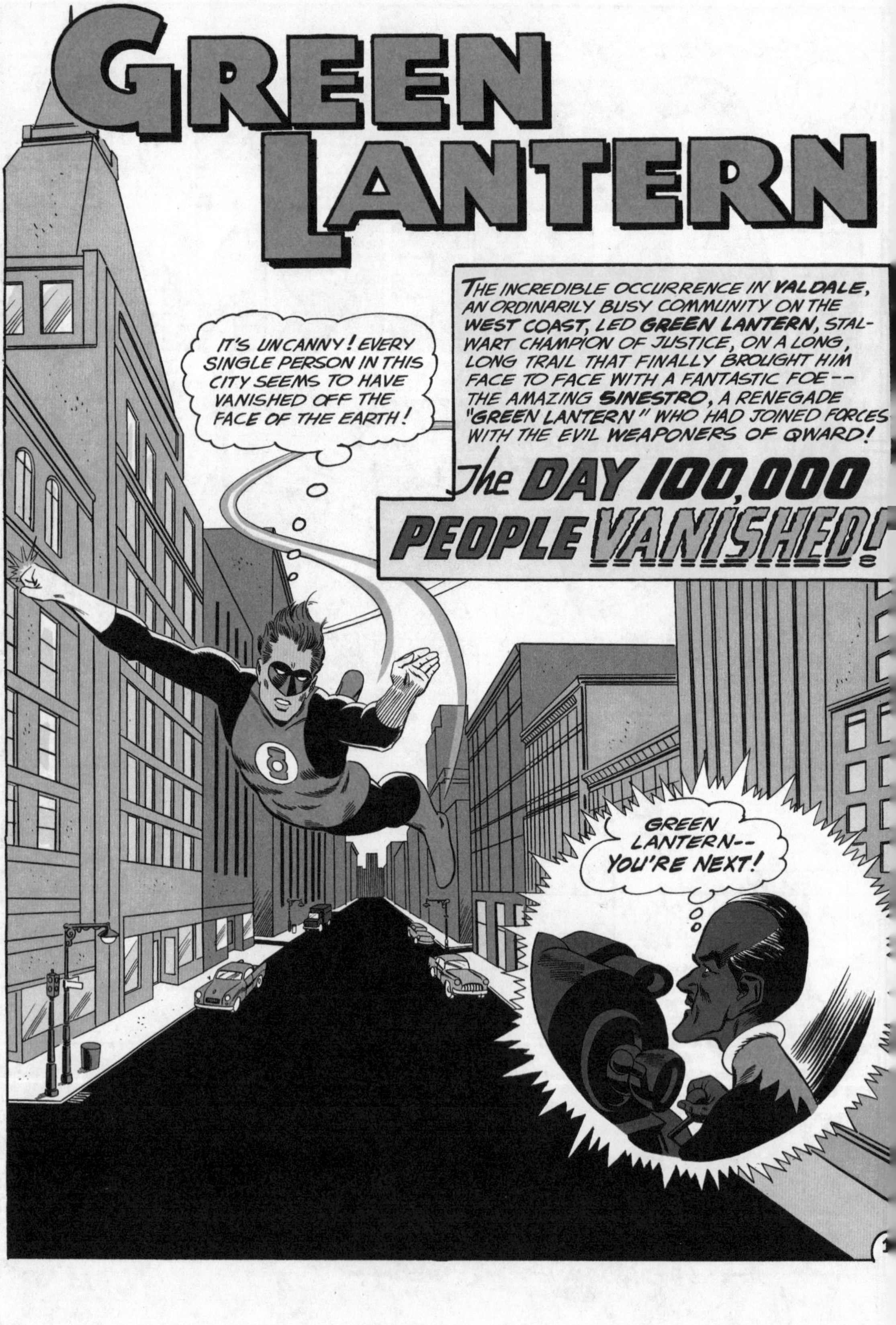
GREEN LANTERN
THE INCREDIBLE OCCURRENCE IN VALDALE, AN ORDINARILY BUSY COMMUNITY ON THE WEST COAST, LED GREEN LANTERN, STALWART CHAMPION OF JUSTICE, ON A LONG, LONG TRAIL THAT FINALLY BROUGHT HIM FACE TO FACE WITH A FANTASTIC FOE-- THE AMAZING SINESTRO, A RENEGADE "GREEN LANTERN" WHO HAD JOINED FORCES WITH THE EVIL WEAPONERS OF QWARD!
The DAY 100,000 PEOPLE VANISHED!
IT'S UNCANNY! EVERY SINGLE PERSON IN THIS CITY SEEMS TO HAVE VANISHED OFF THE FACE OF THE EARTH!
GREEN LANTERN-- YOU'RE NEXT!

AT PRECISELY FOURTEEN MINUTES AFTER NINE ON A BRIGHT MORNING IN THE THRIVING COMMUNITY OF **VALDALE** ON THE WEST COAST, THE RESIDENTS BUSTLE ABOUT THEIR USUAL ACTIVITIES...

FILL 'ER UP, JOE!

GET A MOVE ON, WILLYA?

LOVELY DAY, ISN'T IT, MRS. WILSON?

THONK!

SUDDENLY, THERE IS AN ODD SHIMMERING IN THE AIR, LIKE A **RAIN OF LIGHT**...

AND THE NEXT INSTANT A NOISE LIKE A THUNDERCLAP...

CRAACK!

AND AT EXACTLY NINE FIFTEEN, ONE MINUTE LATER, THE CITY OF **VALDALE**, 100,000 STRONG...

...HAS BECOME A **GHOST TOWN** WITH NOT A SINGLE LIVING HUMAN BEING LEFT IN IT!

2.

WHAT IS THE MEANING OF THIS EXTRAORDINARY EVENT WHICH HORRIFIES THE ENTIRE NATION WHEN IT BECOMES KNOWN? IT IS A *MYSTERY* WHICH BAFFLES *GREEN LANTERN*-- ALIAS *HAL JORDAN,* ACE TEST PILOT--AS MUCH AS ANYONE...

GREEN LANTERN-- DID YOU FIND OUT WHAT HAPPENED AT *VALDALE?*

I EXAMINED THE WHOLE TOWN WITH MY *POWER RING,* PIEFACE--THERE'S NOT A SINGLE CLUE! THE PEOPLE ARE GONE AS IF THEY VANISHED INTO THIN AIR!

JUMPING FISHHOOKS!

WHILE ON THE WAY BACK FROM *VALDALE,* I WAS THINKING-- THE INCREDIBLE DISAPPEARANCE TOOK PLACE AT A LITTLE AFTER NINE O'CLOCK...

THAT'S RIGHT *GL!* BUT WHAT--?

PIEFACE, IT JUST HAPPENS THAT I WAS SUPPOSED TO BE IN *VALDALE* AT THAT *HOUR*--TO TAKE PART IN A CEREMONY OPENING UP A NEW *BOYS SETTLEMENT HOUSE* THERE! I COULDN'T MAKE IT BECAUSE I HAD TO FINISH A CASE I WAS WORKING ON...

GREAT AURORA! THEN *YOU* WOULD HAVE VANISHED TOO--IF YOU HAD KEPT THE APPOINTMENT!

EXACTLY! AND I CAN'T HELP WONDERING-- *EH?*

BEFORE THE *EMERALD GLADIATOR* CAN CONTINUE, AN ODD FEELING PASSES OVER HIM...

THAT'S STRANGE! FOR AN INSTANT MY MIND WENT BLANK AND I COULDN'T REMEMBER WHAT I WAS SAYING! BUT I'M OKAY NOW!

3

AT THAT "BLANK" MOMENT, UNKNOWN TO GREEN LANTERN, HIS ASTRAL SELF--OR ENERGY DUPLICATE--WAS HURTLING THROUGH SPACE...

MEANWHILE, ON THE FAR-FLUNG WORLD OF **OA**, IN THE CENTRAL GALAXY OF THE UNIVERSE, WHERE A GROUP KNOWN SIMPLY AS THE **GUARDIANS** SITS IN COUNCIL...

THE ENERGY-DUPLICATE OF THE POWER BATTERY POSSESSOR IN SECTOR 2814 IS ON THE WAY HERE!

AS A BURST OF LIGHT FLARED BEFORE THE IMPRESSIVE ASSEMBLAGE...

THE--THE **GUARDIANS** OF THE UNIVERSE!

YES! YOUR ENERGY-TWIN REMEMBERS WHAT YOUR CONSCIOUS MIND BACK ON EARTH IS STILL UNAWARE OF, GREEN LANTERN--THAT WE ARE THE **CREATORS** OF **POWER BATTERIES** SUCH AS YOURS...

...AND THAT ONCE BEFORE WE SUMMONED YOU TO US IN A GREAT EMERGENCY!* BUT WE HAVE NOT BROUGHT YOU HERE THIS TIME TO TALK ABOUT OURSELVES--BUT RATHER OF A SITUATION THAT THREATENS **YOU!**

THREATENS-- ME?

*Editor's Note: SEE "PLANET OF DOOMED MEN!" IN GREEN LANTERN #1

WE GUARDIANS DO NOT BESTOW POWER BATTERIES WITHOUT CAREFUL TESTS! BUT THERE ARE MANY POSSESSORS AND MANY WORLDS IN THE COSMOS UNDER OUR CARE! AND IN OUR SELECTIONS WE DID MAKE ONE **MISTAKE!** IT HAPPENED...

"...ON A WORLD CALLED **KORUGAR** IN SECTOR 1417 WHERE WE CHOSE A BEING NAMED **SINESTRO**..."

"...TO BE THE POSSESSOR OF A POWER BATTERY!"

4.

"OUR TESTS SHOWED SINESTRO TO BE A DESERVING ONE AND ABSOLUTELY WITHOUT FEAR! AND INDEED FOR A TIME HE DID SO ACT IN THAT MANNER..."

SINESTRO IS KEEPING DOWN EVIL ON HIS PLANET!

"BUT IN DUE COURSE, AFTER ONE OF OUR PERIODIC CHECKS, A SUBTLE CHANGE CAME OVER THE KORUGARN GREEN LANTERN WHICH WE WERE THEN UNAWARE OF..."

CHARGING MY RING AT THE BATTERY GIVES ME POWER FOR 37 DIORS*--UNLIMITED POWER! THERE IS NOTHING I CAN'T DO WITH IT!

*Editor's Note: THE EQUIVALENT OF 24 EARTH-HOURS!

"A FEELING OF DISSATISFACTION FILLED SINESTRO AS HE STARED ABOUT HIM..."

WHY SHOULD I REMAIN IN THIS SECRET CHAMBER-- HIDDEN HERE FROM MY WORLD? I HAVE A BETTER IDEA--AND A SENSATIONAL WAY TO EMPLOY MY RING!

"USING HIS POWER BEAM, SINESTRO CREATED A SUMPTUOUS HEADQUARTERS FOR HIMSELF, OUTSHINING EVERYTHING ELSE ON HIS PLANET..."

THERE! NOW I HAVE SUITABLE HEADQUARTERS-- THE MOST MAR- VELOUS BUILDING ON KORUGAR!

"FROM THEN ON, THIS GREEN LANTERN DISPENSED JUSTICE FROM HIS NEW HEADQUARTERS! BUT IN A STRANGE WAY..."

WE HAVE TO WAIT TO SEE SINESTRO SOMETIMES FOR DIORDANS*!

AND THEN HE TAKES ONLY THOSE CASES THAT INTEREST HIM--HELPS ONLY A FEW OF US AND IGNORES THE REST!

EVIL RAIDERS THREATENING YOUR SETTLEMENT-- ROBBING YOU?

HOW I AM BORED WITH THESE DIORDAN-LONG COMPLAINTS AND PLEAS FOR MY ASSISTANCE!

*Editor's Note: DIORDAN: 37 DIORS, OR ONE DAY! /5

ALTHOUGH *SINESTRO* DID NOT REALIZE IT, HE WAS ALREADY INFECTED WITH THE VIRUS OF *POWER*--TO WHICH, BY A PSYCHOLOGICAL QUIRK IN HIS BRAIN, HE DID NOT HAVE ENOUGH *RESISTANCE!* AND FROM THEN IT WAS JUST A SHORT STEP TO HIS NEXT ACT...

"ONE OF THE SUPPLICANTS WHOM HE HAD REFUSED TO HELP RE-MONSTRATED WITH HIM, CHARGED HIM WITH LACK OF GOOD WILL..."

YOU ARE NO CHAMPION OF JUSTICE! WE HEARD *GREEN LANTERN* WOULD CRUSH EVIL WHEN IT THREATENED US! BUT INSTEAD YOU HAVE BECOME *POWER-MAD!*

YOU *DARE*--!?

"WITH ONE BURST OF HIS RING, THE KORUGARN GREEN LANTERN STRUCK THE SPEAKER UNCONSCIOUS..."

FOR SHAME! *KI-MON* WAS UNARMED-- HELPLESS!

SILENCE! OR ALL OF YOU WILL GET THE SAME TREATMENT! I AM *GREEN LANTERN*--NO ONE CAN TELL ME WHAT TO DO!

"PRIDE AND A LOVE OF POWER WERE SINESTRO'S UNDOING! SOON IN THE GOVERNING BODY OF HIS WORLD..."

SINCE I HAVE DECIDED TO GOVERN *KORUGAR* MYSELF, I HEREBY DISSOLVE THE HIGH COUNCIL!

HE IS MAKING HIMSELF *DICTATOR!*

"A PALL FELL OVER KORUGAR! NONE KNEW WHEN HE MIGHT INCUR THE NEW MASTER'S DISPLEASURE..."

THREE WHO SPOKE AGAINST GREEN LANTERN THE OTHER *DIORDAN* HAVE DISAPPEARED!

HE HAS BECOME A *LAW UNTO HIMSELF!* WE ARE ENSLAVED!

"BUT FORTUNATELY AT THIS TIME WE GUARDIANS MADE ONE OF OUR PERIODIC SECRET CHECKS..."

SINESTRO HAS MIS-USED THE POWER WE BESTOWED ON HIM!

HE BELIEVED THAT NONE STOOD ABOVE HIM! HE WILL NOW LEARN THAT HE WAS *MISTAKEN!*

6

"BY MEANS KNOWN ONLY TO OUR-SELVES, WE BROUGHT THE KORUGARN BATTERY POSSESSOR BEFORE US..."

SINESTRO, YOU HAVE ABUSED YOUR SACRED TRUST! INSTEAD OF DISPENSING JUSTICE ON YOUR WORLD-- YOU HAVE DIS-PENSED EVIL! UNDER THE CIRCUMSTANCES THERE IS ONLY ONE COURSE OPEN TO US!

"IT WAS THE FIRST AND ONLY TIME WE HAD BEEN FORCED TO TAKE SUCH EXTREME MEASURES..."

SINESTRO OF KORUGAR, YOU HAVE BEEN FOUND UNWORTHY TO BE A BATTERY POSSESSOR! YOU ARE HEREBY STRIPPED OF ALL INSIGNIA AND HONORS--!

YOUR POWER RING IS NO LONGER YOURS!

YOUR BATTERY OF POWER IS NOW RE-TURNING TO US!

EVIL YOU ARE--TO EVIL YOU WILL GO! WE ARE BANISHING YOU TO THE ANTIMATTER UNIVERSE OF QWARD--WHERE ALL IS EVIL AND WHERE YOUR EVIL WILL FIND ONLY OTHER EVIL TO CLASH WITH!

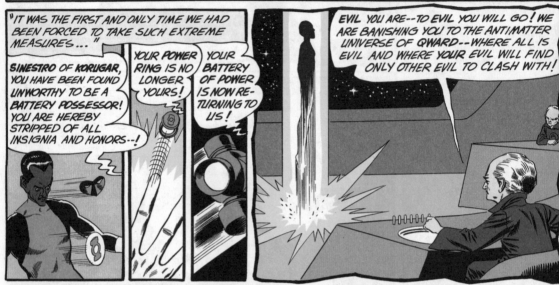

"WE THOUGHT THAT BY SENDING SINESTRO OUT OF OUR UNIVERSE ALTOGETHER WE HAD ENDED HIS MENACE TO US..."

BUT ONCE AGAIN WE WERE WRONG AS FAR AS SINESTRO WAS CONCERNED! WHICH LEADS US TO WHY WE BROUGHT YOU HERE TODAY!

THOUGH WE HAVE NO POWER IN THE ANTI-- MATTER UNIVERSE OF QWARD, WE CAN PEER INTO IT! NOW WE WILL SHOW YOU CERTAIN SCENES WHICH OUR DEVICES HAVE RE-CORDED--SCENES OF INTEREST TO YOU!

"SINESTRO WITH HIS FIERY ENERGY LOST NO TIME IN CONTACTING THE RULERS OF HIS NEW UNIVERSE--THE EVIL WEAPONERS OF QWARD..."

I AM DETERMINED TO BECOME MASTER OF THIS WORLD JUST AS I WAS MASTER OF KORUGAR! THE GUARDIANS WILL NEVER SHAKE MY WILL! I SHALL DEFEAT THEM YET! AND THERE IS ONE WAY TO BEGIN MY STRUGGLE--

7

YOU QWARDIANS HAVE FAILED IN THREE ATTEMPTS TO DESTROY YOUR MORTAL ENEMY, *GREEN LANTERN* OF EARTH! AND THE REASON IS THAT YOU ARE *NOT EVIL ENOUGH!* I SHALL TEACH YOU HOW TO BE THE *ULTIMATE IN EVIL!*

"THE QWARDIANS WERE AWED BY SINESTRO! THEY AGREED EAGERLY TO COOPERATE WITH HIM AND GIVE HIM CERTAIN MATERIALS HE ASKED FOR..."

UNDERSTAND, *WEAPONERS,* THAT *GREEN LANTERN CANNOT* BE HARMED WHILE HIS *POWER RING* IS OPERATING! THEREFORE I HAVE CONSTRUCTED THIS MECHANISM-- A TRULY *EVIL* MECHANISM!

BY *SUPER-RADAR* WE IN *QWARD* CAN DETECT WHAT IS HAPPENING ON EARTH--EVEN THOUGH WE CANNOT SEE DIRECTLY INTO IT! I HAVE LEARNED THAT *GREEN LANTERN* IS DUE TO APPEAR IN THE CITY OF *VALDALE* ON EARTH! DURING THAT TIME HIS RING WILL NOT BE OPERATING!

AT THE *RIGHT MOMENT* I WILL SWITCH ON MY NEW VISO-TELEPORTER--WHICH IS DIRECTED AT *VALDALE*--AND *EVERY VISIBLE* HUMAN BEING IN THE CITY--INCLUDING *GREEN LANTERN,* WILL INSTANTLY BE TRANSPORTED HERE TO *QWARD!*

MARVELOUS, *SINESTRO!* WE WILL HAVE *GREEN LANTERN* IN OUR POWER!

AS THE SCREEN FADES, AND REALIZATION DAWNS ON THE ASTRAL VISITANT...

GREAT STARS! THEN *THAT* EXPLAINS WHAT HAPPENED TO THE PEOPLE OF *VALDALE*! AND I ESCAPED ONLY BY ACCIDENT--BY NOT GOING THERE!

YES! AND NOW THAT WE HAVE TOLD YOU ALL WE KNOW, *GREEN LANTERN* OF EARTH...

...THE REST IS UP TO YOU! YOU MUST DEFEAT YOUR NEW AND VENOMOUS FOE, *SINESTRO*-- AND YOU MUST DO IT BY YOURSELF! FOR OUR JURISDICTION DOES NOT EXTEND TO *QWARD* AND WE CANNOT HELP YOU!

I UNDERSTAND! I WILL DO MY BEST!

GOOD! YOU WILL RETURN TO EARTH NOW TO REJOIN YOUR CORPOREAL BODY! BUT THIS TIME, IN RECOGNITION OF YOUR VALOR AND LOYALTY, WE ARE ALLOWING YOU TO RETAIN A *COMPLETE* MEMORY OF THIS INTERVIEW WITH US!

BACK ON EARTH, ALMOST INSTANTLY, AT THE *FERRIS AIRCRAFT COMPANY*...

GREEN LANTERN--ARE YOU SURE YOU'RE ALL RIGHT?

YES...YES!

I CAN'T TELL PIEFACE ANYTHING ABOUT THE GUARDIANS! THAT'S ONE SECRET I CAN'T SHARE WITH ANYONE!

THE NEXT MOMENT...

JUMPING FISHHOOKS! HE--HE JUST MUMBLED A FEW WORDS TO ME, AND THEN TOOK OFF-- LIKE A STREAK--!

I'VE GOT TO FIND MY WAY *INTO QWARD* WITHOUT A MOMENT'S DELAY! NOT ONLY MUST *SINESTRO* BE DEALT WITH-- BUT ALSO I'VE GOT TO DISCOVER WHAT HAP- PENED TO THE 100,000 INNOCENT PEOPLE OF *VALDALE*!

9

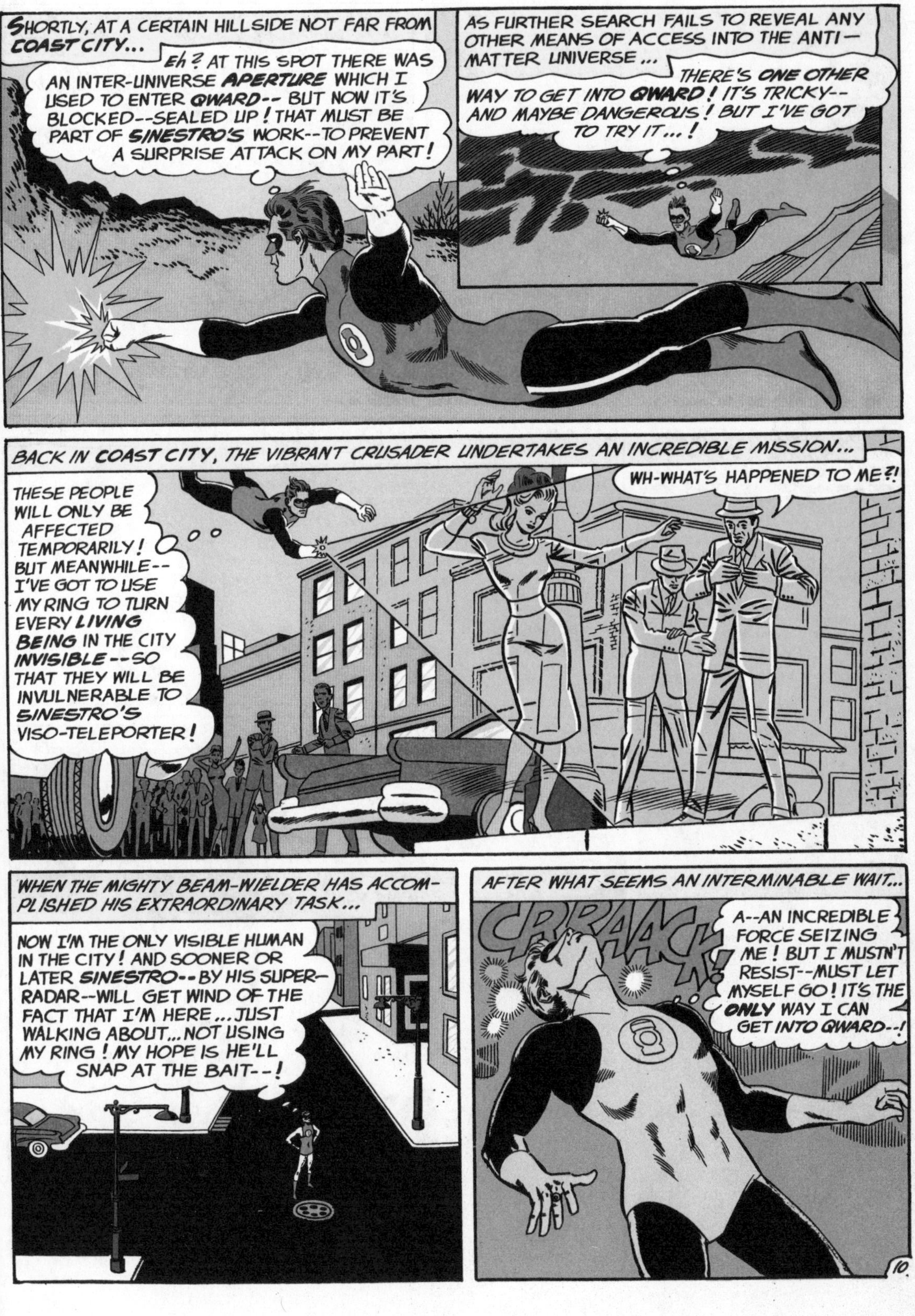
SHORTLY, AT A CERTAIN HILLSIDE NOT FAR FROM COAST CITY...
Eh? AT THIS SPOT THERE WAS AN INTER-UNIVERSE APERTURE WHICH I USED TO ENTER QWARD-- BUT NOW IT'S BLOCKED--SEALED UP! THAT MUST BE PART OF SINESTRO'S WORK--TO PREVENT A SURPRISE ATTACK ON MY PART!
AS FURTHER SEARCH FAILS TO REVEAL ANY OTHER MEANS OF ACCESS INTO THE ANTI-MATTER UNIVERSE...
THERE'S ONE OTHER WAY TO GET INTO QWARD! IT'S TRICKY-- AND MAYBE DANGEROUS! BUT I'VE GOT TO TRY IT...!
BACK IN COAST CITY, THE VIBRANT CRUSADER UNDERTAKES AN INCREDIBLE MISSION...
THESE PEOPLE WILL ONLY BE AFFECTED TEMPORARILY! BUT MEANWHILE-- I'VE GOT TO USE MY RING TO TURN EVERY LIVING BEING IN THE CITY INVISIBLE--SO THAT THEY WILL BE INVULNERABLE TO SINESTRO'S VISO-TELEPORTER!
WH-WHAT'S HAPPENED TO ME?!
WHEN THE MIGHTY BEAM-WIELDER HAS ACCOMPLISHED HIS EXTRAORDINARY TASK...
NOW I'M THE ONLY VISIBLE HUMAN IN THE CITY! AND SOONER OR LATER SINESTRO-- BY HIS SUPER-RADAR--WILL GET WIND OF THE FACT THAT I'M HERE... JUST WALKING ABOUT... NOT USING MY RING! MY HOPE IS HE'LL SNAP AT THE BAIT--!
AFTER WHAT SEEMS AN INTERMINABLE WAIT...
CRRAACK!
A--AN INCREDIBLE FORCE SEIZING ME! BUT I MUSTN'T RESIST--MUST LET MYSELF GO! IT'S THE ONLY WAY I CAN GET INTO QWARD--!
10

Panel 1 caption: AS THE GREEN-CLAD FIGURE VANISHES, IN THE CITY BEHIND HIM...

IT'S UNCANNY! I--I'M INVISIBLE--AND SO IS EVERYONE ELSE IN TOWN! I'M AFRAID TO DRIVE ANOTHER INCH!

Panel 2 caption: THEN SUDDENLY, SINCE GREEN LANTERN HAD COMMANDED HIS RING TO HAVE ONLY A TEMPORARY EFFECT...

GREAT SCOTT! NOW--NOW WE'RE VISIBLE AGAIN!

Panel 3 caption: AT THIS MOMENT, IN THE ANTI-MATTER UNIVERSE OF QWARD, WHERE EVIL IS THE STANDARD OF BEHAVIOR--JUST AS GOOD IS IN OURS...

SINESTRO HAS KEPT HIS PROMISE! HE HAS DELIVERED GREEN LANTERN TO US!

OPEN FIRE! DESTROY HIM!

Panel 4 caption: AS A BATTERY OF DEADLY RADIATION SPURTS AT THE GREEN-CLAD ARRIVAL...

THEY WERE READY FOR ME! I GUESS THEY COUNTED ON MY BEING DAZED WHEN I GOT HERE-- UNABLE TO USE MY POWER RING! BUT THEY DON'T REALIZE I FORE-SAW THIS!

ZZZT!

Panel 5 caption: IN A SPLIT-SECOND, THE GREEN GLADIATOR SETS UP AN IM-PENETRABLE SHIELD BEFORE HIM...

OUR ENERGY BURSTS CAN-NOT REACH HIM! WHAT DO WE DO NOW, SINESTRO?

FEAR NOT! MY EVIL MIND IS EASILY EQUAL TO THIS EMERGENCY--!

HEAR ME, GREEN LANTERN! UNLESS YOU SURRENDER TO US, YOUR COUNTRY-MEN--THE 100,000 PEOPLE OF VALDALE-- WILL BE DESTROYED AT ONCE!

11

AFTER AN AGONIZING MOMENT, THE *EMERALD WARRIOR* REACHES A DECISION...

THIS IS ONE THING I DID **NOT** TAKE INTO ACCOUNT! I HAVE NO CHOICE! I MUST DO AS HE SAYS!

I ACCEPT YOUR TERMS! I WILL PLACE MYSELF IN YOUR POWER--ON ONE CONDITION--

--THAT YOU RELEASE THE PEOPLE OF *VALDALE*, AND SEND THEM BACK WHERE THEY BELONG--SAFE AND SOUND!

AGREED! YOU HAVE MADE A GOOD BARGAIN, *GREEN LANTERN*--100,000 FOR ONE!

AND SOON, BACK IN *VALDALE* WHICH WAS A MOMENT BEFORE ONLY A *GHOST CITY*...

WH-WHAT HAPPENED TO US?

NO ONE KNOWS! BUT THANK GOODNESS WE ARE BACK HOME AGAIN AND ALIVE!

WHILE IN QWARD, TRUE TO HIS PROMISE, *GREEN LANTERN* HAS ALLOWED HIMSELF TO BE CAPTURED...

YOU'VE ENCASED ME IN A *YELLOW BUBBLE* OF PULSATING ENERGY, *SINESTRO*! BUT-- IS **THIS** THE WAY YOU PROPOSE TO DESTROY ME?

PATIENCE, MY EX-COLLEAGUE-- PATIENCE!

AS A FORMER RING-WIELDER MYSELF, I KNOW THAT YOUR *GREEN BEAM* WILL AUTO-MATICALLY PROTECT YOU FROM ALL HARM AS LONG AS YOU ARE CONSCIOUS! THEREFORE, MY PLAN IS SIMPLE! YOU CANNOT ESCAPE FROM OUR *YELLOW ENERGO-SAC--!**

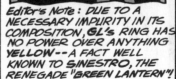

Editor's Note: DUE TO A NECESSARY IMPURITY IN ITS COMPOSITION, *GL's* RING HAS NO POWER OVER ANYTHING *YELLOW*--A FACT WELL KNOWN TO *SINESTRO*, THE RENEGADE "*GREEN LANTERN*"!

FURTHER, OUR SUPER-RADAR INFORMED US **EXACTLY** WHEN YOU LAST CHARGED YOUR RING! WHEN THAT CLOCK STRIKES *SIX*-- YOUR RING WILL RUN *OUT OF POWER!* **THEN** WE SHALL DESTROY YOU!

12

AS THE MINUTES TICK BY WITH MEASURED AND DREADFUL PACE...

SINESTRO, YOU TRULY ARE A *GENIUS OF EVIL!* WE HAVE DECIDED TO MAKE YOU OUR *CHIEFTAIN!*

I ACCEPT! AND AFTER *GREEN LANTERN* IS FINISHED I SHALL LEAD YOU ON A *COUNTERCRUSADE* AGAINST MY ETERNAL ENEMIES--THE *GUARDIANS!*

I MUST ESCAPE FROM HERE AND PREVENT *SINESTRO'S* ATTACK ON THE *GUARDIANS!* BUT HOW CAN I? MY RING WON'T PENETRATE THIS *YELLOW* SURFACE...!

IT SEEMS HOPELESS! AND YET--IN THE TIME I'VE BEEN IN HERE, I'VE NOTICED SOMETHING ABOUT THAT CLOCK! IT WORKS ON THE VIBRATION OF ATOMIC PARTICLES--MY RING HAS BEEN RECEIVING ITS IMPULSES! *Hmm!* I WONDER--!

NOT LONG AFTER, WHEN THE FINAL MOMENT ARRIVES...

THE CLOCK STRIKES *SIX!*

AND SEE--HIS RING IS RUNNING *OUT OF POWER--*JUST AS I SAID IT WOULD!

AS THE MASTER OF EVIL UNLIMBERS AN ENERGY-GUN...

NO NEED FOR THE YELLOW BUBBLE, *GREEN LANTERN!* YOUR HOUR OF DOOM HAS STRUCK--

PERHAPS, SINESTRO...

...AND PERHAPS *NOT!*

AHH--!? HIS RING-- IT IS *STILL WORKING!?*

13

PRESSING HIS ADVANTAGE, GREEN LANTERN HURLS HIMSELF AT HIS STARTLED FOE...

IMPOSSIBLE--!

NO, *SINESTRO!* I KNEW I HAD ONLY *ONE SLIM CHANCE* TO DEFEAT YOUR DIABOLIC SCHEME--BUT IT WAS A CHANCE THAT WORKED!! YOU SEE--

...MY RING COULD NOT PIERCE YOUR YELLOW BUBBLE, BUT I DISCOVERED ONE THING THAT *COULD* GET OUT--THE SUBPARTICLES OF CARBON DIOXIDE *FROM MY OWN BREATH!* AND WHAT I DID WAS TO USE MY GREEN BEAM...

"TO PROPEL THE INVISIBLE CO_2 PARTICLES OUT OF THE BUBBLE AT THE CLOCK..."

THEY DON'T SUSPECT WHAT I'M UP TO! BUT IF I'M RIGHT, THESE PARTICLES I'M SHOOTING AT THE CLOCK WILL *SPEED UP* ITS ATOMIC MECHANISM--AND MAKE IT *RUN FAST!*

AS THE EARTH-CHAMPION PINS HIS ADVERSARY HELPLESSLY TO A WALL...

SO YOU SEE I STILL HAVE *PLENTY OF POWER* LEFT IN MY RING! ENOUGH TO TAKE CARE OF YOU, *SINESTRO*, AND YOUR ALLIES-- THESE EVIL-SERVING MINIONS OF *QWARD!* THIS WILL HOLD YOU WHILE I DEAL WITH THEM!

BEFORE THE *QWARDIANS* CAN RECOVER FROM THEIR SHOCK, A GIGANTIC *GREEN WAVE* SWEEPS THEM AWAY WITH TITANIC FORCE...

I MUST HURRY! ALTHOUGH I MADE THE CLOCK RUN FAST, I DO NOT HAVE TOO MUCH TIME LEFT OUT OF MY TWENTY-FOUR HOURS OF RING POWER! AND I MUST NOT BE CAUGHT HERE IN THIS ANTIMATTER UNIVERSE WITH AN UNCHARGED RING!

As GREEN LANTERN turns once again to his trapped archfoe...

LAUGHING--!?

HA! HA! OF COURSE! YOU AMUSE ME, GREEN LANTERN, AND I WILL TELL YOU WHY! IF I HAD CAUGHT YOU THE WAY YOU HAVE CAUGHT ME, I WOULD HAVE DESTROYED YOU AT ONCE! BUT YOU--

YOUR STUPID CODE PREVENTS YOU FROM KILLING OR HARMING ANYONE IF YOU CAN HELP IT! I KNOW THAT BECAUSE I WORE A UNIFORM LIKE YOURS MYSELF ONCE--BEFORE I LEARNED BETTER! GOOD IS HELPLESS--EVIL ALONE CAN ACT!

AND NOT ONLY THAT, BUT YOU CANNOT EVEN TAKE ME WITH YOU BACK INTO YOUR WORLD TO IMPRISON ME--BECAUSE I WAS BANISHED FOREVER FROM YOUR UNIVERSE BY THE GUARDIANS--AND YOU CANNOT COUNTERMAND THEIR ORDERS! HA! HA! HA!

THAT'S TRUE...

BUT YOU ARE WRONG ABOUT GOOD BEING HELPLESS, SINESTRO! I WILL SHOW YOU HOW WRONG...

Once again the great green beam flares out with invincible force, and instants later...

NO FORCE ON QWARD CAN PENETRATE THE RING-MADE BUBBLE I HAVE CAST AROUND YOU, SINESTRO! ANY EVIL YOU CREATE NOW CAN ONLY BE AGAINST YOURSELF! AND WITH THAT PARTING THOUGHT, I BID YOU A FINAL FAREWELL...!

AT THE SEALED-UP APERTURE BETWEEN THE TWO UNIVERSES SOON AFTER...

I COULDN'T GET THROUGH THIS OPENING FROM OUR SIDE -- BUT BY USING MY RING AND BACKING IT WITH ALL MY *WILL POWER* -- I CAN GET THROUGH FROM THIS SIDE!

AND SHORTLY, IN A CERTAIN FAMILIAR CUBICLE IN THE HANGAR OF THE *FERRIS AIRCRAFT COMPANY*, A SOLEMN OATH IS RENEWED...

I HAD ONLY A *FEW SECONDS* OF POWER LEFT --

IN BRIGHTEST DAY, IN BLACKEST NIGHT, NO EVIL SHALL ESCAPE MY SIGHT! LET THOSE WHO WORSHIP *EVIL'S MIGHT* BEWARE MY POWER -- GREEN LANTERN'S LIGHT!

ON A ONCE-AGAIN PEACEFUL EARTH A BRILLIANT GREEN SHAPE FLARES ALONG...

THE OPENING OF THE *BOYS SETTLEMENT HOUSE* IN *VALDALE* HAS BEEN POST--PONED -- DUE TO THE EXTRAORDINARY EVENTS YESTERDAY -- TO TODAY! AND THIS TIME I'M KEEPING MY APPOINTMENT TO APPEAR THERE!

SOON, A SEA OF YOUTHFUL FACES IS STARING WORSHIP-FULLY UP AT THE *EMERALD GLADIATOR*...

...AND REMEMBER THIS, BOYS, WHEN *RIGHT* IS ON YOUR SIDE, YOU WILL ALWAYS OVERCOME *EVIL* NO MATTER WHERE YOU FIND IT!

The End 16

GREEN LANTERN

WHAT GREEN LANTERN WAS DOING ON THE AIRPLANE IN THE FIRST PLACE IS SOMETHING OF A LONG STORY-- INVOLVING (1) THE MYSTERIOUS, INEXPLICABLE DIS- APPEARANCE OF HIS PAL PIEFACE, THE ESKIMO GREASE- MONKEY; AND (2) THE LONG-AWAITED ARRIVAL FROM ALASKA OF PIE'S CHILDHOOD SWEETHEART!
WE HOPE THAT THESE EXCITING HINTS ARE ENOUGH TO INDUCE YOU TO GO ON WITH THIS TALE THAT WE CALL--

WINGS OF DESTINY

G-GREEN LANTERN! HOW'D HE GET IN HERE--?!

THESE GUNMEN HAVE TAKEN OVER THIS AIRLINER! BUT I'M ABOUT TO TAKE THEM OVER--!

As HAL JORDAN, ACE TEST PILOT, LIES IN HIS BED ONE NIGHT IN A DEEP SLEEP...

...NO, PIEFACE! YOU KNOW I CAN'T USE MY POWER RING FOR TRIVIAL PURPOSES--BUT ONLY TO COMBAT EVIL AND INJUSTICE! STOP BOTHERING ME--

GOLLY, GREEN LANTERN, I'VE ALWAYS WANTED TO FLY! YOU CAN MAKE ME FLY WITH YOUR RING! IS THAT SO MUCH TO ASK OF A GUY'S BEST PAL?

HMMM!

IN HAL'S DREAM HE SEES HIMSELF AS HIS ALTER EGO GREEN LANTERN, BESIEGED BY "PIEFACE," HIS ESKIMO GREASEMONKEY...

ALL RIGHT, PIE! I SUPPOSE THERE IS NO HARM IN IT! BUT JUST THIS ONCE, YOU UNDERSTAND? I'LL TURN YOU INTO A BIRD SO YOU CAN FLY--!

JUMPING FISHHOOKS!

MEANWHILE IN THE DREAM, GREEN LANTERN'S WILL POWER BEGINS TO OPERATE AND...

...UNKNOWN TO THE SLEEPER, HIS CHARGED POWER RING REALLY BEGINS TO OBEY HIS UNCONSCIOUS COMMANDS...

...BEAMING A CHARGE OF ENERGY TO THE ROOM NEXT DOOR WHERE THOMAS KALMAKU (PIEFACE) LIVES...

...AND TURNS HIM WITH THE GREATEST EASE INTO A SEAGULL...

WHAT GOES ON? WHAT GOES ON?

2

IN THE MORNING... GOSH, I SLEPT LATE! I'D BETTER HURRY, GET *PIEFACE*, AND MAKE IT OUT TO THE FIELD!* WE HAVE A BUSY DAY AHEAD OF US--

*Editor's Note; THE *FERRIS* AIRCRAFT COMPANY WHERE HAL JORDAN IS CHIEF TEST PILOT!

SOON... NO ANSWER! I GUESS *PIEFACE* LEFT WITHOUT ME! HE MUST HAVE TRIED TO WAKE ME AND COULDN'T!

KNOCK! KNOCK!

BUT AS HAL TAKES OFF, UNKNOWN TO HIM BE-HIND THE CLOSED DOOR "PIEFACE" IS JUST AWAKENING...

FUNNY! I HAD THE LOOPIEST DREAM LAST NIGHT! ALL ABOUT HOW *GL* GOT IT INTO HIS HEAD TO TURN ME INTO A BIRD!

K-KEK! IMAGINE THAT! *ME* A BIRD! BUT, FUNNY--I FEEL KIND OF ITCHY...

...LIKE I WAS COVERED WITH FEATHERS--OR SOMETHING! I'LL TAKE A LOOK AT MYSELF IN THE MIRROR--

K-KEK! I MUST BE STILL DREAMING --OBVIOUSLY! BUT IN THAT CASE, WHAT AM I DOING UP? I'LL GET BACK INTO BED!

3

WHY AM I PULLING THE COVERS BACK THIS WAY--USING MY **BEAK** INSTEAD OF MY HANDS? FUNNY, I'M BEGINNING TO GET THE QUEEREST FEELING THAT I'M NOT ASLEEP AT ALL...

AND IF I'M NOT ASLEEP THEN THERE'S ONLY ONE CONCLUSION! I'M **NOT** DREAMING! AND IF I'M NOT DREAMING THAT MEANS (K-KEK!) **I AM A BIRD!**

YEOWIE! SOME MEAN VILLAIN HAS DONE THIS--PROBABLY SOME FIEND FROM OUTER SPACE--TRYING TO ELIMINATE ME BEFORE HIS ALIEN RACE INVADES THE EARTH! I GOTTA FIND MY PAL **GREEN LANTERN**-- WARN HIM...

GL CAN CHANGE ME BACK TO MY REGULAR SHAPE! HE CAN DO IT WITH HIS RING--AND THEN TOGETHER THE TWO OF US CAN TAKE ON THE **INVADERS!** I GOTTA FLY **FAST**--!

MEANWHILE AT THE AIRCRAFT COMPANY ON THE OUTSKIRTS OF **COAST CITY**...

STRANGE! THERE'S BEEN NO SIGN OF **PIE-FACE!** I CAN'T IMAGINE WHAT'S HAPPENED TO HIM! AND ESPECIALLY THIS MORNING WHEN THIS TELEGRAM HE'S BEEN WAITING FOR SO LONG HAS FINALLY ARRIVED...

...FROM HIS CHILDHOOD SWEET-HEART, **TERGA**--SAYING THAT SHE'S ARRIVING ON THE TEN O'CLOCK PLANE FROM ALASKA AND THAT HE **MUST MEET HER!** GREAT SCOTT! THE POOR GIRL WILL BE WORRIED TO DEATH IF THERE'S NO ONE THERE! I'VE GOT TO FILL IN FOR **PIE**--!

4

IN THE PRIVACY OF HIS DRESSING ROOM A TRANSFORMATION COMES OVER THE YOUTHFUL PILOT...

NO TIME TO WASTE! I'LL RE-CHARGE MY RING AS *GREEN LANTERN* AND GET OUT TO THE AIRPORT AT ONCE!

IN BRIGHTEST DAY, IN BLACKEST NIGHT, NO EVIL SHALL ESCAPE MY SIGHT! LET THOSE WHO WORSHIP EVIL'S MIGHT BEWARE MY POWER-- *GREEN LANTERN'S LIGHT!*

WHILE POWER-FLYING TO THE AIRPORT...

THAT PESKY *BIRD!* KEEPS FLYING AT ME--! WHAT IN THUNDER IS THE MATTER WITH IT?

HEY, *GL--GL*, YOU MUST LISTEN TO ME!

SUPER-SCIENTIFIC ALIENS...ABOUT TO INVADE THE EARTH! AWFUL EMERGENCY...YOU AND I MUST FIGHT--AFTER YOU TURN ME BACK TO MY REGULAR SHAPE!

THIS BIRD LOOKS LIKE A SEAGULL-- BUT ACTS LIKE A *CUCKOO!*

WITH AN ADDITIONAL BURST OF POWER, THE *EMERALD GLADIATOR* DRAWS SWIFTLY AWAY FROM THE WINGED NUISANCE...

THANK GOODNESS SEAGULLS AREN'T KNOWN FOR SPEED, AND I COULD EASILY GET AWAY FROM IT! NOW TO GET TO THE AIRPORT...

K-KEK!

AND SOON, NEAR THE AIRFIELD, *GREEN LANTERN* SUDDENLY DE-CIDES TO USE HIS RING TO SUM-MON HIS HAL JORDAN CLOTHES TO HIM...

IT'S OCCURRED TO ME I'D BETTER GREET *PIEFACE'S* GIRL FRIEND AS *HAL JORDAN!* THAT WAY IT WILL BE EASIER TO EXPLAIN MY RELATION TO *PIE* AND WHY I'M HERE!

Editor's Note: GREEN LANTERN HAS WILLED HIS CLOTHES TO TRAVEL INVISIBLY FROM HIS HANGAR DRESSING ROOM, TO APPEAR ONLY IN FRONT OF HIM!

PROMPTLY AT TEN...

THERE'S THE PLANE! BUT I DON'T SEE *TERGA*... OR ANYONE WHO REMOTELY FITS HER DESCRIPTION! Eh? WHAT'S THAT...?

...NO MOVE FROM HERE...

5

Panel 1: AS THE ACE TEST PILOT BOARDS THE AIRLINER...

I...NO...MOVE! WANT...SEE THOMAS! NO... MOVE TILL HE COME...

THAT MUST BE *TERGA!* SHE'S ASKING FOR *THOMAS KALMAKU*--THAT'S *PIE'S* SQUARE MONIKER! BUT I DIDN'T REALIZE--SHE CAN HARDLY SPEAK ENGLISH!

Panel 2: BUT BEFORE HAL CAN EVEN APPROACH THE GIRL...

eh? THOSE MEN--BARGED IN HERE--TAKING OVER THE PLANE AT GUN-POINT!

YOU--PILOT! DON'T ASK QUESTIONS! JUST TAKE THE PLANE UP--AND *FAST!*

Panel 3: AS THE PLANE CAPTAIN IS FORCED TO OBEY...

WE'RE ALOFT ALREADY! THOSE GUNMEN MUST BE ESCAPED CON-VICTS OUT TO MAKE A GETAWAY! I'VE GOT TO STOP THEM--BUT I MUST BE CAREFUL! I DON'T WANT *TERGA* TO BE HURT--!

Panel 4: A THOUGHT-COMMAND FROM HAL JORDAN-- AND HIS OUTER GARMENTS FLY OFF...

THOSE CROOKS AREN'T KEEPING TOO CLOSE A WATCH ON ME! I GUESS THEY DON'T THINK I MATTER MUCH! BUT THEY'RE ABOUT TO LEARN DIFFERENTLY!

Panel 5: THE NEXT MOMENT...

FIRST THING I'LL DO IS USE MY RING TO FREEZE THE CON-TROLS--AND MAKE THIS PLANE FLY IN SLOW CIRCLES TO PLAY SAFE--!

G-GREEN LANTERN!? WHERE'D *HE* COME FROM!?

Panel 6: BUT THEN AS AN UNEXPECTED AIR POCKET CAUSES THE CRAFT TO LURCH...

LOOK! *GREEN LANTERN* SLAMMED INTO THAT SEAT--

UHH!

--AND IS CONKING OUT!

6.

QUICK! PLUG HIM! BEFORE HE COMES TO--!

OH!

AT THAT MOMENT, OUTSIDE THE CIRCLING CRAFT...

THERE'S TERGA-- AND MY PAL GREEN LANTERN IN DANGER! IT'S A GOOD THING I SPOTTED THIS PLANE!

AS THE INTREPID BIRD MAKES A SUDDEN ENTRANCE...

HEY!?

GOT THAT HOOD'S ATTENTION JUST BEFORE HE PULLED THAT TRIGGER! BUT TO MAKE SURE HE DOESN'T USE THAT GUN--

CRASH!

JUMPING JETS! THAT BIRD AGAIN--AND LOOKS LIKE IT'S JUST SAVED MY LIFE!

RECOVERING SWIFTLY, THE EMERALD CRUSADER PROPELS HIS GREEN BEAM OUTWARD WITH OVERPOWERING EFFECT...

GREAT GOING, GL! K-KEK!

HE'S GOT US! OUR BUST-OUT IS OVER!

7

LATER, WITH THE CONVICTS BACK IN STATE PRISON WHERE THEY BELONG...

AT LEAST I GOT *TERGA* OFF THE PLANE! SHE SEEMS INCLINED TO TRUST ME! BUT I'D BETTER GET HOLD OF *CAROL* TO CHAPERONE HER, UNTIL WE CAN LOCATE *PIEFACE*! I STILL-- EH?

OOH! BIRD-- GO AWAY...

THAT BIRD! IT'S NOT AFTER ME NOW--IT'S GOING FOR *TERGA*!!

IT'S ALMOST AS IF IT'S HAPPY TO SEE *TERGA*! AS IF IT'S TRYING TO *KISS HER*? EH? JUMPIN' JETS! IS IT POSSIBLE--!?

SUDDENLY, IN BACK OF *GREEN LANTERN'S* MIND A MEMORY STIRS...

MY DREAM LAST NIGHT...USING MY *POWER RING*... TO TURN *PIEFACE INTO A BIRD*!! IS IT POSSIBLE THAT ACTUALLY I--¡GULP!¡ GOT TO FIND OUT!

THEN, AFTER BEAMING A CAGE AROUND THE BIRD...

er--EXCUSE ME A MOMENT, *TERGA*! I'VE-- er--GOT A LITTLE BUSINESS TO TAKE CARE OF! YOU STAY RIGHT THERE... *STAY...THERE...* UNDER- STAND?

Y-YES...

BEHIND THE HANGAR A STARTLING TRANS- FORMATION TAKES PLACE...

PIEFACE! ¡Whew!¡ I MUST MAKE SURE I COMMAND MY *POWER RING* NEVER TO LET SUCH A "*NIGHTMARE*" HAPPEN AGAIN!

HI, *GL*! IT'S GOOD TO SEE YOU AGAIN-- FACE TO FACE!

8

THAT EVENING AFTER THE EMERALD CRUSADER HAS "VANISHED" AND HAL JORDAN HAS AGAIN POPPED UP...

IT WAS A GOOD IDEA OF YOURS, HAL, TO ARRANGE THIS *DOUBLE DATE* WITH *TERGA* AND *PIEFACE!* I'M ENJOYING THEM--

SO AM I, CAROL! * THEY ARE A WONDERFUL COUPLE...

*Editor's Note! CAROL FERRIS, IN THE ABSENCE OF HER FATHER, IS IN SOLE CHARGE OF THE FERRIS AIRCRAFT COMPANY WHERE HAL WORKS! NOMINALLY, THEREFORE, SHE IS HAL'S BOSS-- BUT ACTUALLY, AND MAINLY, SHE IS HIS ROMANTIC INTEREST!

...AND SHE'S SO LOYAL TO HIM! YOU KNOW THEY HAD THE *HARDEST TIME* GETTING HER OFF THE PLANE--BECAUSE HE WASN'T THERE!

YES, AND I GATHER FROM HER TALK THAT SHE SPEAKS ONLY A FEW WORDS OF ENGLISH...

--AND SHE'S USING MOST OF THEM NOW!

THOMAS... YOU... ME... LOVE!

The End

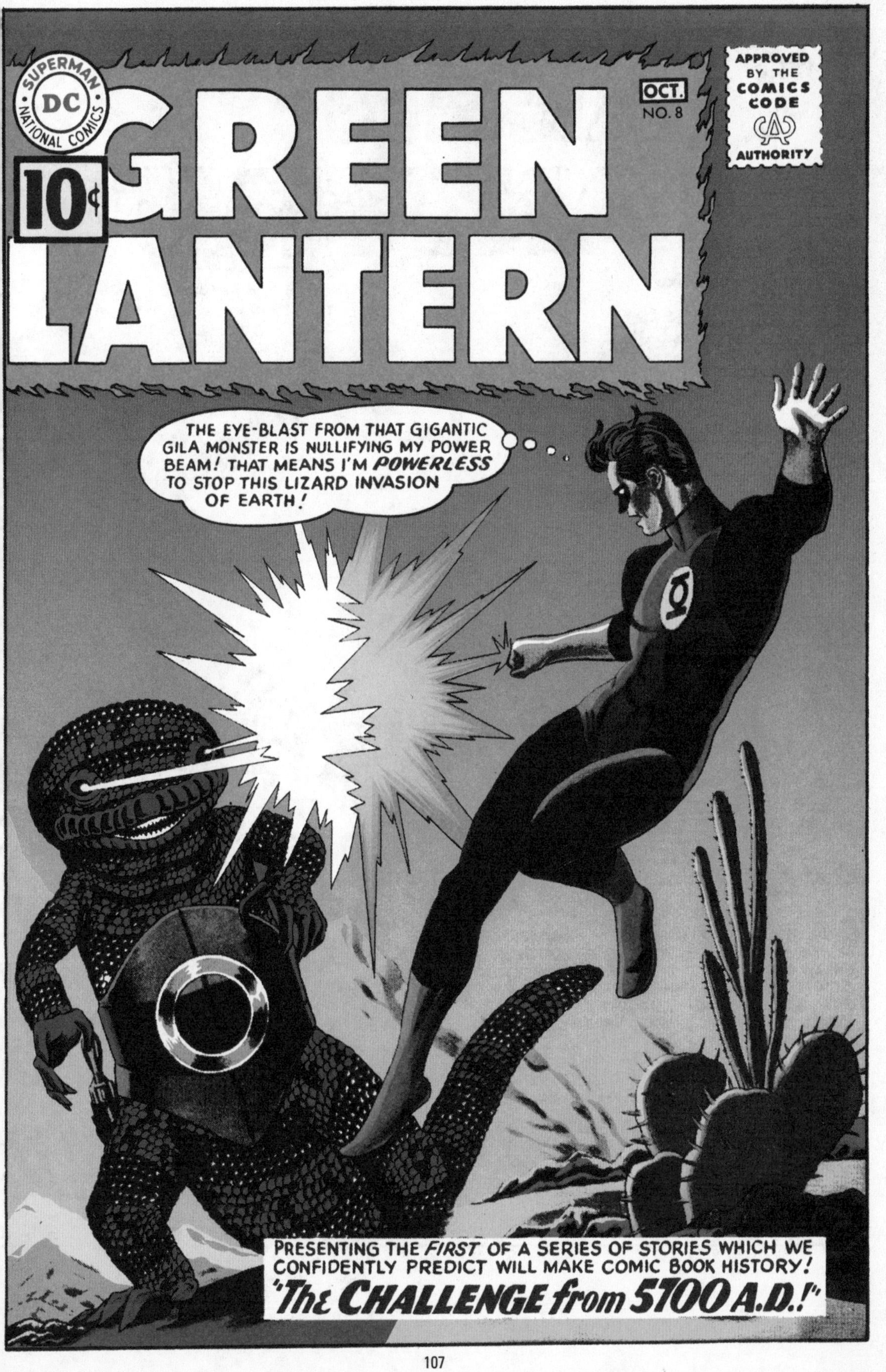
SUPERMAN
DC
NATIONAL COMICS
10¢
GREEN LANTERN
OCT.
NO. 8
APPROVED BY THE COMICS CODE AUTHORITY
THE EYE-BLAST FROM THAT GIGANTIC GILA MONSTER IS NULLIFYING MY POWER BEAM! THAT MEANS I'M POWERLESS TO STOP THIS LIZARD INVASION OF EARTH!
PRESENTING THE FIRST OF A SERIES OF STORIES WHICH WE CONFIDENTLY PREDICT WILL MAKE COMIC BOOK HISTORY!
"The CHALLENGE from 5700 A.D.!"

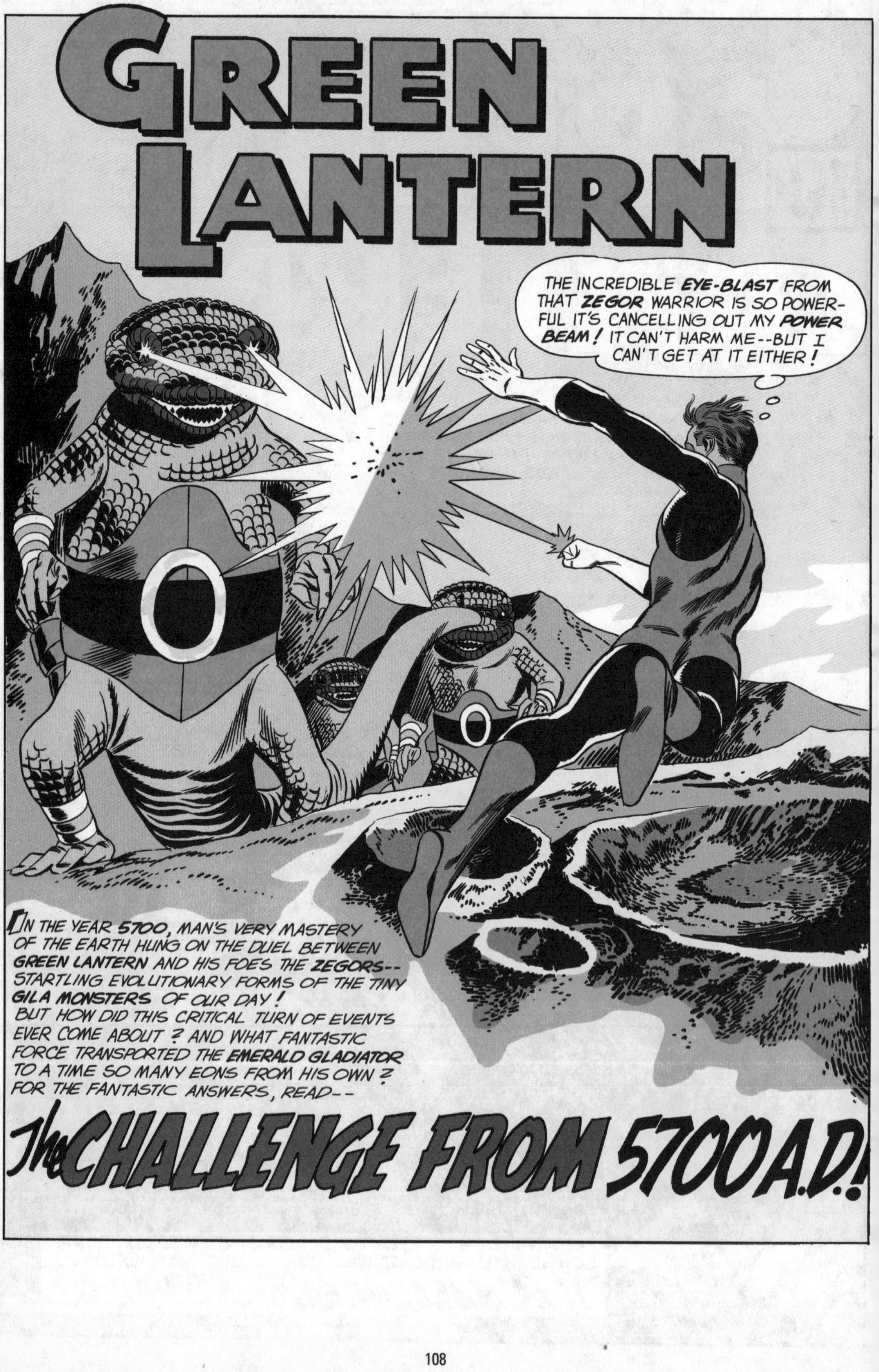
GREEN LANTERN
THE INCREDIBLE EYE-BLAST FROM THAT ZEGOR WARRIOR IS SO POWERFUL IT'S CANCELLING OUT MY POWER BEAM! IT CAN'T HARM ME--BUT I CAN'T GET AT IT EITHER!
IN THE YEAR 5700, MAN'S VERY MASTERY OF THE EARTH HUNG ON THE DUEL BETWEEN GREEN LANTERN AND HIS FOES THE ZEGORS--STARTLING EVOLUTIONARY FORMS OF THE TINY GILA MONSTERS OF OUR DAY! BUT HOW DID THIS CRITICAL TURN OF EVENTS EVER COME ABOUT? AND WHAT FANTASTIC FORCE TRANSPORTED THE EMERALD GLADIATOR TO A TIME SO MANY EONS FROM HIS OWN? FOR THE FANTASTIC ANSWERS, READ--
The CHALLENGE FROM 5700 A.D.!

IN THE YEAR **5700** IN **STAR CITY**, EARTH, AN IMPRESSIVE PLASTI—STEEL STRUCTURE HOUSES THE EXECUTIVE OFFICES OF THE SOLAR SYSTEM GOVERNMENT..

IN THIS MIGHTY EDIFICE, ONE SPACIOUS CHAMBER IS SET ASIDE FOR THE USE OF THE ALL POWERFUL **SOLAR DIRECTOR** HIMSELF...HIGH ABOVE THE VAULTING AERIAL-WAYS OF THE CITY...

AND AT THE IMPOSING DESK IN THIS ROOM SITS THE MAN WHO WIELDS MORE AUTHORITY OVER THE PEOPLE OF EARTH THAN ANY INDIVIDUAL WHO EVER LIVED...

...NONE OTHER, DEAR READER, THAN YOUR FRIEND AND MINE, **GREEN LANTERN** OF OUR OWN DAY AND AGE!

NOW THAT I HAVE BEEN MADE **SOLAR DIRECTOR**, I MUST SELECT FOR MY AIDES THE **BEST** TALENTS AVAILABLE--IN ORDER TO DEFEAT THE TERRIBLE THREAT THAT CONFRONTS THE EARTH!

BUT WAIT--WE CAN HEAR YOU GASP, READER--THIS IS THE YEAR **5700**! HOW CAN **GREEN LANTERN** BE IN **STAR CITY**? HOW CAN **HE** OF ALL PEOPLE BE THE GREAT **SOLAR DIRECTOR**? **HOW** COULD THIS POSSIBLY HAVE COME ABOUT? WELL, IN ORDER TO EXPLAIN, IT MIGHT BE A GOOD IDEA, WITH YOUR PERMISSION, READER...

...TO TURN THE CALENDAR BACK TO A MEETING OF THE HIGH COUNCIL OF SOLAR DELEGATES, SITTING IN **SOLAR HALL**, **STAR CITY**, IN A SESSION OF THE GRAVEST EMERGENCY...

FELLOW SOLARITES*, WE ARE MET IN THIS CRISIS TO CONSIDER A NEW CANDIDATE FOR THE CRUCIAL POST OF **SOLAR DIRECTOR**! MANY CANDIDATES HAVE BEEN CONSIDERED--

YES! BUT NONE OF THEM WAS **EQUAL** TO THE **JOB**!

*Editor's Note: BY 5700 A.D., CENTURIES OF LIVING ON THE OTHER SOLAR SYSTEM PLANETS THEY HAVE COLONIZED HAS ALTERED EARTHMEN AND CHANGED THEM ACCORDING TO THE CLIMATIC CONDITIONS OF THEIR NEW HOMES.

BEFORE I REVEAL THE LATEST CANDIDATE, I MUST REMIND YOU THAT NOT LONG AGO OUR SCIENCE DEVELOPED THE ABILITY TO PEER AT WILL INTO THE *PAST*--IN EFFECT, TO VIEW HISTORY AS IT HAPPENS--BY THE INVENTION OF THE *TIMESCOPE* !

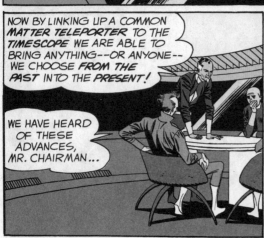

NOW BY LINKING UP A COMMON *MATTER TELEPORTER* TO THE *TIMESCOPE* WE ARE ABLE TO BRING ANYTHING--OR ANYONE--WE CHOOSE *FROM THE PAST* INTO THE *PRESENT* !

WE HAVE HEARD OF THESE ADVANCES, MR. CHAIRMAN...

...BUT WHAT HAVE THEY TO DO WITH OUR CHOICE FOR A *SOLAR DIRECTOR* ?

I AM COMING TO THAT, *RAF TAMIN* ! IN THE COURSE OF OUR RESEARCHES INTO THE *PAST* WE CAME ACROSS A TRULY *AMAZING INDIVIDUAL* ...

"...IN THE FARAWAY *20th CENTURY* NAMED *GREEN LANTERN* ! MY SECRETARY, *IONA VANE*, AND I STUDIED HIM CLOSELY ON THE *TIMESCOPE*..."

HE IS ABSOLUTELY FEARLESS !

HE IS A CHAMPION OF CHAMPIONS !

SINCE WE HAVE NOT BEEN ABLE TO FIND A GREAT LEADER IN OUR OWN ERA, I PROPOSE THE FOLLOWING: THAT WE BRING THIS ANCIENT HERO *GREEN LANTERN* TO OUR TIME AND MAKE *HIM* OUR *SOLAR DIRECTOR* !

WHAT AN ASTONISHING PROPOSAL !

AFTER THE MATTER HAS BEEN WEIGHED CAREFULLY, AND EVERY FACET OF *GREEN LANTERN'S* LIFE HAS BEEN EXAMINED...

WE AGREE, CHAIRMAN DASOR ! YOU HAVE FOUND OUR *SOLAR DIRECTOR* ! BUT *HURRY*--THERE IS VERY LITTLE TIME--!

EVERYTHING IS READY, FELLOW SOLARITES-- EXCEPT FOR ONE PROBLEM..

3

TO TRAVEL IN TIME CAUSES AN INDIVIDUAL'S MEMORY TO BE **COMPLETELY WIPED OUT!** IF **GREEN LANTERN** CAME HERE WITHOUT HIS "LIFE-HISTORY" HE WOULD BE DAZED-- OF LITTLE USE, TO US!

BUT **HOW** CAN SUCH AN OBSTACLE BE OVERCOME?

SIMPLY! MISS VANE HERE HAS PREPARED A FICTITIOUS PERSONAL HISTORY FOR **GREEN LANTERN**! HE WILL **BELIEVE** HE IS A MAN OF OUR TIME WHILE HE IS HERE! IN THAT WAY HE WILL BE ABLE TO FUNCTION PERFECTLY!

AS CHAIRMAN DASOR GOES OVER THE DATA PREPARED BY HIS ATTRACTIVE SECRETARY...

THIS IS VERY CONVINCING, MISS VANE! **GREEN LANTERN** WILL BELIEVE THAT HE IS A FAMOUS SPACE-EXPLORER IN OUR ERA WHO HAS SPENT YEARS AMONG THE **ASTEROIDS**-- AND WHO HAS JUST BEEN SUMMONED BACK TO EARTH TO DEAL WITH THE DREADFUL MENACE THAT PERILS US! BUT WAIT--!

THERE IS ONE THING YOU HAVE OMITTED, MISS VANE! A YOUNG MAN LIKE **GREEN LANTERN** WOULD CERTAINLY HAVE A **ROMANTIC INTEREST**! WITHOUT THAT, HIS MIND MIGHT BE DISSATISFIED-- MIGHT FEEL THAT SOMETHING IS WRONG!

Y-YOU'RE RIGHT, CHAIRMAN DASOR!

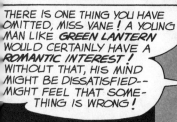

OBVIOUSLY! AND SINCE I HAPPEN TO KNOW THAT **YOU** ARE UNMARRIED AND UNATTACHED, **IONA**, IT OCCURS TO ME THAT **YOU** CAN BE HIS ROMANTIC INTEREST!

M-ME!?

AFTER THE MATTER HAS BEEN SWIFTLY SETTLED...

THEN ALL IS ARRANGED! COME WITH ME, GENTLEMEN--!

I-- HARDLY KNOW THIS **GREEN LANTERN**! BUT-- I CAN'T LET MY PERSONAL FEELINGS STAND IN THE WAY OF THE **SAFETY OF HUMAN CIVILIZATION!**

4

NATURALLY AT THIS MOMENT, IN THE **20th** CENTURY, GREEN LANTERN HIMSELF COULD HARDLY SUSPECT THAT HIS NAME WOULD FIGURE IN A TOP SECRET CONFERENCE IN AN ERA CENTURIES REMOVED FROM HIS OWN! IN FACT, DEAR READER, IF WE MAY SWITCH AT THIS TIME TO THE EMERALD GLADIATOR, WE FIND HIM AT A TASK...

...WHICH OCCUPIES HIM SEVERAL TIMES A WEEK... CHARGING HIS MIGHTY **POWER RING**...

IN BRIGHTEST DAY, IN BLACKEST NIGHT, NO EVIL SHALL ESCAPE MY SIGHT! LET THOSE WHO WORSHIP EVIL'S MIGHT BEWARE MY POWER--**GREEN LANTERN'S LIGHT!**

AND AS THE GREEN-CLAD FIGURE BURSTS FROM THE REAR OF THE HANGAR WHERE IN HIS SECRET IDENTITY HE IS **HAL JORDAN**, ACE TEST PILOT...

I'VE GOT TO GET TO THE OCEANFRONT AS SOON AS POSSIBLE! ACCORDING TO THE LATEST BROADCASTS AN INCREDIBLE SEA MONSTER HAS BEEN SIGHTED THERE AND IS THREATENING LIVES AND PROPERTY! NO ONE KNOWS WHERE IT COULD HAVE COME FROM!

...AND THE ONLY CLUE IS THAT WHILE THE **NAVY** WAS SEARCHING FOR A **LOST SPACE-CAPSULE**... THE MONSTER SUDDENLY APPEARED IN THE **SAME** AREA! BUT WHAT COULD BE THE CONNECTION BETWEEN THOSE TWO EVENTS IS **ANYBODY'S GUESS!**

SHORTLY...

THERE IT IS! AND GREAT SCOTT--!

IT'S CAPSIZING THAT SHIP! I'VE GOT TO STOP IT!

AND AS FATE WILLS IT, THIS IS THE VERY MOMENT WHEN IN 5700 A.D. A LEVER IS PRESSED..

ACCORDING TO OUR CALCULATIONS IT WILL TAKE ABOUT *FIVE SECONDS* FOR THE *TIME-PULSE* TO TRAVEL DOWN THROUGH THE AGES TO *1961! IONA,* BEGIN THE COUNTDOWN!

FIVE... FOUR...

WILL IT WORK? WILL WE REALLY BE ABLE TO BRING *GREEN LANTERN* TO OUR ERA?

DOWN, DOWN, THROUGH THE LONG CENTURIES OF HISTORY THE *TIME-PULSE* SPEEDS WITH INEXPRESSIBLE SWIFTNESS...

THREE... TWO

ONE... ZERO!

eh? A QUEER NUMBNESS COMING OVER ME!

AND SIMULTANEOUSLY, BEFORE THE *GREEN GLADIATOR'S* THOUGHTS CAN GO ANY FURTHER, THERE IS A *SNAP* IN HIS MIND! AND...

WE DID IT! *GREEN LANTERN IS HERE!* THIS IS A CRITICAL MOMENT! THE TRANSITION HAS MADE HIS MIND TEMPORARILY A BLANK! NOW HIS PSEUDO— HISTORY MUST BE FED INTO IT *AT ONCE!*

...YOU ARE CALLED *GREEN LANTERN*...BUT SECRETLY YOU ARE *POL MANNING*... FAMED ASTEROID-EXPLORER IN THE 57th CENTURY...

AS THE TEMPORARILY BLANK MIND OF THE **EMERALD CRUSADER** GREEDILY SUCKS IN THE INFORMATION BEING FED TO IT...

MY ALTER EGO IS **POL MANNING**, EXPLORER...

NOT EVEN **IONA VANE**, THE GIRL IN YOUR LIFE, KNOWS YOUR SECRET IDENTITY, **GREEN LANTERN**!

AS SOON AS YOU HEARD OF OUR MORTAL STRUGGLE AGAINST THE **ZEGORS** YOU IMMEDIATELY RETURNED TO EARTH TO AID US IN OUR BATTLE! YOU HAVE ALREADY LEARNED THAT WE ELECTED YOU OUR **SOLAR DIRECTOR**!

AFTER THE LAST BIT OF DATA INVOLVING THE CAREER OF **POL MANNING—GREEN LANTERN**, TOGETHER WITH THE NECESSARY MEMORY PICTURES, HAS ENTERED THE TIME-VOYAGER'S BRAIN...

HE IS RETURNING TO NORMAL NOW! HE WILL SPEAK...!

GREETINGS... GREETINGS TO THE HIGH SOLAR COUNCIL! AND **IONA**--

IONA, IT'S BEEN TWO LONG MONTHS-- SINCE WE LAST SAW EACH OTHER!

MMM! THIS PLAY-ACTING ISN'T GOING TO BE AS DIFFICULT FOR ME AS I THOUGHT! HE **IS** ATTRACTIVE!

BUT I MUSTN'T FORGET THAT I'M JUST A PAWN IN A MUCH BIGGER GAME THAN MERE ROMANCE!

OH-- YES!

GREEN LANTERN, YOU--YOU MUST LISTEN TO CHAIRMAN **DASOR**!

RELUCTANTLY, GRIMLY, THE STALWART GREEN-CLAD FIGURE TURNS...

NOW--TELL ME ALL ABOUT THE **ZEGORS**, CHAIRMAN DASOR! I RECEIVED ONLY SKETCHY REPORTS ON MY--ER-- TRAVELS!

HIS MIND IS WORKING PERFECTLY! HE'S EVEN CONCEALING HIS SECRET IDENTITY FROM US!

VERY WELL, **GREEN LANTERN**...

*B*UT WHILE THE NEW **SOLAR DIRECTOR** IN **5700 A.D.** IS BRIEFED ON THE DREADFUL DANGER TO EARTH WHICH HE HAS COME HOME TO FIGHT AGAINST, LET US PAUSE FOR A MOMENT, READER, TO REVIEW THIS STARTLING SITUATION!

*W*E KNOW, READER, THAT THE MAN NOW SITTING IN THE CHAMBER OF THE HIGH COUNCIL IN **STAR CITY** IS REALLY UNDER HIS MASK HAL JORDAN OF THE 20th CENTURY!
BUT SO WELL HAS THE BRAIN–DATA MACHINE OF THIS ERA WORKED THAT HE BELIEVES HE IS SOMEONE ELSE ENTIRELY-- AND HAS NO DOUBTS ABOUT IT!

...THEN THE **ZEGORS** HAVE RISEN FROM THE INTERIOR OF THE EARTH, TO THREATEN **MANKIND'S MASTERY** OF OUR **PLANET**?

EXACTLY, **GREEN LANTERN!** AND IT IS A CHALLENGE WE COULD NEVER HAVE FORESEEN...

"WE KNEW THAT THE **GILA MONSTERS*** HAD VANISHED ABOUT THE YEAR **2000**, AND WE ASSUMED THEY HAD BECOME EXTINCT.."

Editor's Note: LIZARDS ABOUT 18 INCHES LONG, COVERED WITH BEAD-LIKE SKIN, FOUND ONLY IN THE SOUTHWEST DESERT OF THE U.S.

"WHAT WE DID NOT KNOW WAS THAT THE CREATURES HAD MERELY RETREATED DEEP UNDERGROUND WHERE THEIR NATURAL RESISTANCE TO HEAT..."

"ENABLED THEM TO FLOURISH AND EVOLVE INTO A **NEW** AND **FORMIDABLE** CIVILIZATION OVER THE CENTURIES..."

"OUR FIRST SIGN OF THE THREAT CAME WHEN AN ARCHEOLOGIST, DR. VANCE BARNARD, AND HIS PARTY WERE WORKING IN THE ARIZONA DESERT SOME MONTHS AGO..."

LOOK! IN THE NAME OF THE NINE PLANETS--!

S-SOMETHING COMING OUT OF ITS EYES-- EEEAHH...

"AND EVEN AS THE CRY OF THE ARCHEOLOGIST LINGERED ON THE SULTRY DESERT AIR..."

DR. BARNARD! | HE'S VANISHED!

EEEAAGH!

"ONLY ONE OF THAT PARTY MANAGED TO ESCAPE, REACHING AN OUTLYING POST OF OUR CONTINENTAL PATROL..."

IT'S AN INCREDIBLE TALE! BUT WE'LL SEND OUT A FORCE TO INVESTIGATE AT ONCE!

"THE PATROL SQUAD WAS ARMED WITH THE LATEST WEAPONS! IT DID THEM NO GOOD, FOR BY THAT TIME..."

MORE OF THE CREATURES!

OUR HIGH-SPEED NUCLEAR BLASTS-- BOUNCING RIGHT OFF THEM!

"AND THEN..."

GREAT SKYHOOKS! SOMETHING--SOME QUEER FORCE-- SHOOTING OUT OF THEIR EYES--!

W-WIPED OUT HALF OUR FORCE IN AN INSTANT!

RUN! THESE THINGS CAN'T BE STOPPED!

"THAT WAS THE BEGINNING! WE SOON FOUND THAT NOT EVEN HYDRO- MISSILES COULD HALT THE ZEGORS, AS THEY CALL THEM-- SELVES..."

THEY'VE BEEN ADVANCING SLOWLY! BY NOW THEY CONTROL A SIZABLE PART OF THE COUNTRY! AND WE'VE BEEN FORCED ON THE DEFENSIVE, GREEN LANTERN!

I SEE!

9

So there you have it! Now, reader, you understand how **GREEN LANTERN** of our time came to be the **SOLAR DIRECTOR** of Earth in 5700 A.D.! In his very first hours on the job, the new chief...

...REVEALS THE EXECUTIVE GENIUS WHICH IN PART HAS WON HIM THE HIGH POST!

CHAIRMAN DASOR, I WANT A FULL REPORT OF THE EXACT MILITARY SITUATION AS SOON AS POSSIBLE!

HERE'S A LIST OF POSSIBILITIES FOR YOUR CABINET, **GREEN LANTERN**!

But desk work alone does not suit the temperament of the new **DIRECTOR**...

IONA, I'VE DECIDED TO USE MY **POWER RING** TO GET A FIRSTHAND LOOK AT THE **ZEGOR** ADVANCES!

PLEASE-- BE CAREFUL, **GREEN LANTERN**!

I WILL! SEE YOU SOON!

FORTUNATELY THE BRAIN-DATA IMPLANT ALLOWED HIM TO RETAIN ALL THE INFORMATION ABOUT HIS ORIGINAL ABILITY AS **GREEN LANTERN**-- AND THE USE OF HIS AMAZING **POWER BEAM**!

AND SOON, NOT FAR FROM THE EARTH NERVE-CENTER OF **STAR CITY**...

ZEGORS! NOTIFY! HEAD-QUARTERS!

THE ENEMY-- ADVANCING TOWARD THIS MILITARY OUTPOST!

AS THE STREAKING FIGURE WHIPS DOWN TOWARD THE SCENE...

THERE'S THAT **EYE-BLAST** DASOR DESCRIBED TO ME--GOING AT THAT BRAVE SOLDIER! AND--**GREAT THUNDER**!!

10

THE SOLDIER JUST SEEMED TO EVAPORATE, AS IF BLOWN AWAY BY THE WIND! AND NOW THE CREATURE IS TURNING TOWARD ME--!

OUT OF THE RING OF THE *EMERALD WARRIOR* A BEAM OF OVERPOWERING ENERGY SPURTS...

BUT THE NEXT MOMENT...

GOOD GOSH! THE TWO FORCES-- THE EYE-BLAST OF THAT *ZEGOR* AND MY POWER BEAM--ARE CANCELLING EACH OTHER OUT! HE CAN'T GET THROUGH TO ME--BUT NEITHER CAN I GET THROUGH TO HIM!

AS THE CREATURE SLINKS OFF...

GETTING AWAY! I COULD GO AFTER IT--BUT I CAN'T FIGHT ALL OF THESE *ZEGORS* ONE BY ONE! ACCORDING TO THE REPORTS THERE ARE HUNDREDS--THOUSANDS OF THEM!

ON THE WAY BACK TO *STAR CITY*, A GRIMLY SERIOUS *GREEN LANTERN* TAKES THOUGHT...

THERE MUST BE SOME WAY TO DEFEAT THIS *LIZARD INVASION* THREATENING MAN'S MASTERY OF THE PLANET! UNLESS THEY'RE STOPPED... HUMANS WILL BECOME FUGITIVES --FORCED TO HIDE OUT LIKE ANIMALS! HMMM! THAT EYE-BLAST SEEMS TO BE THEIR MAIN WEAPON...

11

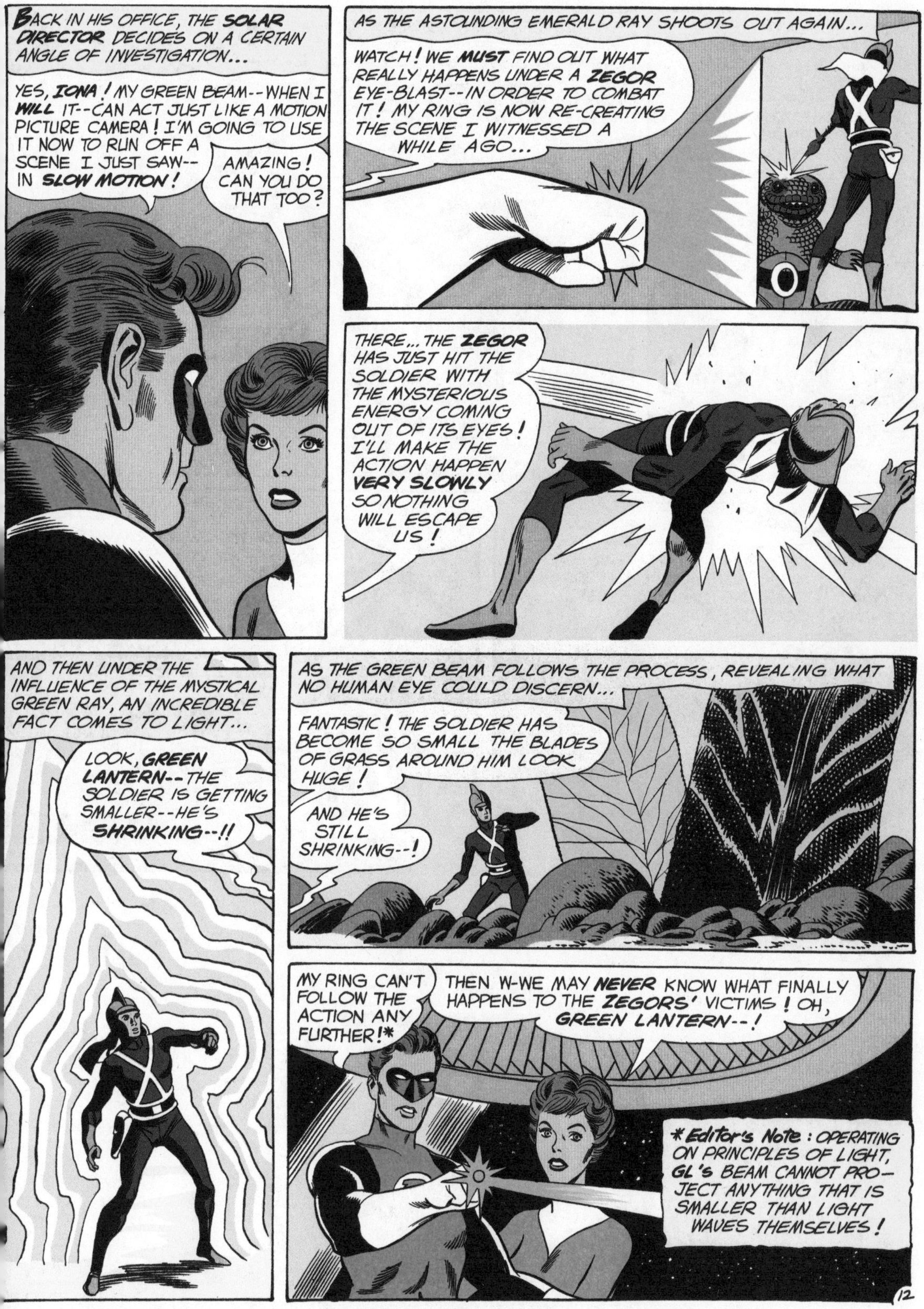
BACK IN HIS OFFICE, THE SOLAR DIRECTOR DECIDES ON A CERTAIN ANGLE OF INVESTIGATION...
YES, IONA! MY GREEN BEAM--WHEN I WILL IT--CAN ACT JUST LIKE A MOTION PICTURE CAMERA! I'M GOING TO USE IT NOW TO RUN OFF A SCENE I JUST SAW-- IN SLOW MOTION!
AMAZING! CAN YOU DO THAT TOO?
AS THE ASTOUNDING EMERALD RAY SHOOTS OUT AGAIN...
WATCH! WE MUST FIND OUT WHAT REALLY HAPPENS UNDER A ZEGOR EYE-BLAST--IN ORDER TO COMBAT IT! MY RING IS NOW RE-CREATING THE SCENE I WITNESSED A WHILE AGO...
THERE... THE ZEGOR HAS JUST HIT THE SOLDIER WITH THE MYSTERIOUS ENERGY COMING OUT OF ITS EYES! I'LL MAKE THE ACTION HAPPEN VERY SLOWLY SO NOTHING WILL ESCAPE US!
AND THEN UNDER THE INFLUENCE OF THE MYSTICAL GREEN RAY, AN INCREDIBLE FACT COMES TO LIGHT...
LOOK, GREEN LANTERN--THE SOLDIER IS GETTING SMALLER--HE'S SHRINKING--!!
AS THE GREEN BEAM FOLLOWS THE PROCESS, REVEALING WHAT NO HUMAN EYE COULD DISCERN...
FANTASTIC! THE SOLDIER HAS BECOME SO SMALL THE BLADES OF GRASS AROUND HIM LOOK HUGE!
AND HE'S STILL SHRINKING--!
MY RING CAN'T FOLLOW THE ACTION ANY FURTHER!*
THEN W-WE MAY NEVER KNOW WHAT FINALLY HAPPENS TO THE ZEGORS' VICTIMS! OH, GREEN LANTERN--!
*Editor's Note: OPERATING ON PRINCIPLES OF LIGHT, GL's BEAM CANNOT PROJECT ANYTHING THAT IS SMALLER THAN LIGHT WAVES THEMSELVES!
12

AT THAT MOMENT, THE COMMUNICATOR ON **GREEN LANTERN'S** DESK COMMANDS HIS ATTENTION...

SOLAR DIRECTOR, THIS IS CHAIRMAN DASOR! A REPORT OF A LONE **ZEGOR** SCOUT... IN **STAR CITY**...

IN THIS CITY!?

AND ALMOST SIMULTANEOUSLY...

G-GREEN LANTERN! HELP!

IONA! WHAT--?

THE **ZEGOR**-- IT'S BLASTED **IONA**!

WITH INCREDIBLE, OVERMASTERING FURY, THE **GREEN GLADIATOR'S** RING BURSTS OUT...

THAT'S ONE OVERGROWN LIZARD THAT WON'T BE TAKING OVER THE EARTH! BUT **IONA**! I **CAN'T** LET HER **VANISH** LIKE THE OTHERS! GOT TO SAVE HER!

VOOMP!

ON THE IMPULSE OF THE MOMENT, **GL** ACTS QUICKLY.

GOT TO USE MY RING TO SHRINK MYSELF...

...INTO ATOMIC SIZE!

IT'S THE ONLY WAY...

I CAN FOLLOW **IONA**... SAVE HER...

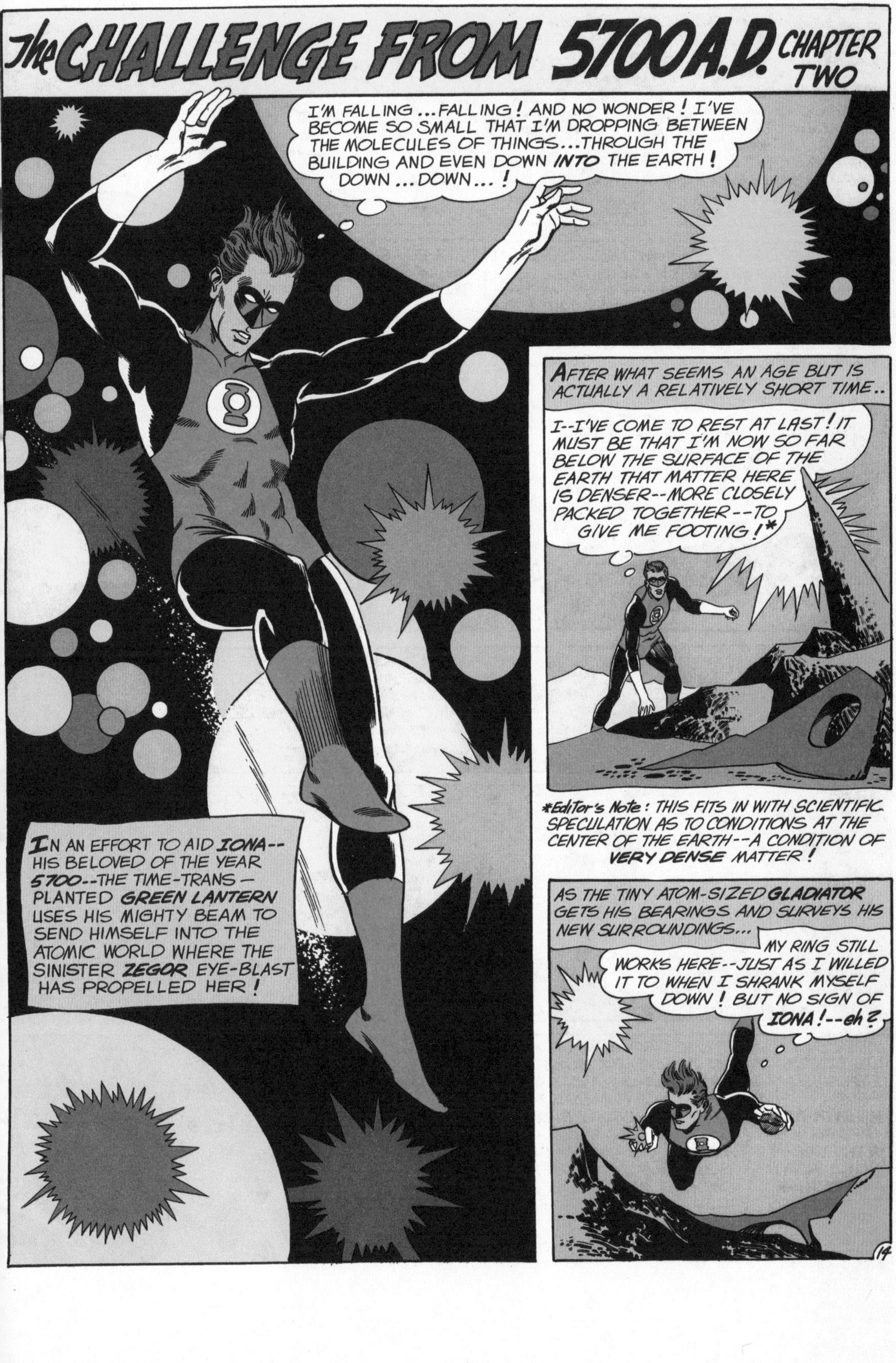

The CHALLENGE FROM 5700 A.D. CHAPTER TWO
I'M FALLING...FALLING! AND NO WONDER! I'VE BECOME SO SMALL THAT I'M DROPPING BETWEEN THE MOLECULES OF THINGS...THROUGH THE BUILDING AND EVEN DOWN INTO THE EARTH! DOWN...DOWN...!
IN AN EFFORT TO AID IONA--HIS BELOVED OF THE YEAR 5700--THE TIME-TRANS-PLANTED GREEN LANTERN USES HIS MIGHTY BEAM TO SEND HIMSELF INTO THE ATOMIC WORLD WHERE THE SINISTER ZEGOR EYE-BLAST HAS PROPELLED HER!
AFTER WHAT SEEMS AN AGE BUT IS ACTUALLY A RELATIVELY SHORT TIME..
I--I'VE COME TO REST AT LAST! IT MUST BE THAT I'M NOW SO FAR BELOW THE SURFACE OF THE EARTH THAT MATTER HERE IS DENSER--MORE CLOSELY PACKED TOGETHER--TO GIVE ME FOOTING!*
*Editor's Note: THIS FITS IN WITH SCIENTIFIC SPECULATION AS TO CONDITIONS AT THE CENTER OF THE EARTH--A CONDITION OF VERY DENSE MATTER!
AS THE TINY ATOM-SIZED GLADIATOR GETS HIS BEARINGS AND SURVEYS HIS NEW SURROUNDINGS...
MY RING STILL WORKS HERE--JUST AS I WILLED IT TO WHEN I SHRANK MYSELF DOWN! BUT NO SIGN OF IONA!--eh?
14

As a strange phenomenon becomes apparent to the swift-moving green figure...

THAT'S ODD! MY RING IS REVEALING MYSTERIOUS ENERGY PULSATIONS TRAVELING UPWARD TOWARD THE SURFACE! BUT NO SUCH ENERGY HAS EVER BEEN DETECTED BY SCIENCE...!

In the mind of the keen-witted crusader another fact suddenly links up...

SOMETHING HAS JUST OCCURRED TO ME! WHEN I USED MY RING TO RE-CREATE THAT SCENE WITH THE ZEGOR AND THE SOLDIER A WHILE BACK I NOTICED SOMETHING THAT ONLY FAINTLY REGISTERED AT THE TIME...

"...A BARELY VISIBLE ENERGY TRAVELING TOWARD THE ZEGOR... COMING UP FROM SOMEWHERE BELOW...!"

"NATURALLY I COULDN'T HAVE SEEN THIS ENERGY MYSELF! BUT MY RING CAUGHT IT, AND IN PROJECTING THE SCENE, DUPLICATED IT!"

IF I'M RIGHT, MAYBE I HAVE FOUND A WAY TO DEFEAT THE ZEGORS! BUT BEFORE I DO ANYTHING ELSE I'VE GOT TO FIND IONA!

AND SOON, TO THE INDOMITABLE CRUSADER'S INTENSE RELIEF...

IONA!

GREEN LANTERN! YOU TRAPPED HERE--TOO?!

AFTER GL HAS BRIEFLY EXPLAINED HIS VOLUNTARY APPEARANCE IN THE SUB-ATOMIC WORLD AND IN TURN HAS LEARNED CERTAIN THINGS FROM THE GIRL...

ALL THOSE WHO WERE STRICKEN BY THE ZEGOR EYE-BLASTS ARE DOWN HERE--AND SAFE! THIS MEANS I CAN USE MY RING TO RETURN EVERY-ONE TO THE SURFACE-- AND TO THEIR ORIGINAL SIZE! BUT THEN THEY'D ONLY BE IN DANGER AGAIN--

15

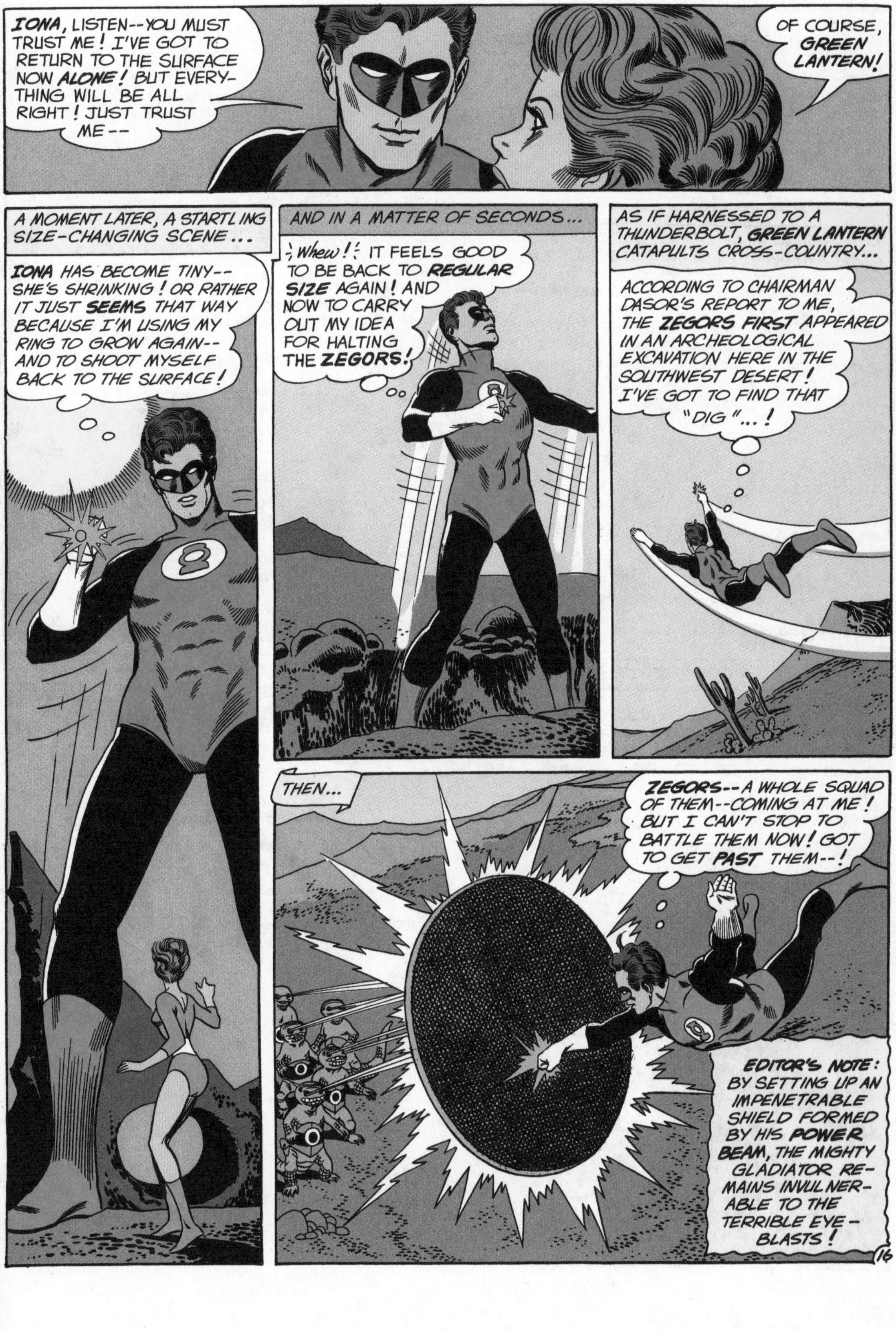

IONA, LISTEN--YOU MUST TRUST ME! I'VE GOT TO RETURN TO THE SURFACE NOW ALONE! BUT EVERY-THING WILL BE ALL RIGHT! JUST TRUST ME--
OF COURSE, GREEN LANTERN!
A MOMENT LATER, A STARTLING SIZE-CHANGING SCENE...
IONA HAS BECOME TINY--SHE'S SHRINKING! OR RATHER IT JUST SEEMS THAT WAY BECAUSE I'M USING MY RING TO GROW AGAIN--AND TO SHOOT MYSELF BACK TO THE SURFACE!
AND IN A MATTER OF SECONDS...
Whew! IT FEELS GOOD TO BE BACK TO REGULAR SIZE AGAIN! AND NOW TO CARRY OUT MY IDEA FOR HALTING THE ZEGORS!
AS IF HARNESSED TO A THUNDERBOLT, GREEN LANTERN CATAPULTS CROSS-COUNTRY...
ACCORDING TO CHAIRMAN DASOR'S REPORT TO ME, THE ZEGORS FIRST APPEARED IN AN ARCHEOLOGICAL EXCAVATION HERE IN THE SOUTHWEST DESERT! I'VE GOT TO FIND THAT "DIG"...!
THEN...
ZEGORS--A WHOLE SQUAD OF THEM--COMING AT ME! BUT I CAN'T STOP TO BATTLE THEM NOW! GOT TO GET PAST THEM--!
EDITOR'S NOTE: BY SETTING UP AN IMPENETRABLE SHIELD FORMED BY HIS POWER BEAM, THE MIGHTY GLADIATOR RE-MAINS INVULNER-ABLE TO THE TERRIBLE EYE-BLASTS!
16

AND SOON...

GOT THROUGH ALL RIGHT! AND THERE IT IS-- THE EXCAVATION--THE OPENING IN THE EARTH WHERE THE *ZEGORS* FIRST APPEARED!

WITH GRIM DETERMINATION, THE *EMERALD-CLAD WARRIOR* PLUMMETS TOWARD THE CREVICE...

THOSE ODD *ENERGY BEAMS*-- COMING UP IN FULL FORCE FROM THE OPENING! THIS *PROVES* I'M ON THE *RIGHT TRACK!*

WITHOUT A MOMENT'S HESITATION, THE FEARLESS CRUSADER PLUNGES DOWNWARD, FOLLOWING HIS TRAIL...

DASOR SAID THE *ZEGORS* ROSE UP FROM THE CENTER OF THE EARTH! THIS MUST BE THE PATH THEY USED TO THE SURFACE--THIS LONG CORRIDOR LIKE A *MINE SHAFT!* BUT HOW LONG WILL IT KEEP GOING DOWN? AND WHERE WILL IT LEAD ME?

SOON, AFTER THE GREAT POWER BEAM HAS PROPELLED ITS WIELDER ALONG WITH PRECIPITATE SPEED...

I'VE COME OUT INTO AN ENORMOUS CAVERN! AND GREAT SCOTT--! THERE'S A CITY--A WHOLE CIVILIZATION DOWN HERE!-- INCLUDING THE STRUCTURE I'M LOOKING FOR--THE BUILDING WHERE THOSE ENERGY RAYS ARE COMING FROM!

17

AS **GREEN LANTERN** HURTLES TOWARD HIS OBJECTIVE, RING BLAZING, HIS APPEARANCE IS THE INSTANT SIGNAL FOR A COMBINED ATTACK BY THE DENIZENS OF THE CITY...

ZEGORS--COMING AT ME FROM ALL SIDES! I--I CAN'T FIGHT OFF ALL THOSE EYE-BLASTS AT ONCE! BUT THERE'S ANOTHER WAY TO DEAL WITH THIS SITUATION!

IN THE SPLIT-MOMENT, AS THE EYE-RAYS BLAZE TOWARD THE GREEN-CLAD INTRUDER, THE **POWER BEAM** FLARES OUT WITH OVERPOWERING MIGHT...

TURNING MY **GREEN BEAM** INTO A **HUGE LIGHTNING BOLT** HAS SPLIT THAT "ENERGY" BUILDING LIKE AN EGGSHELL!

CRRAACK!

IT WORKED--JUST AS I FIGURED! THE **ZEGORS** CAN'T EMPLOY THEIR **EYE-BLAST** ANY MORE! THE POWER FOR IT CAME TO THEM FROM A SOURCE IN THAT BUILDING!

RUNNING FOR IT! BUT I WON'T PURSUE THEM! IT'S THE ONES UP ON THE SURFACE THAT MUST BE HANDLED FIRST! NOW TO GET BACK TO **STAR CITY**...

18

SOON AFTER, IN THE CAPITAL...

GREEN LANTERN, YOU--YOU'VE BROUGHT ALL OF US WHO WERE REDUCED IN SIZE BY THE ZEGORS BACK TO NORMAL AGAIN-- AND RETURNED US HERE TO THE SURFACE OF THE EARTH!

YES, IONA! IT WAS NOT SO DIFFICULT-- WITH MY POWER RING!

AND NOW IS THE TIME WHEN WE NEED EVERY AVAILABLE PERSON TO COMBAT THE ZEGORS! THEY MUST HAVE OTHER WEAPONS BESIDES THEIR EYE-BLASTS--AND THEY'LL USE THEM! CALL A MEETING OF MY PRINCIPAL AIDES, IONA!

YES, SIR!

SHORTLY...

BY MY CALCULATIONS IT SHOULD TAKE THREE EARTHMEN FIRING NUCLEAR PISTOLS AT THE SAME INSTANT TO KNOCK OUT ONE ZEGOR! THEIR POWERS OF RESISTANCE ARE ENORMOUS-- BUT THAT SHOULD DO IT! SPREAD THE WORD-- OUR FORCES ARE TO OPERATE IN TEAMS OF THREE!

THEY'RE TO SYNCHRONIZE THEIR MOVEMENTS --AND PRACTICE FIRING THEIR WEAPONS SIMULTANEOUSLY! IS THAT CLEAR?

YES, MR. SOLAR DIRECTOR! THE ORDER SHALL GO OUT AT ONCE!

AS THE MANEUVER ORIGINATED BY THE INSPIRED SOLAR DIRECTOR TURNS THE TIDE AGAINST THE DREAD INVADERS...

IT WORKED! OUR THREE SHOTS TOGETHER BLASTED THE LIZARD!

COME ON! WE'LL FIND MORE OF THEM--WIPE THEM OUT--OR DRIVE THEM BACK WHERE THEY CAME FROM!

19

SHORTLY, OVER THE **TELEX INTERPLANETARY NETWORK** OF 5700 A.D. ...

...AND THE **ZEGORS** HAVE SURRENDERED UNCONDITIONALLY! UNDER THE LEADERSHIP OF THE NEW **SOLAR DIRECTOR**, **GREEN LANTERN**, EARTH FORCES EVERYWHERE HAVE BEEN COMPLETELY VICTORIOUS! THE REMNANTS OF THE **ZEGORS** HAVE BEEN ALLOWED TO RETURN TO THEIR HALF-DESTROYED UNDERGROUND CITY...

MEANWHILE, THE NEW **SOLAR DIRECTOR** IS PUTTING SOME FINAL TOUCHES TO THE VICTORY...

I'M SURE THE **ZEGORS** WILL NEVER CHALLENGE MANKIND AGAIN! BUT JUST IN CASE THEY EVER DO TRY ANYTHING-- THIS ALARM SYSTEM I'M LAYING DOWN WITH MY RING WILL INSTANTLY WARN THE EARTH-- AND ALLOW IT TIME TO MEET THE THREAT!

AT THAT MOMENT, BACK IN **STAR CITY**...

GREEN LANTERN IS ON HIS WAY BACK HERE! NOW IS THE TIME WHEN WE MUST **RETURN** HIM TO HIS OWN ERA! IN **23** HOURS, HE HAS ACCOMPLISHED EVERYTHING WE COULD HAVE ASKED OF HIM-- AND WILL FOR-EVER BE ENSHRINED IN OUR HISTORY AND OUR MEMORY!

BUT CHAIRMAN DASOR--

CAN'T YOU LET **GREEN LANTERN** STAY WITH US A WHILE LONGER? ANOTHER FEW DAYS AT LEAST!

I'M SORRY, **IONA**! WE HAVE NO RIGHT TO KEEP HIM HERE A SECOND LONGER THAN ABSOLUTELY NECESSARY! BE-SIDES, OUR RESEARCH TELLS US THAT HIS **POWER RING** MUST BE RECHARGED EVERY 24 HOURS OR IT WILL FAIL TO WORK!

MOREOVER, HIS OWN ERA NEEDS HIM! OF COURSE-- HE WILL RETURN THERE AT THE SPLIT-INSTANT HE WAS TRANSPORTED TO OUR CENTURY! THERE WILL BE NO LOSS--NO TIME-LAPSE BETWEEN! THAT IS NECESSARY TO FULFILL THE RIGID LAWS OF TIME-TRAVEL!

IN THE SAME MANNER HE WILL REMEMBER **ABSOLUTELY NOTHING** OF THIS PERIOD IN HIS CAREER!

HE--HE'S **GONE**!

CLICK!

20

At that moment... S-SOMETHING HAPPENING--!?

SLICK

WITH NO INTERVAL AT ALL, OR POSSIBLY THAT OF AN ATOM'S PULSE...

UHH--THE QUEER NUMBNESS I FELT--IT CAME AND WENT LIKE--LIKE A FLASH! BUT I HAVE NO TIME TO THINK ABOUT IT NOW! GOT TO HALT THAT FANTASTIC SEA MONSTER!

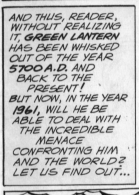

AND THUS, READER, WITHOUT REALIZING IT, *GREEN LANTERN* HAS BEEN WHISKED OUT OF THE YEAR *5700 A.D.* AND BACK TO THE PRESENT! BUT NOW, IN THE YEAR *1961,* WILL HE BE ABLE TO DEAL WITH THE INCREDIBLE MENACE CONFRONTING HIM AND THE WORLD? LET US FIND OUT...

AS THE VIBRANT FIGURE DARTS AT HIS OUTSIZE FOE...

eh? MY RING HAS *NO EFFECT* ON IT-- NONE AT ALL! STRANGE! I CAN'T UNDERSTAND--IT'S *NOT* YELLOW--!*

*Editor's Note: DUE TO A NECESSARY IMPURITY IN HIS POWER BATTERY, *GREEN LANTERN'S* POWER RING HAS NO EFFECT ON ANYTHING YELLOW! BUT WHAT WILL HE DO NOW?

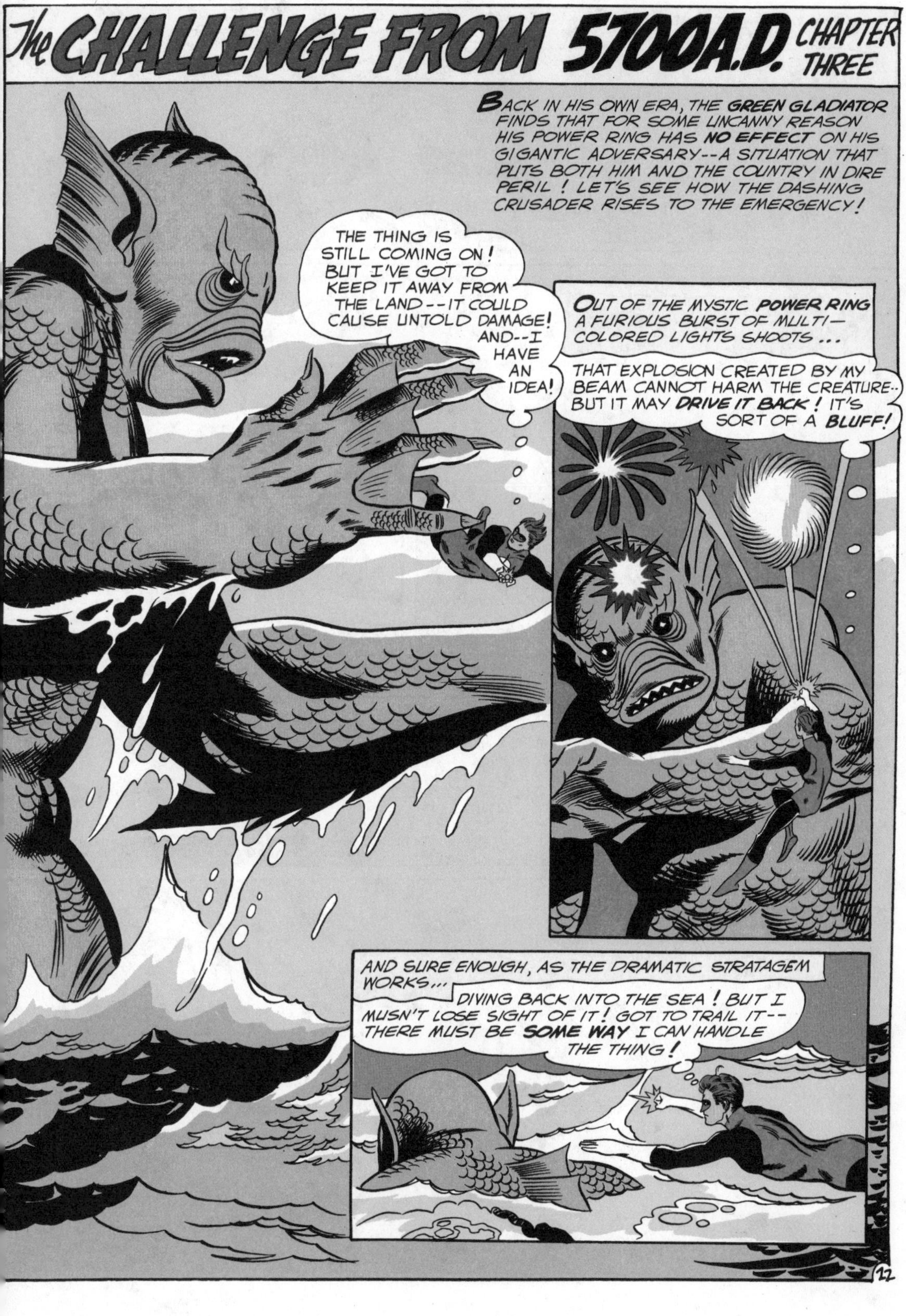
The CHALLENGE FROM 5700 A.D. CHAPTER THREE
BACK IN HIS OWN ERA, THE GREEN GLADIATOR FINDS THAT FOR SOME UNCANNY REASON HIS POWER RING HAS NO EFFECT ON HIS GIGANTIC ADVERSARY--A SITUATION THAT PUTS BOTH HIM AND THE COUNTRY IN DIRE PERIL! LET'S SEE HOW THE DASHING CRUSADER RISES TO THE EMERGENCY!
THE THING IS STILL COMING ON! BUT I'VE GOT TO KEEP IT AWAY FROM THE LAND--IT COULD CAUSE UNTOLD DAMAGE! AND--I HAVE AN IDEA!
OUT OF THE MYSTIC POWER RING A FURIOUS BURST OF MULTI-COLORED LIGHTS SHOOTS...
THAT EXPLOSION CREATED BY MY BEAM CANNOT HARM THE CREATURE.. BUT IT MAY DRIVE IT BACK! IT'S SORT OF A BLUFF!
AND SURE ENOUGH, AS THE DRAMATIC STRATAGEM WORKS...
DIVING BACK INTO THE SEA! BUT I MUSN'T LOSE SIGHT OF IT! GOT TO TRAIL IT--THERE MUST BE SOME WAY I CAN HANDLE THE THING!
12

Enclosing himself in a ring-made oxygen bubble to enable him to breathe, GREEN LANTERN catapults under the surface...

THERE IT GOES! IT SEEMS TO BE HEADING FOR THE OCEAN DEEPS!

As the huge aquatic apparition spurts downward...

WITH MY RING I CAN FOLLOW IT EASILY! BUT WAIT A SECOND--! MY RING IS REVEALING SOMETHING!

Under the influence of the EMERALD RAY a strange fact becomes clear...

NO WONDER MY RING HAS NO EFFECT ON THE CREATURE! IT'S GIVING OFF AN INVISIBLE GOLDEN LIGHT-- A SORT OF INFRA-YELLOW COLOR--!*

*EDITOR'S NOTE: JUST AS INFRARED IS INVISIBLE RED LIGHT, SO INFRAYELLOW IS CONSIDERED INVISIBLE YELLOW LIGHT!

In the keen brain of the EMERALD CRUSADER, as he grimly trails his giant quarry, several facts instantly link up...

THIS IS THE SPOT WHERE THE NAVY CAPSULE DISAPPEARED! THE CAPSULE PENETRATED OUTER SPACE--AND IT MUST HAVE PICKED UP SOME UNKNOWN RADIATION-- WHICH REACTED WITH THE CHEMICALS IN THE SEA WATER TO SPAWN THIS CREATURE! THAT WOULD EXPLAIN ITS INVISIBLE GOLDEN COLOR--THE SEA IS FULL OF GOLD IN CHEMICAL SOLUTION!

Then...

GREAT THUNDER! ONE OF OUR NEW ATOMIC SUBMARINES HAS COME ALONG--POSSIBLY SEARCHING FOR THE LOST CAPSULE--AND THE CREATURE IN ITS FURY HAS SEIZED IT!

IT SEEMS DETERMINED TO DESTROY THAT SUB! I'VE GOT TO SAVE IT! BUT HOW? MY RING CAN'T AFFECT THE MONSTER WITH ITS INVISIBLE, GOLDEN COLOR--EH? MAYBE-- THAT'S MY CLUE!

AS THE GREAT POWER BEAM AGAIN IS SET TO WORK WITH FEVERISH HASTE...

ONE CHANCE!

ALTHOUGH MY RING CAN'T AFFECT THE CREATURE DIRECTLY, I MAY BE ABLE TO USE IT AGAINST THE THING INDIRECTLY-- BY CREATING THESE CHEMICAL RETORTS FOR THE MANUFACTURE OF ACIDS..!

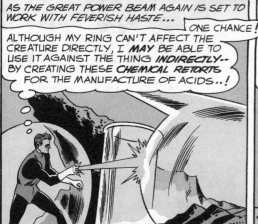

FANTASTICALLY, GL HAS MADE A SMALL CHEMICAL LABORATORY ON THE OCEAN'S FLOOR...

ACCORDING TO WHAT I REMEMBER OF SCIENCE, ONLY ONE SUBSTANCE CAN DISSOLVE GOLD-- THE MIXTURE OF HYDROCHLORIC AND NITRIC ACIDS KNOWN AS AQUA REGIA!* I'VE GOT TO MANUFACTURE A QUANTITY OF IT QUICKLY!

*Editor's Note: IN ANCIENT TIMES AQUA REGIA, OR ROYAL WATER, WAS SO CALLED BECAUSE IT ALONE COULD DISSOLVE GOLD, THE KING OF METALS!

AND SOON...

NOW TO USE MY RING TO HURL THIS ACID AT THE MONSTER BEFORE IT SUCCEEDS IN SHAKING THAT SUB APART!

THEN, AFTER A BREATHTAKING MOMENT OF SUSPENSE...

¡WHEW!¡ FOR AN INSTANT IT WAS TOUCH AND GO-- BUT NOW THE AQUA REGIA HAS TAKEN EFFECT AND IT'S DISSOLVING THE CREATURE-- FORCING IT TO RELEASE THE SUB--AND UTTERLY DESTROYING IT!

SHORTLY, IN A TOP-LEVEL CONFERENCE WITH HIGH NAVY BRASS...

NO DOUBT YOU'RE RIGHT, **GREEN LANTERN**-- THAT OUR CAPSULE PICKED UP SOME UNKNOWN RADIATION THAT SPAWNED THE CREATURE! BUT WE'RE TAKING STEPS TO INSURE THAT IT NEVER HAPPENS AGAIN! AND PLEASE ACCEPT THE NATION'S GRATITUDE FOR SAVING THAT SUB!

AS A FAMILIAR FIGURE ZOOMS HOMEWARD..

TIME FOR **HAL JORDAN** TO GET BACK ON HIS **TEST PILOT JOB** AT THE **FERRIS AIRCRAFT COMPANY!** BUT--WAIT A SECOND! THAT'S ODD--**MY RING** FEELS AS IF IT NEEDS RECHARGING!

AND SOON, BEHIND CLOSED DOORS AT THE AIRCRAFT COMPANY HANGAR...

IT **DID** NEED RECHARGING! BUT I CAN'T UNDERSTAND--MY ENCOUNTER WITH THE **SEA MONSTER** ONLY TOOK AN HOUR--AND I CHARGED IT JUST BEFORE I SET OFF! *Hmm!* THAT **IS** STRANGE!

GREEN LANTERN WOULD PERHAPS THINK IT EVEN STRANGER IF HE COULD AT THIS MOMENT PEER INTO THE WORLD OF THE FUTURE...5700 A.D...

HE CAN'T REMEMBER ME--HE DOESN'T EVEN KNOW I EXIST! BUT I'LL **NEVER FORGET HIM**--NEVER!

THIS IS **NOT THE END,** READER! WATCH FOR ANOTHER THRILLING **FUTURE - GREEN LANTERN** STORY IN A FORTH-COMING ISSUE!

The End

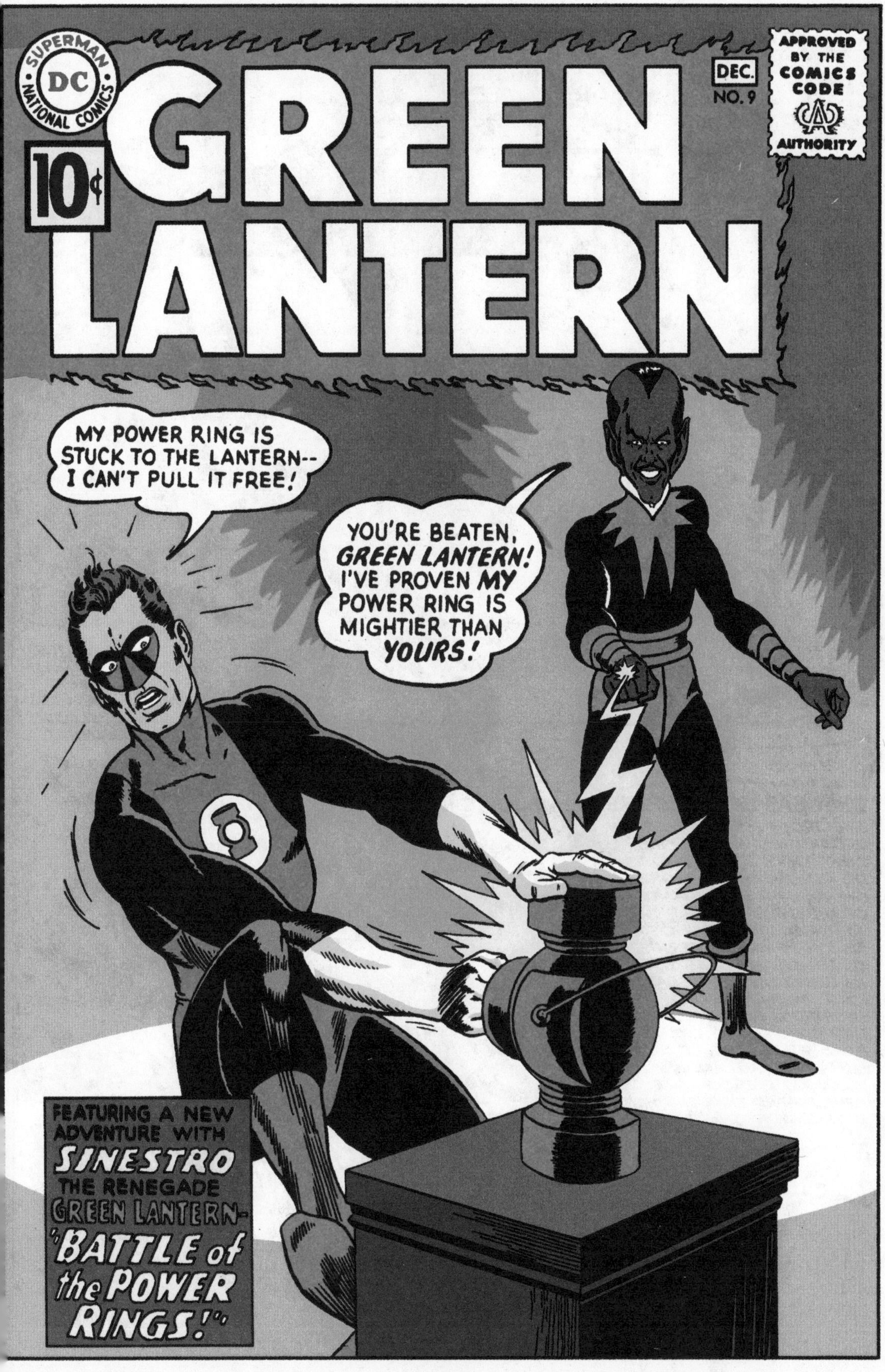

SUPERMAN DC NATIONAL COMICS
10¢
GREEN LANTERN
DEC. NO. 9
APPROVED BY THE COMICS CODE AUTHORITY
MY POWER RING IS STUCK TO THE LANTERN-- I CAN'T PULL IT FREE!
YOU'RE BEATEN, GREEN LANTERN! I'VE PROVEN MY POWER RING IS MIGHTIER THAN YOURS!
FEATURING A NEW ADVENTURE WITH SINESTRO THE RENEGADE GREEN LANTERN- "BATTLE of the POWER RINGS!"

GREEN LANTERN

IT'S FANTASTIC! THE MORE POWER I THROW BEHIND MY GREEN BEAM, THE STRONGER SINESTRO'S YELLOW BEAM BECOMES!

WHAT HAS GONE BEFORE: SINESTRO, A RENEGADE GREEN LANTERN, WHO MISUSED HIS GREAT POWER, WAS EXILED TO THE ANTI-MATTER WORLD OF QWARD, BY THE GUARDIANS OF THE UNIVERSE -- THE MYSTERIOUS BEINGS WHO BESTOW POWER BATTERIES ON DESERVING ONES SUCH AS GREEN LANTERN OF EARTH! BUT ONCE ON QWARD, SINESTRO'S RESTLESSLY EVIL MIND SOUGHT ONLY ONE THING: TO REVENGE HIMSELF ON THE GUARDIANS! AND ALL HIS VENOMOUS ENERGIES ARE BENT TOWARD THAT END HERE, IN THIS STORY THAT WE CALL...

The BATTLE of the POWER RINGS!

AS THE EMERALD GLADIATOR SPEEDS OVER COAST CITY...

THERE'S A REPORT THAT THE **PACKER GANG** -- THAT PREYS ON VALUABLE FREIGHT CARGO -- WILL STRIKE TONIGHT! I'VE GOT TO GET DOWN TO THE RAILROAD YARDS AT ONCE...

AND I CAN'T WASTE ANY TIME-- BECAUSE RIGHT AFTERWARD I HAVE AN ALL-IMPORTANT MEETING TO ATTEND--ONE THAT I WOULDN'T WANT TO MISS FOR ALL THE WORLDS IN THE GALAXY! eh--?

SUDDENLY...

MY **POWER RING** -- SOMETHING'S WRONG WITH IT! IT'S NOT PUTTING OUT ENOUGH JUICE TO KEEP ME AIRBORNE!

SHORTLY, AS GREEN LANTERN MANAGES TO LAND WITHOUT HARM...

¿*Whew!*¿ THAT'S NOT THE **FIRST** TIME THIS WEEK THIS HAS HAPPENED! AGAIN AND AGAIN DURING THE PAST FEW DAYS MY GREEN BEAM ABRUPTLY SEEMED TO LOSE POWER! NOT ALTOGETHER--BUT ENOUGH TO BOTHER ME!

I CAN'T IMAGINE WHAT COULD BE CAUSING THIS! USUALLY THE POWER PICKS UP AGAIN A BIT... BUT NO TIME TO WORRY ABOUT THAT NOW! HERE'S THE FREIGHT YARD...

...AND THERE'S THE **PACKER GANG** -- AT WORK ON THAT FREIGHT CAR THEY'VE OPENED!

DESPITE UNEASINESS ABOUT HIS UNRELIABLE RING, THE **GREEN-CLAD CRUSADER** PLUNGES AT THE MARAUDERS...

GREEN LANTERN!?

I DON'T KNOW WHETHER MY RING CAN STOP **BULLETS** IN ITS WEAKENED STATE! BUT I'LL BET I'M ABOUT TO FIND OUT--!

I'LL JUST USE MY RING TO PROTECT MYSELF UNTIL THOSE HOODS RUN OUT OF AMMUNITION! NO SENSE TAKING **UNNECESSARY** CHANCES...!

AND SOON, WITH THE LAST LEAD PELLET FIRED...

NOW IT'S MY TURN, BOYS!

AFTER THE HAPLESS GUNMEN HAVE BEEN HANDED OVER TO THE AUTHORITIES...

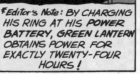

POLICE

POLICE

FUNNY... MY RING'S IN **FULL FORCE** AGAIN! I'D LIKE TO GET TO THE BOTTOM OF THIS--BUT IT WILL HAVE TO WAIT UNTIL **AFTER** THE **MEETING!** NOTHING TAKES PRIORITY OVER **THAT!**

BUT BEFORE I START OUT I'LL CHARGE MY RING-- JUST TO MAKE SURE! I'VE BEEN CHARGING IT REGULARLY*... AND I KNOW IT'S NOT THAT WHICH HAS CAUSED IT TO FAIL...

I'M BACK AT THE **FERRIS** AIR-CRAFT COMPANY...

*Editor's Note: BY CHARGING HIS RING AT HIS **POWER BATTERY**, GREEN LANTERN OBTAINS POWER FOR EXACTLY TWENTY-FOUR HOURS!

SOON, IN THE DRESSING ROOM OF ACE TEST PILOT HAL JORDAN, THE EMERALD GLADIATOR'S CIVILIAN ALTER EGO...

IN BRIGHTEST DAY, IN BLACKEST NIGHT, NO EVIL SHALL ESCAPE MY SIGHT! LET THOSE WHO WORSHIP EVIL'S MIGHT BEWARE MY POWER--GREEN LANTERN'S LIGHT!

SOMETHING'S **WRONG!** SOMEONE.. IS IN THIS ROOM!!

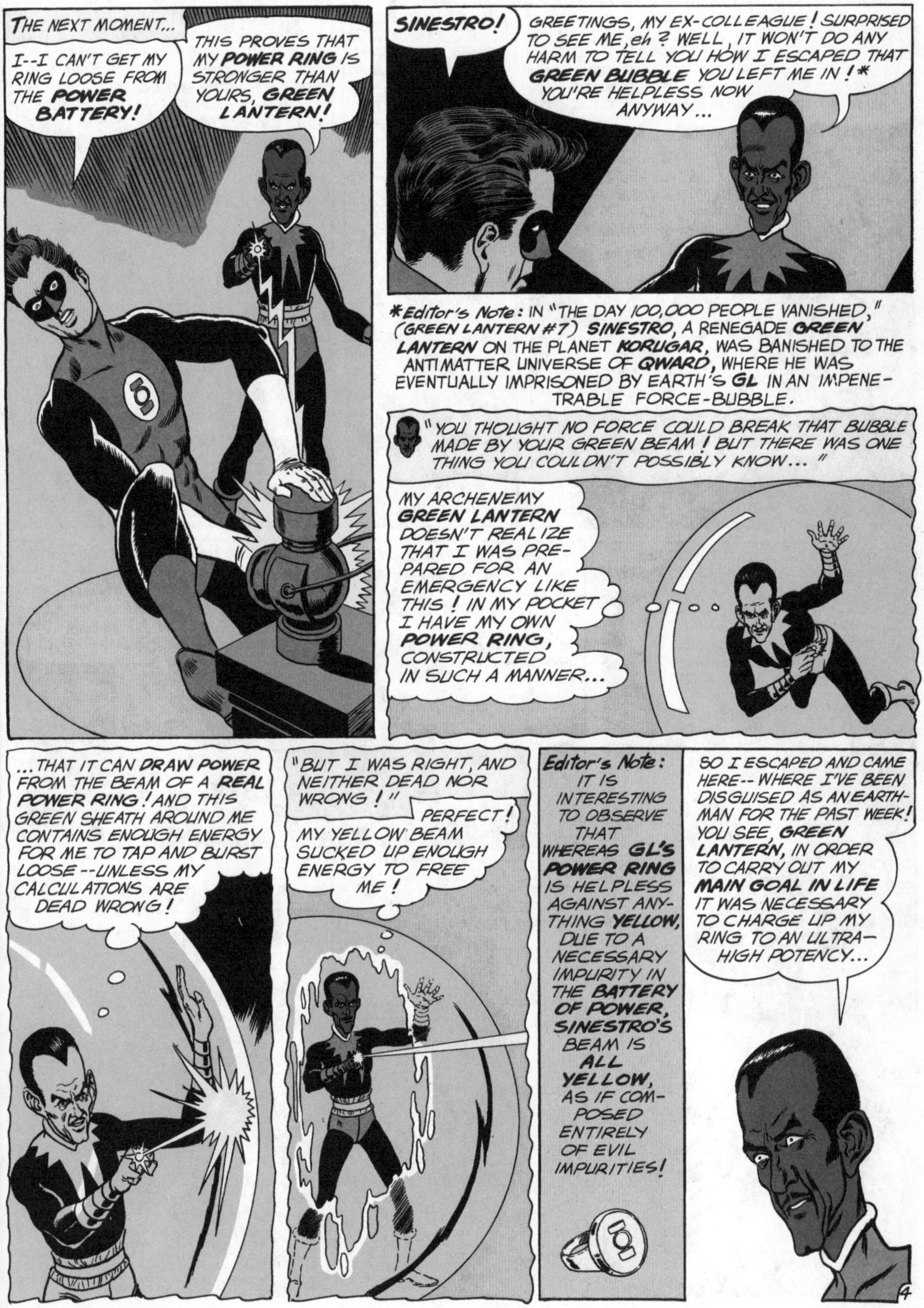

THE NEXT MOMENT...
I--I CAN'T GET MY RING LOOSE FROM THE POWER BATTERY!
THIS PROVES THAT MY POWER RING IS STRONGER THAN YOURS, GREEN LANTERN!
SINESTRO!
GREETINGS, MY EX-COLLEAGUE! SURPRISED TO SEE ME, eh? WELL, IT WON'T DO ANY HARM TO TELL YOU HOW I ESCAPED THAT GREEN BUBBLE YOU LEFT ME IN!* YOU'RE HELPLESS NOW ANYWAY...
*Editor's Note: IN "THE DAY 100,000 PEOPLE VANISHED," (GREEN LANTERN #7) SINESTRO, A RENEGADE GREEN LANTERN ON THE PLANET KORUGAR, WAS BANISHED TO THE ANTIMATTER UNIVERSE OF QWARD, WHERE HE WAS EVENTUALLY IMPRISONED BY EARTH'S GL IN AN IMPENETRABLE FORCE-BUBBLE.
"YOU THOUGHT NO FORCE COULD BREAK THAT BUBBLE MADE BY YOUR GREEN BEAM! BUT THERE WAS ONE THING YOU COULDN'T POSSIBLY KNOW..."
MY ARCHENEMY GREEN LANTERN DOESN'T REALIZE THAT I WAS PREPARED FOR AN EMERGENCY LIKE THIS! IN MY POCKET I HAVE MY OWN POWER RING, CONSTRUCTED IN SUCH A MANNER...
...THAT IT CAN DRAW POWER FROM THE BEAM OF A REAL POWER RING! AND THIS GREEN SHEATH AROUND ME CONTAINS ENOUGH ENERGY FOR ME TO TAP AND BURST LOOSE--UNLESS MY CALCULATIONS ARE DEAD WRONG!
"BUT I WAS RIGHT, AND NEITHER DEAD NOR WRONG!"
PERFECT! MY YELLOW BEAM SUCKED UP ENOUGH ENERGY TO FREE ME!
Editor's Note: IT IS INTERESTING TO OBSERVE THAT WHEREAS GL'S POWER RING IS HELPLESS AGAINST ANYTHING YELLOW, DUE TO A NECESSARY IMPURITY IN THE BATTERY OF POWER, SINESTRO'S BEAM IS ALL YELLOW, AS IF COMPOSED ENTIRELY OF EVIL IMPURITIES!
SO I ESCAPED AND CAME HERE--WHERE I'VE BEEN DISGUISED AS AN EARTHMAN FOR THE PAST WEEK! YOU SEE, GREEN LANTERN, IN ORDER TO CARRY OUT MY MAIN GOAL IN LIFE IT WAS NECESSARY TO CHARGE UP MY RING TO AN ULTRA-HIGH POTENCY...
4

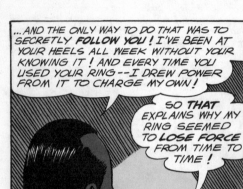

...AND THE ONLY WAY TO DO THAT WAS TO SECRETLY **FOLLOW YOU!** I'VE BEEN AT YOUR HEELS ALL WEEK WITHOUT YOUR KNOWING IT! AND EVERY TIME YOU USED YOUR RING--I DREW POWER FROM IT TO CHARGE MY OWN!

SO **THAT** EXPLAINS WHY MY RING SEEMED TO **LOSE FORCE** FROM TIME TO TIME!

AS SINESTRO, THE RENEGADE GREEN LANTERN, GLOWERS AT HIS PREY...

EXACTLY! THUS, **MY POWER RING** GAINED AS **YOURS LOST!** BY MEANS OF MY RING I LEARNED THAT YOU ARE DUE TO ATTEND A MEETING OF ALL THE **GREEN LANTERNS** OF THE GALAXY! THAT IS WHY I AM HERE!

YOU WILL **NOT** ATTEND THAT MEETING, **GREEN LANTERN**--BUT I WILL IN YOUR PLACE! IT IS PART OF MY SCHEME TO DESTROY MY ETERNAL ENEMIES--THE **GUARDIANS OF THE UNIVERSE!**

THE **GUARDIANS** IN DANGER!? I'VE GOT TO GET LOOSE!!

WITH TREMENDOUS EFFORT THE **GREEN GLADIATOR** STRAINS AGAINST THE FORCE HOLDING HIM...

C-CAN'T PULL MY RING FREE! BUT WAIT--THERE MAY BE **ANOTHER** WAY TO GET AT MY SATANIC-FACED FOE!

SUDDENLY, **GREEN LANTERN** SPRINGS A SURPRISE MANEUVER...

HE FOUND A WAY TO BREAK FREE... **BY SLIPPING HIS FINGER OUT OF THE RING!**

I'D JUST AS SOON TAKE CARE OF YOU WITH MY **BARE** HANDS, SINESTRO!

SNAP!

IF YOU CAN REACH ME, GREEN LANTERN!

HE'S JUST A FEW FEET AWAY! GOT TO KEEP STRUGGLING AGAINST THAT YELLOW BEAM!

BUT NO UNAIDED HUMAN FORCE CAN OVERCOME THE BALEFUL POWER OF *SINESTRO'S* YELLOW BEAM ! AND DESPITE THE INCREDIBLE EFFORTS OF THE *EMERALD CRUSADER*...

ONE LAST LUNGE...

UH--FALLING SHORT...

GOING DOWN...

DOWN...

END OF THE LINE, *GREEN LANTERN!* YOU'RE FINISHED!

THEN, AS THE EVIL RAY IS PUT TO A FINAL, GRIM USE...

GREEN LANTERN, YOU CAN *NEVER* BREAK OUT OF THAT CAGE FORMED BY MY *YELLOW BEAM!* REMEMBER THAT-- YOU CAN *NEVER* BREAK OUT OF THERE !

NOW TO USE MY RING TO ALTER MY APPEARANCE-- AND BECOME AN *ABSOLUTE REPLICA* OF MY EX-- COLLEAGUE !

AND MOMENTS LATER...

GREEN LANTERN OF EARTH IS DUE TO ARRIVE SHORTLY ON THE FAR- OFF PLANET OF *YQUEM!* "HE" WILL ARRIVE AT THE MEETING --HA HA-- AS *SCHEDULED* !

MEANWHILE ON THE WORLD OF *YQUEM* IN A CENTRALLY-LOCATED AREA OF THE GALAXY...

ARE WE ALL HERE ?

ONLY *GREEN LANTERN OF EARTH* IS STILL MISSING !

WE WILL WAIT A LITTLE LONGER FOR HIM..

WHILE THE ASSEMBLAGE WAITS--THE FIRST GALAXY- WIDE CONFERENCE OF ALL *POWER BATTERY POSSESSORS,* MEETING TO EXCHANGE NOTES AND BENEFIT BY EACH OTHER'S EXPERIENCE--LET US EXAMINE A FEW OF THE MEMBERS OF THIS UNIQUE BAND, AND IDENTIFY SOME OF THEM FOR FUTURE REFER- ENCE...

⑥

GREEN LANTERN OF XAOS, A WORLD WHERE INSECTS RULE AND WHERE THE HUMAN RACE IS UNKNOWN!

GREEN LANTERN OF BARRIO III, A PLANET OF CRYSTAL LIFE—FORMS, ULTRA—SENSITIVE, WITH 13 SENSES INSTEAD OF THE USUAL 6 OF HUMANS!

GREEN LANTERN OF ROJIRA, ONE OF THE MOST ADVANCED, AGED AND SUPER-SCIENTIFIC CIVILIZATIONS!

GREEN LANTERN OF T4IR, WHERE LIFE HAS CULMINATED IN A SHAPE ALTOGETHER DIFFERENT FROM MANKIND!

GREEN LANTERN OF AEROS, A WATER-WORLD INHABITED BY VARIOUS FORMS OF FISH LIFE!

YET DESPITE THEIR DIVERSITY, ALL THE **GREEN LANTERNS** ARE HIGHLY INTELLIGENT AND EQUALLY ADEPT AT PROJECTING THEIR THOUGHTS TO OVERCOME THE **LANGUAGE BARRIER**...

SOMEONE IS ARRIVING NOW!

I CAN MAKE HIM OUT! IT IS **GREEN LANTERN OF EARTH!**

GREETINGS, MY ILLUSTRIOUS COLLEAGUES! SORRY I AM LATE--BUT A--er--LAST-MINUTE MATTER CAME UP BACK ON MY WORLD THAT I HAD TO ATTEND TO!

OUR NUMBER IS COMPLETE..

...SO LET US BEGIN THE MEETING!

THEY'RE ALL HERE! THIS FITS IN WITH MY PLANS-- THAT THEY DON'T SUSPECT!

WE WILL NOW HEAR AN ACCOUNT BY **GREEN LANTERN OF BARRIO III** CONCERNING AN OUTBREAK OF EVIL ON HIS PLANET AND HOW HE DEALT WITH IT!

FELLOW GREEN LANTERNS UHH!!

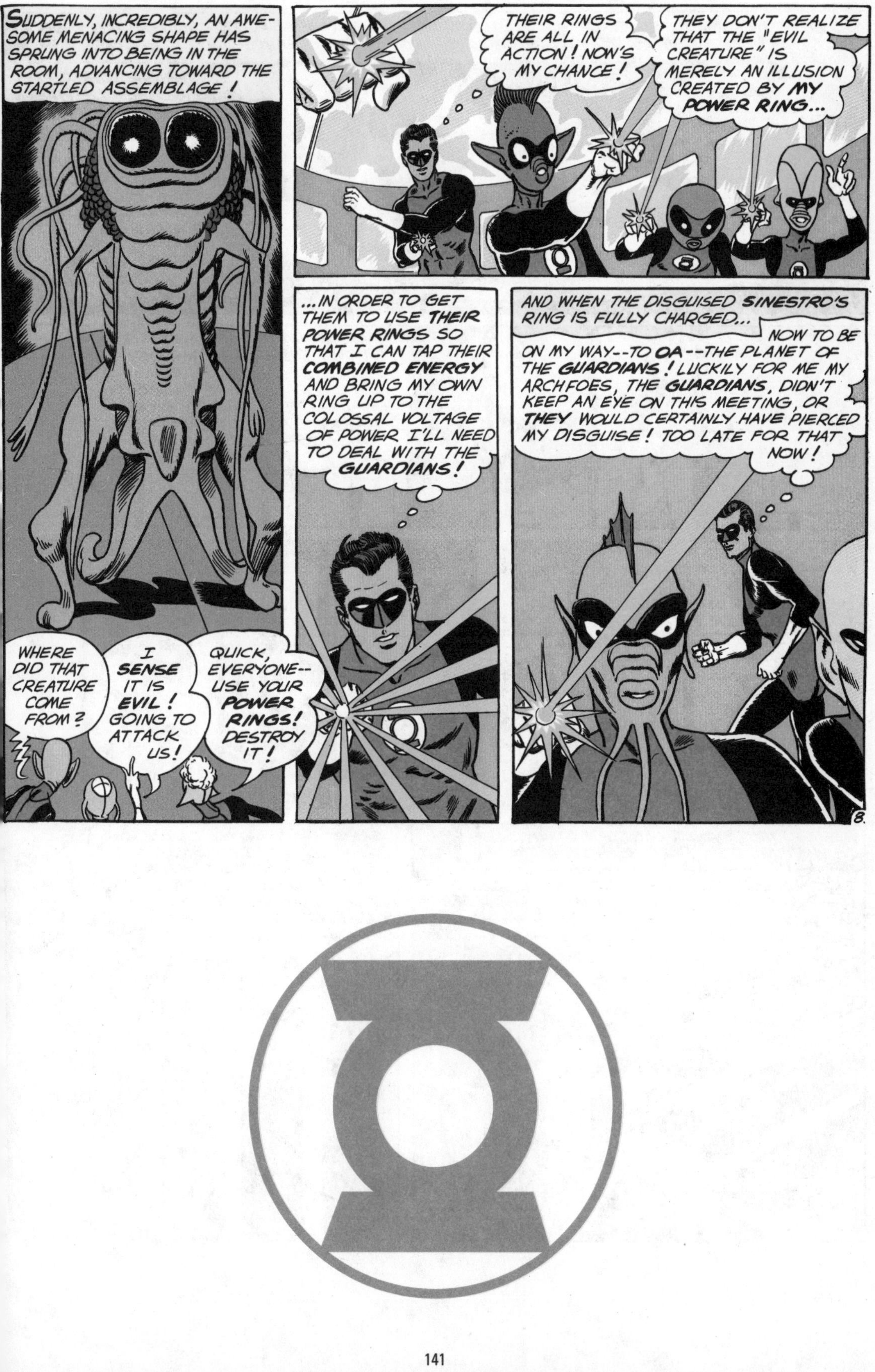
SUDDENLY, INCREDIBLY, AN AWESOME MENACING SHAPE HAS SPRUNG INTO BEING IN THE ROOM, ADVANCING TOWARD THE STARTLED ASSEMBLAGE!
WHERE DID THAT CREATURE COME FROM?
I SENSE IT IS EVIL! GOING TO ATTACK US!
QUICK, EVERYONE-- USE YOUR POWER RINGS! DESTROY IT!
THEIR RINGS ARE ALL IN ACTION! NOW'S MY CHANCE!
THEY DON'T REALIZE THAT THE "EVIL CREATURE" IS MERELY AN ILLUSION CREATED BY MY POWER RING...
...IN ORDER TO GET THEM TO USE THEIR POWER RINGS SO THAT I CAN TAP THEIR COMBINED ENERGY AND BRING MY OWN RING UP TO THE COLOSSAL VOLTAGE OF POWER I'LL NEED TO DEAL WITH THE GUARDIANS!
AND WHEN THE DISGUISED SINESTRO'S RING IS FULLY CHARGED...
NOW TO BE ON MY WAY--TO OA--THE PLANET OF THE GUARDIANS! LUCKILY FOR ME MY ARCHFOES, THE GUARDIANS, DIDN'T KEEP AN EYE ON THIS MEETING, OR THEY WOULD CERTAINLY HAVE PIERCED MY DISGUISE! TOO LATE FOR THAT NOW!
8.

SOON, AFTER USING HIS RING TO CAST A *YELLOW PALL* OVER THE WORLD OF *YQUEM* AND THUS PREVENT PURSUIT, *SINESTRO*--DISDAINING DISGUISE NOW--CLEAVES AGAIN THROUGH THE VOID...

THEIR *POWER RINGS* PROTECT THE *GREEN LANTERNS* FROM DESTRUCTION, OR I WOULD HAVE TRIED TO FINISH THEM OFF--INSTEAD OF JUST BLINDING THEM BY THE *YELLOW CLOUD* I'VE LEFT BEHIND ME! BUT ANYWAY--I'M OUT AFTER *BIGGER GAME!!*

MEAN-WHILE WHAT OF THE EN-TRAPPED *GREEN LANTERN* ON *EARTH?*...

THAT *COMMAND OF SINESTRO'S*--SAYING I COULD *NEVER GET FREE*--SEEMS TO HAVE *PARALYZED* MY WILL! SOMEHOW HE USED HIS *YELLOW BEAM* TO PLANT AN ULTRA-POWERFUL *SUGGESTION* IN MY BRAIN!

AND I CAN'T USE MY OWN RING TO COUNTERACT THE EFFECT ON MY MIND--BECAUSE IT'S STILL STUCK TO THE *POWER BATTERY*--AND NO WAY FOR ME TO REACH IT!

DESPERATELY, *GREEN LANTERN* STRUGGLES AGAINST HIS OWN PARALYSIS OF WILL...

I KNOW I COULD GET LOOSE IF ONLY I COULD OVERCOME THAT *WILL-COMMAND* OF *SINESTRO'S*, BUT I CAN'T SEEM TO--WAIT--WHAT WERE *SINESTRO'S* EXACT WORDS AGAIN--?

"GREEN LANTERN, YOU CAN NEVER BREAK OUT..."! THAT GIVES ME AN IDEA! IF *GREEN LANTERN* CAN'T ESCAPE FROM THIS CAGE--*MAYBE HAL JORDAN* CAN!! GOT TO STRIP OFF MY UNIFORM AND TRY IT...

THE NEXT MOMENT, AS THE INSPIRATION OF THE GLADIATOR WORKS LIKE A CHARM...

MADE IT! THIS IS ONE TIME MY *DOUBLE IDENTITY* REALLY CAME IN HANDY! AS HAL JORDAN I'M IMMUNE TO ANY MENTAL SUGGESTIONS GIVEN TO *GREEN LANTERN!*

SWIFTLY, THE *EMERALD CRUSADER* DONS HIS UNIFORM AGAIN, AND THEN...

NOW MY RING CAME LOOSE, ALL RIGHT! IT MUST HAVE BEEN THE SHOCK OF SEEING SINESTRO HERE THAT PREVENTED ME FROM GETTING IT LOOSE BEFORE! I CAN'T BELIEVE HIS RING IS *STRONGER* THAN MINE!

AND AS SOON AS I FIND SINESTRO I'LL *PROVE* THAT MY RING IS STRONGER THAN HIS! GOOD HAS TO BE ABLE TO DEFEAT EVIL! AND SINESTRO IS *PURE EVIL!*

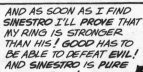
As GL CATAPULTS HIMSELF THROUGH THE VOID AT BREAK-NECK PACE, ON THE MYSTERIOUS WORLD OF OA, HOME OF THE GUARDIANS...

MY ARCHFOES HAVE THEIR DEFENSES ALL RIGHT! ONE FORCE-FIELD AFTER ANOTHER BARS THE WAY TO THEIR CITADEL! BUT MY YELLOW BEAM IS POWERFUL ENOUGH NOW TO BREAK THROUGH ANY-THING!

THE LAST BARRIER-- I'M BREAKING THROUGH TO THE GUARDIANS!

LOOKS LIKE I ARRIVED HERE *JUST* IN TIME!

GOOD THING I DECIDED TO COME *STRAIGHT* HERE INSTEAD OF FIRST CHECKING THE MEETING ON YQUEM!

YOU!? FOOL, DO YOU THINK TO STOP ME NOW!?

10.

AS TWO TREMENDOUS ENERGY-FORCES, ONE YELLOW, THE OTHER GREEN, CLASH IN TITANIC COMBAT...

SO IT'S *MY POWER RING* AGAINST YOURS, *eh, GREEN LANTERN?* WE'LL SEE WHO WINS!

IT'S INCREDIBLE! THE MORE FORCE I PUT BEHIND *MY* GREEN BEAM, THE STRONGER HIS BE-COMES--BECAUSE HIS RING IS *ABSORBING POWER* FROM MINE, AS HE WAS GOOD ENOUGH TO EXPLAIN TO ME!

YOU'RE ALMOST FINISHED, *GREEN LANTERN!* YOU CAN'T WITHSTAND ME!

RALLYING HIS GREAT WILL POWER, THE *EMERALD CRUSADER* OF EARTH FORCES THE INTENSITY OF HIS WILL-- BACKED BEAM UP TO UN-PRECEDENTED HEIGHTS...

THERE *MUST* BE A LIMIT TO THE AMOUNT OF *POWER* HIS RING CAN HOLD! MY ONLY CHANCE IS TO *EXCEED THAT LIMIT*--TO FILL HIS RING SO FULL OF ENERGY THAT IT WILL COLLAPSE LIKE AN OVERCHARGED BATTERY! GOT TO KEEP POURING IT ON!

AND THE NEXT MOMENT...

UHH!

DID IT! HIS RING IS BURSTING-- FLYING TO PIECES UNDER THE PRESSURE!!

YOU--YOU BEAT ME!

NOW WE KNOW WHOSE POWER RING WAS STRONGER, SINESTRO!

LOOK--!

AFTER THE OTHER *GREEN LANTERNS,* ARRIVING POST-HASTE FROM *YQUEM,* ARE BRIEFED ON WHAT HAS HAPPENED.

SO HE WAS OUT TO ATTACK THE *GUARDIANS!* WE SUSPECTED SOMETHING LIKE THAT AFTER HIS *"EVIL CREATURE"* TURNED OUT TO BE JUST AN *ILLUSION!* THAT'S WHY WE TRAILED HIM HERE AS FAST AS WE COULD!

NO DOUBT YOU WOULD HAVE ARRIVED IN TIME TO STOP HIM-- IF I HADN'T REACHED HIM FIRST TO DO THE JOB, MY FELLOW *GREEN LANTERNS!* BUT NOW-- WE'D BETTER MAKE A *FULL REPORT* TO THE GUARDIANS!

AND SOON, IN THE MIGHTY CITADEL OF THE *GUARDIANS--* JUSTICE-LOVING SENTINELS OF THE UNIVERSE--A STRANGE SCENE TAKES PLACE, AS ALL THE ASSEMBLED *GREEN LANTERNS* CHARGE THEIR *POWER RINGS* AT THE *CENTRAL POWER BATTERY* FROM WHICH ALL THE SMALLER INDIVIDUAL *POWER BATTERIES* ALL OVER THE COSMOS DRAW THEIR *MYSTIC ENERGY...*

BY COMING UP HERE TO SAVE US, THE *GREEN LANTERNS* USED UP A GOOD DEAL OF *RING ENERGY!* NOW, BY CHARGING THEIR RINGS AT OUR *MAIN POWER BATTERY* THEY WILL OBTAIN ENOUGH POWER TO SUSTAIN THEM UNTIL THEY REACH THEIR OWN *POWER BATTERIES* AGAIN!

YES! BUT WE STILL HAVE TO DECIDE WHAT TO DO WITH *SINESTRO...*

12.

SOON AFTER, THE RECHARGED **POWER RINGS** OF THE ASSEMBLED **GREEN LANTERNS** ARE PUT TO A COMBINED USE...

ALL TOGETHER NOW... USE YOUR **GREEN BEAMS** WITH ALL YOUR POWER!!

THERE GOES **SINESTRO**, EXILED INTO SPACE..

AT THE TERRIFIC SPEED WITH WHICH HE HAS BEEN PROPELLED INTO SPACE, **SINESTRO** WILL ORBIT THE UNIVERSE--A JOURNEY THAT WILL TAKE **EIGHTEEN BILLION YEARS** TO COMPLETE! WE DON'T HAVE TO WORRY ABOUT HIM ANYMORE!

AND SO THE ARCHVILLAIN OF THE COSMOS BEGINS HIS **LAST JOURNEY**, LOCKED INSIDE A SEALED GREEN CAPSULE ARCING HELPLESSLY THROUGH THE VOID...

The End

BUT IS THIS REALLY THE END OF **SINESTRO**--OR WILL HIS SUPER-EVIL MIND FIND SOME WAY TO AVERT HIS FATE? THIS IS A QUESTION THAT ONLY **TIME**--AND A FUTURE ISSUE OF **GREEN LANTERN**-- WILL TELL! 13

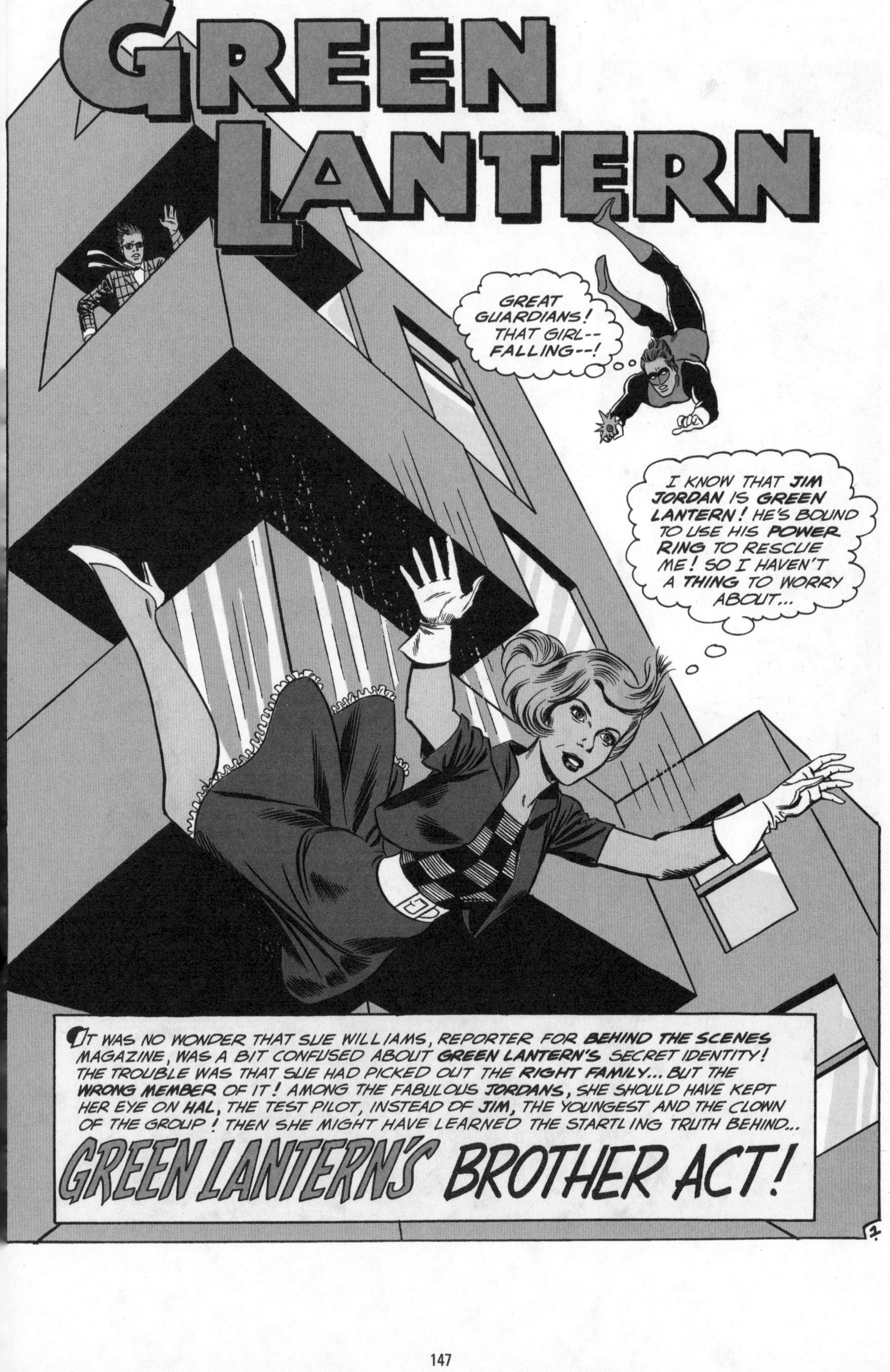
GREEN LANTERN
GREAT GUARDIANS! THAT GIRL-- FALLING--!
I KNOW THAT JIM JORDAN IS GREEN LANTERN! HE'S BOUND TO USE HIS POWER RING TO RESCUE ME! SO I HAVEN'T A THING TO WORRY ABOUT...
IT WAS NO WONDER THAT SUE WILLIAMS, REPORTER FOR BEHIND THE SCENES MAGAZINE, WAS A BIT CONFUSED ABOUT GREEN LANTERN'S SECRET IDENTITY! THE TROUBLE WAS THAT SUE HAD PICKED OUT THE RIGHT FAMILY... BUT THE WRONG MEMBER OF IT! AMONG THE FABULOUS JORDANS, SHE SHOULD HAVE KEPT HER EYE ON HAL, THE TEST PILOT, INSTEAD OF JIM, THE YOUNGEST AND THE CLOWN OF THE GROUP! THEN SHE MIGHT HAVE LEARNED THE STARTLING TRUTH BEHIND...
GREEN LANTERN'S BROTHER ACT!
1

IN THE NEWSPAPERS ON THE WEST COAST, A CERTAIN *FAMILY RE-UNION* IS GIVEN A BIG SPREAD..

Morning Mail 5¢

ONCE AGAIN THE THREE JORDAN BROTHERS COME TOGETHER TO HELP ELECT BROTHER JACK TO OFFICE!

THE POST

AS USUAL THE JORDAN FAMILY WILL BE IN THIS ELECTION ALL THE WAY!

Coast

OPPONENT CLAIMS FOE SAYS HE IS UP AGAINST A TRIO OF JORDANS--NOT JUST ONE!

BUT WHILE THE ENTIRE PACIFIC AREA BUZZES WITH THE LATEST NEWS ABOUT THE FABULOUS JORDANS, LET US, DEAR READER, EXAMINE THE *THREE BROTHERS* A BIT MORE CLOSELY...

FIRST, THERE IS THE *OLDEST BROTHER JACK*--NOW RUNNING FOR DISTRICT ATTORNEY ON A REFORM TICKET! LIKE ALL JORDANS, HE HAS TREMENDOUS ENERGY-- AND A BRILLIANT LEGAL MIND!

SECOND, LET US EXAMINE THE YOUNGEST OF THE TRIO--*JIM JORDAN!* JIM, INCLINED TO BE FUN-LOVING AND HAPPY-GO-LUCKY, IS THE "PET" OF THE OTHER TWO--BUT ALSO VERY SERIOUS ABOUT ELECTING JACK!

AND FINALLY WE COME TO THE *MIDDLE BROTHER--HAL JORDAN,* FAMED FLIER AND TEST PILOT! BUT NOT EVEN HIS TWO BROTHERS KNOW THAT HAL IN HIS *SECRET IDENTITY* IS THE EVEN MORE FAMOUS *GREEN LANTERN!*

SOME DAYS EARLIER, *HAL JORDAN* HAD ALERTED HIS PAL AND CONFIDANT, *PIEFACE,* HIS ESKIMO GREASEMONKEY...

...SO IF ANY EMERGENCY COMES UP FOR ME, EITHER AS HAL JORDAN *OR GREEN LANTERN*-- YOU'LL KNOW WHERE TO REACH ME, *PIE?*

CHECK, HAL! DON'T WORRY! I'LL COVER YOU!

WHICH EXPLAINS HAL'S PRESENCE NOW AT A TYPICAL FAMILY CONFAB IN HIS BROTHER JACK'S HOUSE NEAR *COAST CITY...*

I'D LIKE TO KNOW WHAT YOU TWO THINK MY CHANCES REALLY ARE IN THIS ELECTION?

WE'RE A SHOO-IN, JACK! WE CAN'T MISS!

SHUCKS,

2

YOU WERE ALWAYS THE IMPETUOUS ONE, JIM! WHAT DO YOU THINK, HAL?

WELL, THE OPPOSITION IS TOUGH, JACK! I WOULDN'T TAKE THEM TOO LIGHTLY!

NOW WE'RE GETTING SOMEWHERE! THE "OUTFIT"-- THE MACHINE THAT RUNS POLITICS IN THIS STATE-- WILL DO ANYTHING TO KEEP THEMSELVES IN POWER! AND I MEAN ANYTHING! WE'LL HAVE TO BE ON OUR TOES EVERY MINUTE TILL ELECTION DAY!

NOW, I'VE GOT THREE SPEAKING DATES TODAY--BUT THOSE PUBLICITY "FLIERS" HAVE TO BE CIRCULATED ALL OVER THE COUNTY! IT'S A DRUDGE JOB BUT--

SAY NO MORE! WE'LL DO IT!

AFTER THE BUSY CANDIDATE HAS LEFT...

HAL, I JUST REMEMBERED! I'VE GOT A DATE WITH A REPORTER OF A POPULAR MAGAZINE TO GIVE JACK PUBLICITY! AND I'M LATE NOW!

THAT'S ALL RIGHT, JIM! YOU GO AHEAD! I'LL TAKE CARE OF THE LEAFLETS!

JIM FEELS BAD ABOUT PASSING THE "DRUDGE JOB" TO ME! HE THINKS I'VE GOT TO LUG THE LEAFLETS DOWN TO THE AIRPORT, HIRE A PLANE AND SO ON! HE DOESN'T KNOW I HAVE ...OTHER IDEAS!

AND SOON HIGH IN THE SKY ABOVE COAST COUNTY, A STRIKING EMERALD FIGURE IS WHIRLING FASTER THAN ANY PLANE COULD GO...

THEORETICALLY, I'M ONLY SUPPOSED TO USE MY POWER RING TO COMBAT EVIL... BUT IF THE OUTFIT WE JORDANS ARE OUT TO BEAT IN THIS ELECTION ISN'T EVIL ...I DON'T KNOW WHAT IS!

WITH HIS POWER BEAM, THE GREEN-CLAD CRUSADER SCATTERS HIS LEAFLETS OVER THE COUNTY IN A MATTER OF MINUTES...

GOT TO STAY HIGH ENOUGH SO THAT I'M NOT SPOTTED! IF I'M CONNECTED WITH THIS CAMPAIGN, MY SECRET IDENTITY MIGHT BE EXPOSED! WELL, THERE GOES THE LAST OF THE LEAFLETS EXPOSING THE CROOKED *OUTFIT!* I CAN GET BACK TO "HEAD-QUARTERS" NOW AND SEE WHAT ELSE THERE IS TO DO...

MEANWHILE IN A HOTEL ROOM NEARBY...

CHIEF, LISTEN, I'VE GOT EXCITING NEWS! I MAY BE ABLE TO GIVE YOU A BIGGER STORY THAN THE JACK JORDAN ELECTION CAMPAIGN YOU ASSIGNED ME TO COVER!

WHAT'S *THAT,* SUE?

YOU MAY REMEMBER, CHIEF, I SAID THAT IF I EVER SAW A PICTURE OF *GREEN LANTERN* IN HIS CIVILIAN IDENTITY *I'D RECOGNIZE HIM?* WELL, I'M CONVINCED NOW I *KNOW* WHO HE IS-- BECAUSE I'VE GOT THE PICTURE RIGHT IN FRONT OF ME!

MORNING STAR 5¢

JACK JORDAN FAVOR...

THE PICTURE OF THE *THREE* JORDAN BROTHERS IN ALL THE NEWSPAPERS! YOU MUST HAVE SEEN IT--!

SURE I'VE SEEN IT, BUT--SUE WILLIAMS, ARE YOU TRYING TO TELL ME THAT *JACK JORDAN* IS *GREEN LANTERN?*

NO, NOT *JACK* JORDAN! IT'S THE ONE YOU'D *LEAST* EXPECT--NATURALLY!

YOU MEAN HIS BROTHER *HAL,* THE TEST PILOT!?

4.

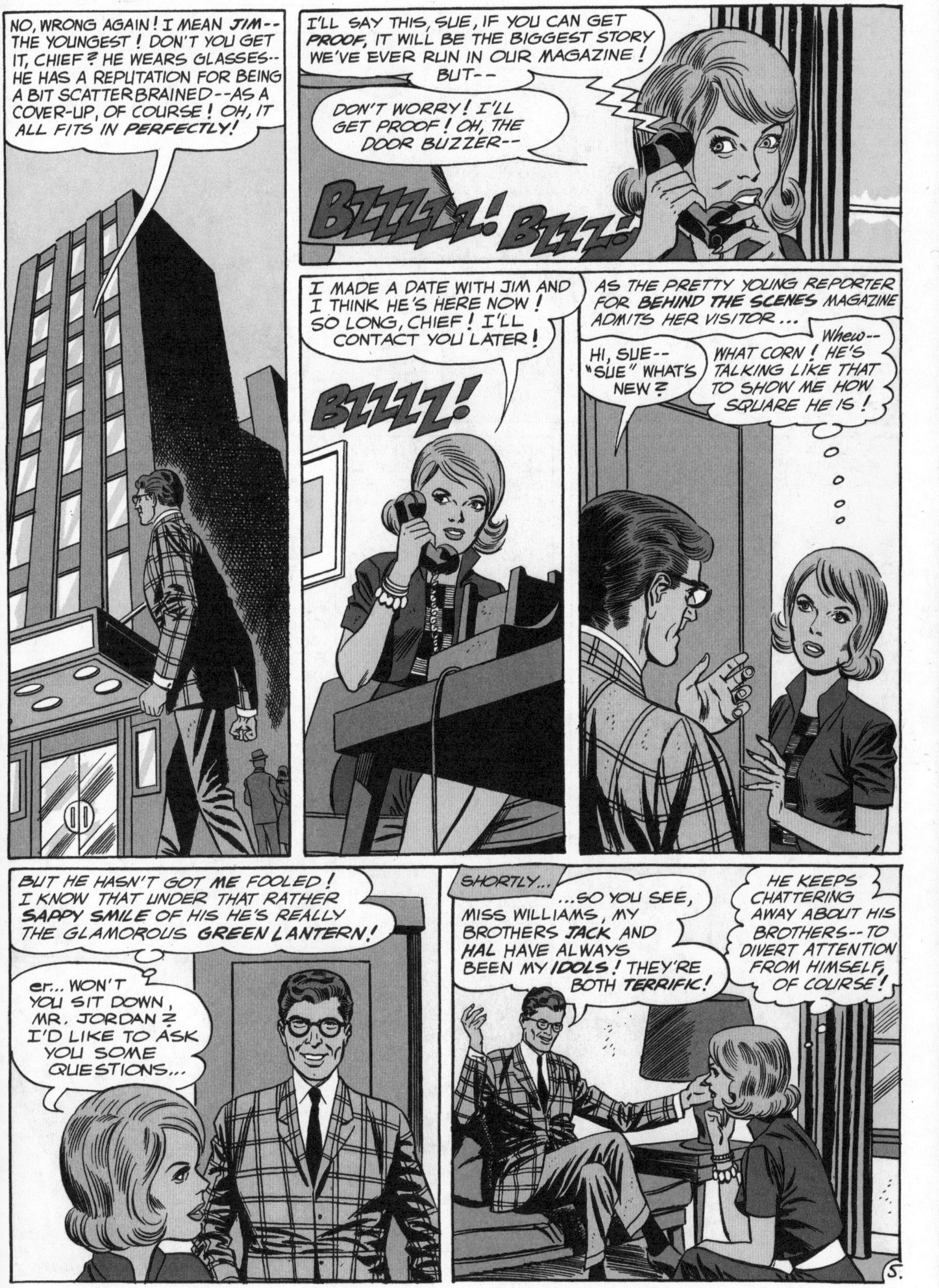

NO, WRONG AGAIN! I MEAN JIM-- THE YOUNGEST! DON'T YOU GET IT, CHIEF? HE WEARS GLASSES-- HE HAS A REPUTATION FOR BEING A BIT SCATTERBRAINED--AS A COVER-UP, OF COURSE! OH, IT ALL FITS IN PERFECTLY!
I'LL SAY THIS, SUE, IF YOU CAN GET PROOF, IT WILL BE THE BIGGEST STORY WE'VE EVER RUN IN OUR MAGAZINE! BUT--
DON'T WORRY! I'LL GET PROOF! OH, THE DOOR BUZZER--
BZZZZZ! BZZZ!
I MADE A DATE WITH JIM AND I THINK HE'S HERE NOW! SO LONG, CHIEF! I'LL CONTACT YOU LATER!
BZZZZ!
AS THE PRETTY YOUNG REPORTER FOR BEHIND THE SCENES MAGAZINE ADMITS HER VISITOR...
HI, SUE-- "SUE" WHAT'S NEW?
Whew-- WHAT CORN! HE'S TALKING LIKE THAT TO SHOW ME HOW SQUARE HE IS!
BUT HE HASN'T GOT ME FOOLED! I KNOW THAT UNDER THAT RATHER SAPPY SMILE OF HIS HE'S REALLY THE GLAMOROUS GREEN LANTERN!
er... WON'T YOU SIT DOWN, MR. JORDAN? I'D LIKE TO ASK YOU SOME QUESTIONS...
SHORTLY...
...SO YOU SEE, MISS WILLIAMS, MY BROTHERS JACK AND HAL HAVE ALWAYS BEEN MY IDOLS! THEY'RE BOTH TERRIFIC!
HE KEEPS CHATTERING AWAY ABOUT HIS BROTHERS--TO DIVERT ATTENTION FROM HIMSELF, OF COURSE!
5.

I SEE I'LL HAVE TO DO SOMETHING DRASTIC! HE'S TOO SMART TO GIVE HIMSELF AWAY! AND I HAVE AN IDEA SWIPED FROM *LOIS LANE'S* ROUTINE WITH *SUPERMAN!* IT'S *RISKY*-- BUT IT'S A *SUREFIRE* WAY TO GET THE PROOF I NEED!

LET'S GO OUT ON THE TERRACE, MR. JORDAN! IT'S COOLER!

AS THE PLUCKY NEWSGIRL PUTS HER DARING SCHEME INTO EFFECT...

ISN'T THERE A WONDERFUL VIEW FROM UP HERE? BY LEANING OUT FAR ENOUGH YOU CAN ACTUALLY SEE *SIERRA MOUNTAINS*--OH!!

THE NEXT INSTANT...

THIS WILL DO IT! HE'S GOT TO RESCUE ME! I DON'T HAVE A THING IN THE WORLD TO WORRY ABOUT! I'VE GOT HIM *TRAPPED!*

AT THAT VERY MOMENT, A LEAFLET-DISTRIBUTOR IS RETURNING TO THE CITY...

GREAT GUARDIANS! * THAT GIRL-- FALLING TOWARD THE GROUND!

*Editor's Note: THE ALIEN RACE IN FAROFF SPACE FROM WHOM *GREEN LANTERN* DRAWS HIS MIGHTY POWER!

LIKE A BLAZE OF EMERALD LIGHTNING, *GREEN LANTERN* STREAKS TOWARD THE SCENE OF DANGER...

≈Whew!≈ I JUST BARELY HAD TIME TO SAVE HER!

WELL, I MUST SAY GL SHAVED IT *RATHER CLOSE!* FOR A MOMENT OR TWO I ALMOST BEGAN TO THINK... BUT NO POINT WORRYING NOW! OBVIOUSLY MY *STUNT* HAS WORKED LIKE A *CHARM!*

6.

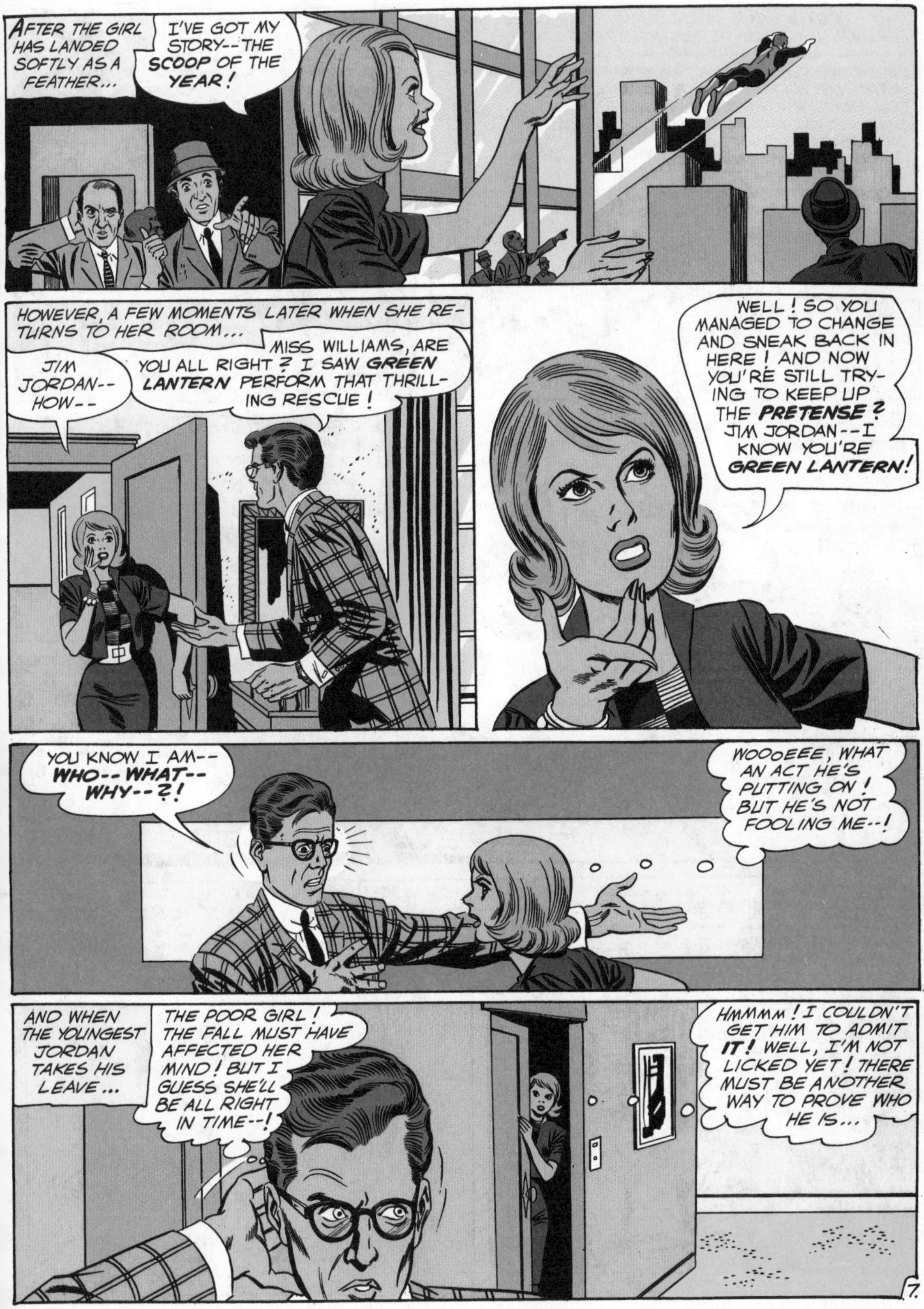
AFTER THE GIRL HAS LANDED SOFTLY AS A FEATHER...
I'VE GOT MY STORY-- THE SCOOP OF THE YEAR!
HOWEVER, A FEW MOMENTS LATER WHEN SHE RETURNS TO HER ROOM...
MISS WILLIAMS, ARE YOU ALL RIGHT? I SAW GREEN LANTERN PERFORM THAT THRILLING RESCUE!
JIM JORDAN-- HOW--
WELL! SO YOU MANAGED TO CHANGE AND SNEAK BACK IN HERE! AND NOW YOU'RE STILL TRYING TO KEEP UP THE PRETENSE? JIM JORDAN--I KNOW YOU'RE GREEN LANTERN!
YOU KNOW I AM-- WHO--WHAT-- WHY--?!
WOOoEEE, WHAT AN ACT HE'S PUTTING ON! BUT HE'S NOT FOOLING ME--!
AND WHEN THE YOUNGEST JORDAN TAKES HIS LEAVE...
THE POOR GIRL! THE FALL MUST HAVE AFFECTED HER MIND! BUT I GUESS SHE'LL BE ALL RIGHT IN TIME--!
HMMMM! I COULDN'T GET HIM TO ADMIT IT! WELL, I'M NOT LICKED YET! THERE MUST BE ANOTHER WAY TO PROVE WHO HE IS...
7

THAT EVENING NEAR *JACK JORDAN'S* HOME, THE JORDAN HEADQUARTERS IN THE ELECTION...

I'M GOING TO SET UP A *TWENTY-FOUR HOUR* WATCH OVER *JIM JORDAN!* I'LL WATCH HIM *EVERY SECOND!* SOONER OR LATER SOME EMERGENCY IS BOUND TO COME UP REQUIRING HIM TO CHANGE TO HIS *GREEN LANTERN* IDENTITY! AND WHEN HE DOES...

...I'LL CATCH HIM RED-HANDED! AND IF AN EMERGENCY DOESN'T COME UP, I'LL FAKE ONE! I'LL THINK OF *SOMETHING* TO BREAK THIS-- eh?..

AT THAT MOMENT...

WHAT'S ALL THIS?

DON'T ASK QUESTIONS, PAL! THIS AIN'T A INFORMATION BUREAU! *GET IN THE CAR!*

AND SECONDS AFTERWARD...

G-GOLLY! THOSE ARE *GANGSTERS!* THEY FORCED *JACK JORDAN* INTO THAT CAR AT GUNPOINT!

WITH THE SPEED OF A STARTLED DEER, SUE STREAKS INTO THE HOUSE...

JIM JORDAN! LISTEN-- THERE ISN'T A MOMENT TO LOSE! GET INTO YOUR *GREEN LANTERN* COSTUME AT ONCE!

MISS WILLIAMS!?

OH, THE POOR GIRL...

FOR GOODNESS' SAKE, THIS IS NO TIME FOR *PLAY-ACTING!* GET MOVING!

THAT FALL REALLY DID AFFECT HER MIND! I'M GOING TO HAVE TO DO SOMETHING ABOUT GETTING HER TO SEE A DOCTOR!

In an adjoining room where Sue's voice easily carries...

I TELL YOU YOUR BROTHER JACK HAS BEEN SEIZED BY GUNMEN! HE'S IN TERRIBLE DANGER! THEY'RE TAKING HIM FOR A RIDE!

GREAT JUPITER! JACK--IN DANGER!?

On the instant, a grim Hal Jordan explodes into motion...

IT MUST BE THE OUTFIT! JACK SAID THEY'D STOP AT NOTHING TO WIN THE ELECTION-- AND HE WAS RIGHT!

NO USE! HE WON'T BECOME GREEN LANTERN IN FRONT OF ME--THAT'S WHAT IT IS! I'LL GO OUT-- AND GIVE HIM A CHANCE! EVIDENTLY HE'S MORE INTERESTED IN PRO-TECTING HIS IDENTITY-- THAN IN SAVING HIS BROTHER!

And moments later outside...

I THOUGHT SO! AS LONG AS MY BACK WAS TURNED-- HE SWITCHED TO HIS GREEN LANTERN COSTUME! I WONDER JUST WHO JIM JORDAN THINKS HE'S KIDDING!

Meanwhile...

WHO'S PAYING YOU FOR THIS JOB? WHAT'S HIS NAME?

YOU'RE A REGULAR GROUCHO THE QUESTION-ASKER, AIN'T YOU? BETTER SHADDUP!

AW, WHAT ARE WE WAITIN' FOR, PUNCHY? LET'S TAKE CARE OF HIM NOW!

NO, THIS HAS GOTTA BE DONE RIGHT, LOOIE--LIKE THEY USED TO DO IT IN THEM OLD GANGSTER MOVIES, REMEMBER?

"SCARFACE"! THE PUBLIC ENEMY! RAT-TAT-TAT! AH, THEM WERE THE GOOD OLD DAYS! WHAT DO THE MUGS YOU SEE NOW ON TELEVISION KNOW ABOUT BUMPING SOMEBODY OFF?

UH--THIS IS A GOOD PLACE...

THEN, ON A LONELY ROAD...

I WARN YOU TWO! THE ENTIRE LEGAL MACHINERY OF THIS STATE WILL HUNT YOU DOWN-- YOU'LL BE BROUGHT TO JUSTICE!

SAY, THAT SOUNDS GOOD! HE TALKS JUST LIKE THE HERO DID IN THEM OLD MOVIES!

IT PUTS ME IN THE RIGHT MOOD! YEAH, OKAY, JORDAN! TURN AROUND AND START WALKIN'! GIT!

WHY DO WE HAVE TO DRAG THIS OUT, PUNCHY?

WHY?! FOR THE SUSPENSE, YOU SAP! ANOTHER FEW FEET AND HE'LL LOOK BACK-- AND THAT'S WHEN HE GETS IT! DON'T YOU REMEMBER ANYTHIN' LOOIE?

GOT TO MAKE A DIVE FOR THOSE BUSHES...

HE'S RUNNING!

THE CRUM! HE AIN'T FOLLOWING THE SCRIPT! LET HIM HAVE IT!

AT THAT VERY MOMENT, ABOVE..

I SPOTTED THAT AUTO A FEW SECONDS AGO FROM THE AIR! AND-- THE GUNMEN THAT GIRL TALKED ABOUT-- THEY'RE ABOUT TO SHOOT JACK!

10

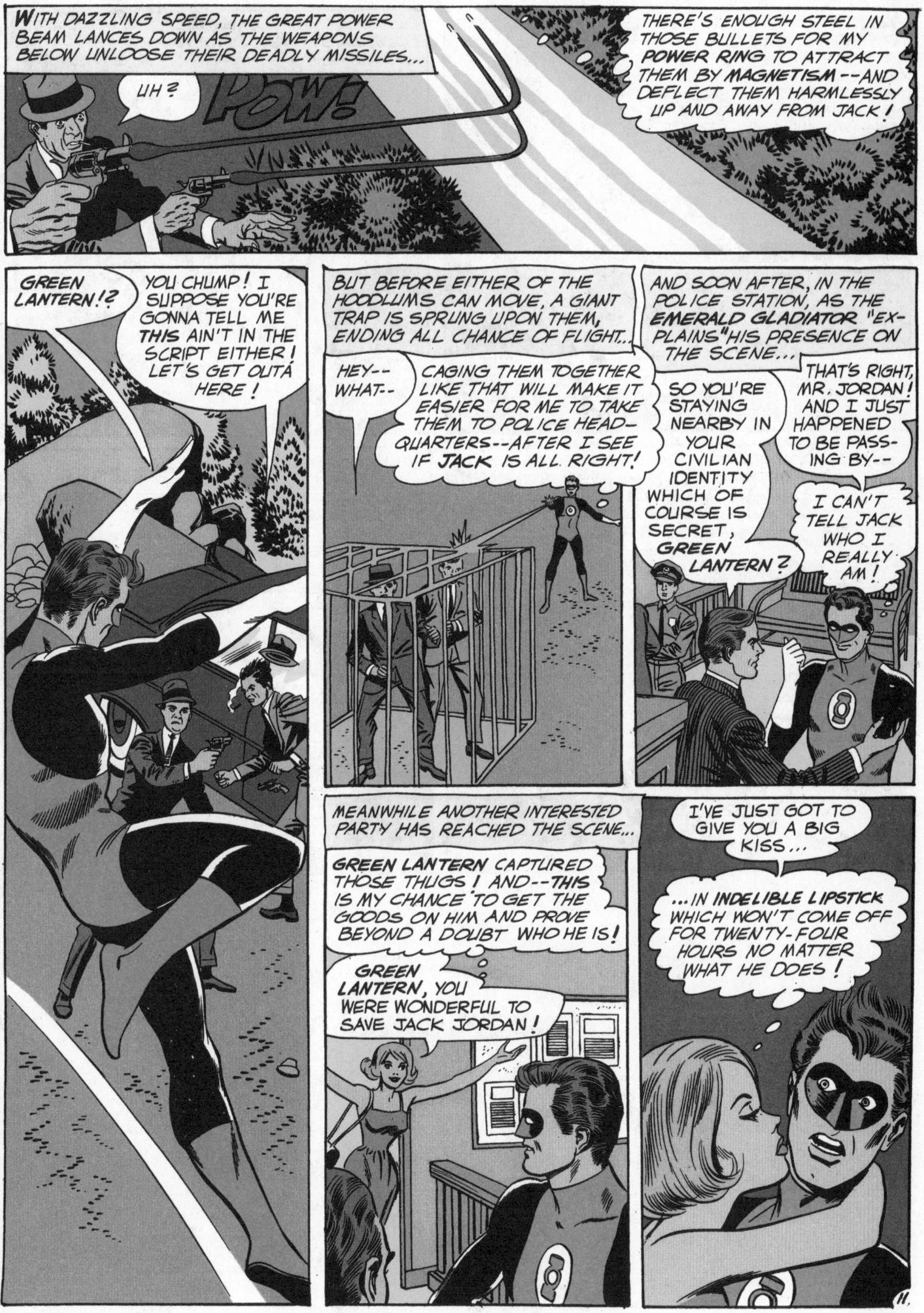
WITH DAZZLING SPEED, THE GREAT POWER BEAM LANCES DOWN AS THE WEAPONS BELOW UNLOOSE THEIR DEADLY MISSILES...
UH?
POW!
THERE'S ENOUGH STEEL IN THOSE BULLETS FOR MY POWER RING TO ATTRACT THEM BY MAGNETISM--AND DEFLECT THEM HARMLESSLY UP AND AWAY FROM JACK!
GREEN LANTERN!?
YOU CHUMP! I SUPPOSE YOU'RE GONNA TELL ME THIS AIN'T IN THE SCRIPT EITHER! LET'S GET OUTA HERE!
BUT BEFORE EITHER OF THE HOODLUMS CAN MOVE, A GIANT TRAP IS SPRUNG UPON THEM, ENDING ALL CHANCE OF FLIGHT...
HEY-- WHAT--
CAGING THEM TOGETHER LIKE THAT WILL MAKE IT EASIER FOR ME TO TAKE THEM TO POLICE HEAD-QUARTERS--AFTER I SEE IF JACK IS ALL RIGHT!
AND SOON AFTER, IN THE POLICE STATION, AS THE EMERALD GLADIATOR "EX-PLAINS" HIS PRESENCE ON THE SCENE...
SO YOU'RE STAYING NEARBY IN YOUR CIVILIAN IDENTITY WHICH OF COURSE IS SECRET, GREEN LANTERN?
THAT'S RIGHT, MR. JORDAN! AND I JUST HAPPENED TO BE PASS-ING BY--
I CAN'T TELL JACK WHO I REALLY AM!
MEANWHILE ANOTHER INTERESTED PARTY HAS REACHED THE SCENE...
GREEN LANTERN CAPTURED THOSE THUGS! AND--THIS IS MY CHANCE TO GET THE GOODS ON HIM AND PROVE BEYOND A DOUBT WHO HE IS!
GREEN LANTERN, YOU WERE WONDERFUL TO SAVE JACK JORDAN!
I'VE JUST GOT TO GIVE YOU A BIG KISS...
...IN INDELIBLE LIPSTICK WHICH WON'T COME OFF FOR TWENTY-FOUR HOURS NO MATTER WHAT HE DOES!
11

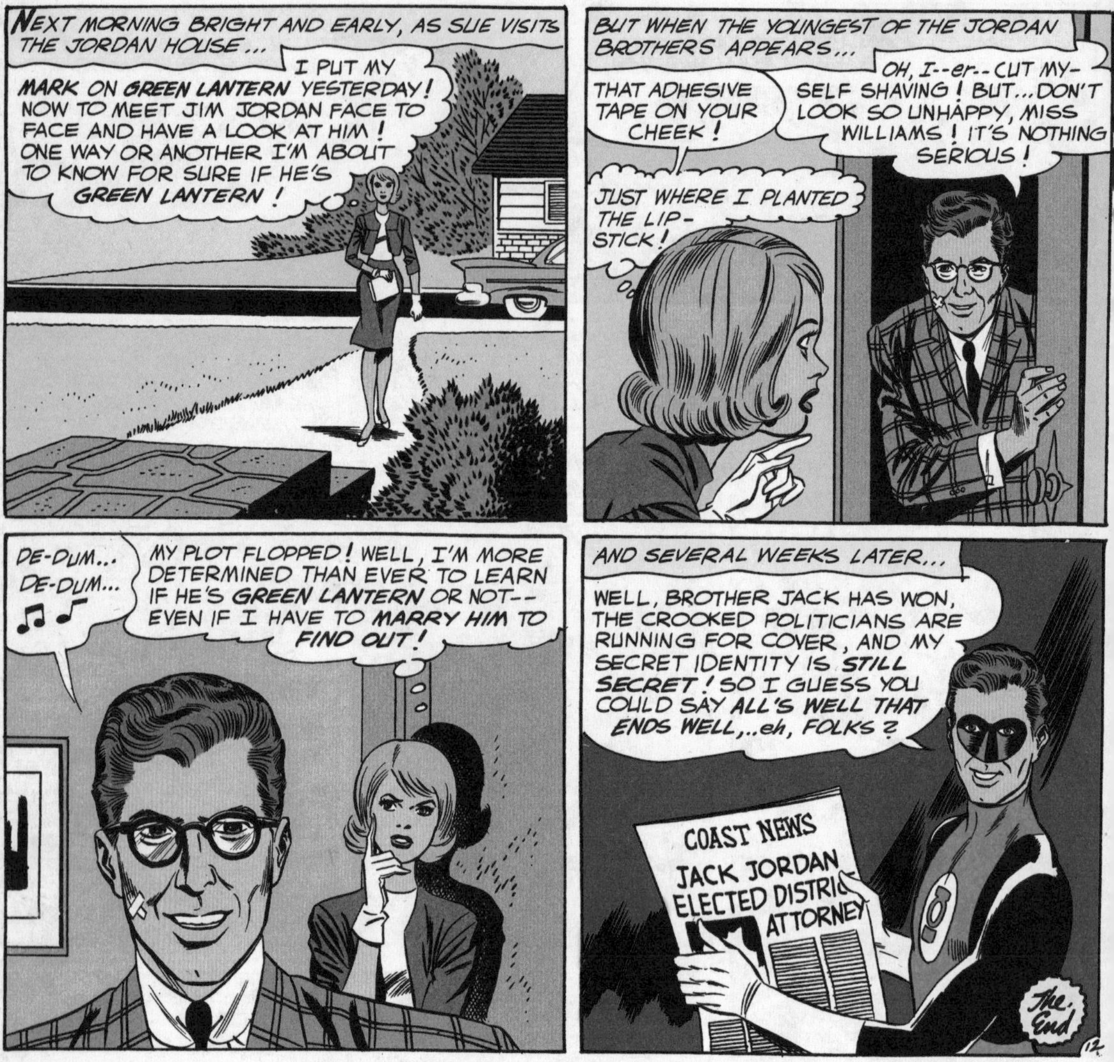
NEXT MORNING BRIGHT AND EARLY, AS SUE VISITS THE JORDAN HOUSE...
I PUT MY MARK ON GREEN LANTERN YESTERDAY! NOW TO MEET JIM JORDAN FACE TO FACE AND HAVE A LOOK AT HIM! ONE WAY OR ANOTHER I'M ABOUT TO KNOW FOR SURE IF HE'S GREEN LANTERN!
BUT WHEN THE YOUNGEST OF THE JORDAN BROTHERS APPEARS...
THAT ADHESIVE TAPE ON YOUR CHEEK!
OH, I--er--CUT MY-SELF SHAVING! BUT...DON'T LOOK SO UNHAPPY, MISS WILLIAMS! IT'S NOTHING SERIOUS!
JUST WHERE I PLANTED THE LIP-STICK!
DE-DUM... DE-DUM...
MY PLOT FLOPPED! WELL, I'M MORE DETERMINED THAN EVER TO LEARN IF HE'S GREEN LANTERN OR NOT--EVEN IF I HAVE TO MARRY HIM TO FIND OUT!
AND SEVERAL WEEKS LATER...
WELL, BROTHER JACK HAS WON, THE CROOKED POLITICIANS ARE RUNNING FOR COVER, AND MY SECRET IDENTITY IS STILL SECRET! SO I GUESS YOU COULD SAY ALL'S WELL THAT ENDS WELL,..eh, FOLKS?
COAST NEWS
JACK JORDAN ELECTED DISTRIC ATTORNEY
The End
12

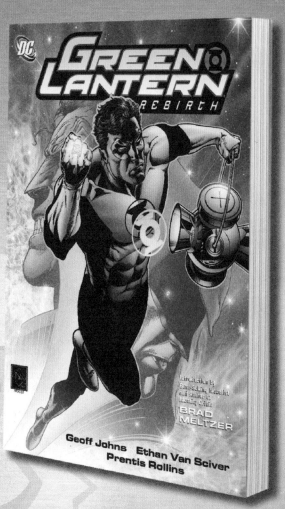

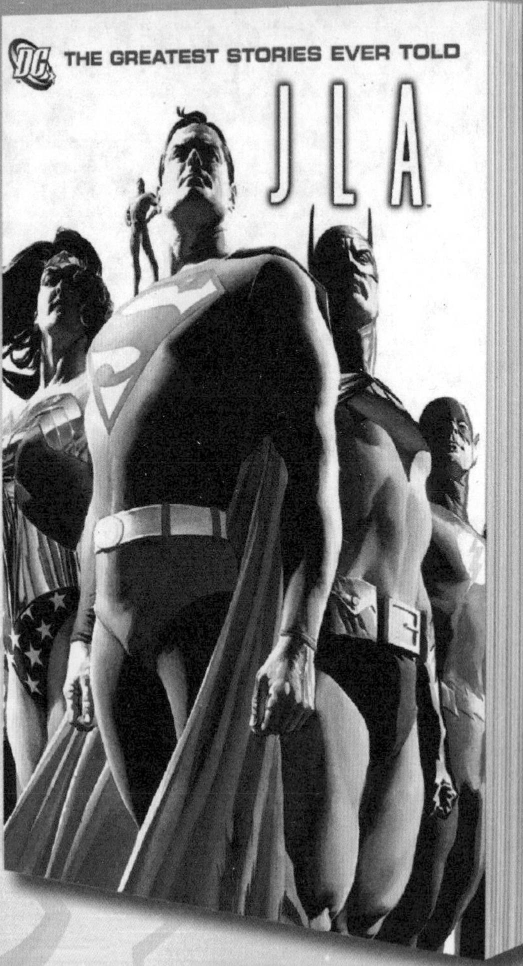
DC
THE GREATEST STORIES EVER TOLD
JLA

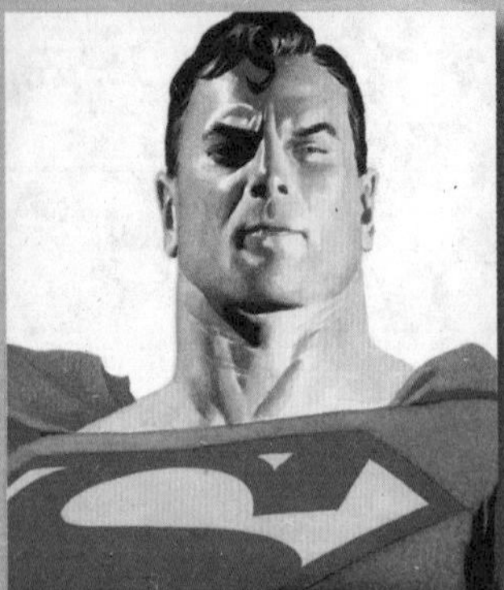
SUPERMAN
THE GREATEST STORIES EVER TOLD
DC

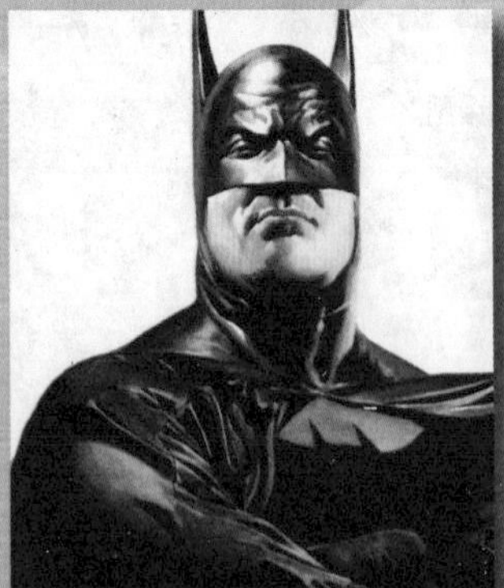
BATMAN
THE GREATEST STORIES EVER TOLD
DC

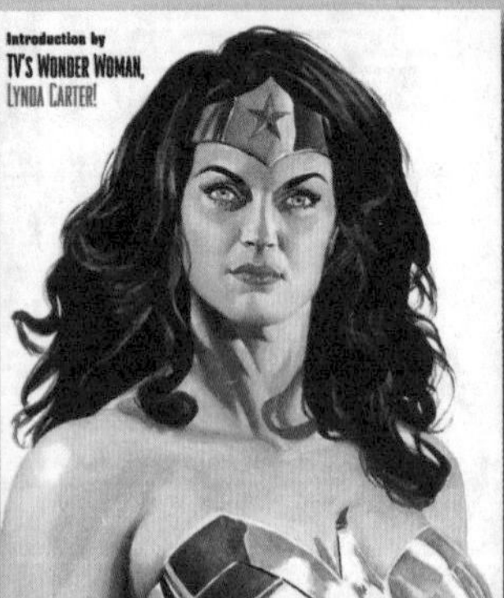
Introduction by
TV'S WONDER WOMAN,
LYNDA CARTER!
WONDER WOMAN
THE GREATEST STORIES EVER TOLD
DC